The End of Modernity

The End of Modernity

*Nihilism and Hermeneutics in
Post-modern Culture*

GIANNI VATTIMO

Translated and with an Introduction
by Jon R. Snyder

Polity Press

First published in Italian as *La fine della modernità* © Garzanti Editore s.p.a. 1985

English translation first published 1988 by Polity Press in association
with Basil Blackwell

Editorial Office:
Polity Press, Dales Brewery, Gwydir Street,
Cambridge CB1 2LJ, UK

Basil Blackwell Ltd
108 Cowley Road, Oxford OX4 1JF, UK

British Library Cataloguing in Publication Data

Vattimo, Gianni
    The end of modernity : nihilism and
    hermeneutics in post-modern culture.
    1. Philosophy. Postmodernism
    I. Title II. La fine della modernità.
    English
    190

ISBN 0-7456-0453-6

Typeset in Plantin 11 on 13 pt
by Hope Services, Abingdon
Printed in Great Britain by
Billing & Sons Ltd, Worcester

Contents

Translator's Introduction

The idea of 'post-modernity' lies at the centre of contemporary intellectual debate in the West. The critics and supporters of post-modernity have engaged in often heated exchanges over the course of the past decade, particularly regarding painting, architecture, ballet, theatre, cinema, literature and philosophy.[1] There is a widely shared sense that Western ways of seeing, knowing and representing have irreversibly altered in recent times; but there is little consensus over what this might mean or what direction Western culture is now taking. Has modernity really come to a close, or has it simply undergone a change of appearance? Do the global spread of information-systems technology, the pervasive influence of the mass media, and the deindustrialization of Western economies signal a permanent shift in the course of culture and society, or can they be accounted for as a part of the logic of modernity itself? If we agree that we are now at a point in history that is at the end of modernity, is it fair to assume that the problems which plague modernity will somehow be left behind along with it? Much is at stake in this debate, and the outcome will have profound consequences for the future. Yet the concept upon which the discourse on post-modernity depends – namely the 'end of modernity' as the moment of closure of the civilization of modernity – has not yet been given the full and careful analysis it deserves. The signal contribution of Gianni Vattimo's *The End of Modernity* is its attempt to develop a philosophical basis for understanding the closure of modernity

and its consequences for the arts and sciences. This is an
ambitious undertaking, but from Vattimo's perspective one
that is firmly rooted in the tradition of nineteenth- and
twentieth-century European philosophy, with whose insights
into the nature of the human subject and of human society we
are still struggling to come to terms. His concern for the
philosophical tradition, however, is accompanied by an
abiding awareness of the failure of philosophy to get to grips
with the alienating conditions of contemporary technological
civilization. In all spheres of human activity, as in the world of
nature that has been so drastically altered by modern
civilization, the 'desert' is growing rapidly, and this situation
demands a positive response from contemporary thought. The
present book provides one philosopher's appraisal of the role
philosophy may play in shaping a constructive vision of
human existence at the end of modernity.

The essays collected in this volume display the wide
range of Vattimo's thought and his thoroughly international
approach to the discipline of philosophy. While a number
were originally written for conferences and special issues of
scholarly journals, altogether they form a coherent and
consistent mosaic design of his interests and ideas over the
past decade. My chief aim in this introduction will be to
provide a preliminary account of this design through a
description of the central themes of the essays included in the
volume. In this way I hope to bring to light the value and
significance of Vattimo's principal philosophical concepts for
readers who might otherwise find them elusive. One particular
difficulty readers may encounter is the fact that *The End of
Modernity* is principally a work of *theoretical* philosophy,
offering relatively little illustration of the main argument.
Although Vattimo highlights the usefulness of other philosophers and theorists – particularly Friedrich Nietzsche and
Martin Heidegger – for thinking about post-modernity, he
rarely supplies here a thorough, detailed reading of their texts,
usually limiting himself to a reference to a single aphorism,
sentence or passage. He has performed thorough readings in

his many published books on Nietzsche and Heidegger, and in *The End of Modernity* may quite rightly take for granted the familiarity of the majority of his Italian audience with these books. Apart from a few scattered articles in specialized journals, however, Vattimo's writings are still largely unknown to the English-speaking world. It would thus seem appropriate to provide at the outset some contextual information for readers unfamiliar with the ideas of Nietzsche, Heidegger and others with whose work Vattimo engages in this volume, but to which he often refers in shorthand fashion. However, I have in the following pages deliberately avoided a critical analysis of Vattimo's own theory of post-modernity; although I believe that a number of his ideas and interpretations are open to question, this is not the place to present my own reservations.

Gianni Vattimo was born in Turin, Italy, in 1936. After completing the *liceo classico*, with its rigorous programme of classical studies, he studied philosophy with Luigi Pareyson at the University of Turin in the mid-to-late 1950s. Pareyson had been among the very first intellectuals in Italy to discover existentialism in the early 1940s, despite Italy's cultural isolation under the fascist regime. He published *La filosofia dell'esistenza e C. Jaspers* (*The Philosophy of Existence and Karl Jaspers*) in 1940, and *Studi sull'esistenzialismo* (*Studies on Existentialism*) in 1943. In the years following the end of the war, which in Italy were marked by a concerted effort to create a new, more cosmopolitan culture out of the ashes of Fascism, Pareyson helped to introduce Heidegger's work, together with the discipline of hermeneutics, into contemporary Italian philosophy. After Vattimo completed his doctoral thesis under Pareyson's direction, he pursued his philosophical studies with Hans-Georg Gadamer and Karl Löwith (both of whom had been Heidegger's students at Marburg in the 1920s) at the University of Heidelberg in West Germany. It was around this time in the early 1960s that the focus of Vattimo's research turned to nineteenth- and twentieth-century European philosophy, most notably hermeneutics and ontology, a field in which he has worked exclusively ever since. Beginning with his *Essere, storia e linguaggio in Heidegger* (*Being, History, and Language in Heidegger*) in 1963, with its somewhat traditional Heideggerian existentialism, he produced a series of studies of Heidegger, Schleiermacher and Nietzsche culminating in the present work, which appeared in Italy in 1985 with the title *La fine della modernità*.[2] In 1966 Vattimo first gained a measure of international recognition with a highly praised paper presented at the Royaumont colloquium on Heidegger. When Pareyson retired from teaching in Turin, Vattimo – who had served as his assistant for many years – succeeded him as Professor of Aesthetics; since 1982 Vattimo has been Professor of Theoretical Philosophy there. Like so many members of his generation in Europe, Vattimo was profoundly affected by the student revolt of 1968 and its aftermath. His 1974 book on Nietzsche, *Il soggetto e la maschera* (*The Subject and the Mask*), reflects the themes of the 1968 revolt in its celebration of 'the death of the [bourgeois] subject' and in its blend of Marxian and Nietzschean concepts. For a time in this same period Vattimo played an active role in the politics of the Radical party in Turin, one of the smallest but most vocal of Italy's many political parties of the Left. Since the late 1970s, he has emerged as one of Italy's most prominent and popular contemporary philosophers, chiefly because of his writings concerning *il pensiero debole* or, as it is best translated, 'weak thought'. Vattimo's theses on the 'weakness' of thinking and Being at the end of modernity have provoked considerable controversy in Italy throughout the 1980s, and the publication in late 1983 of a volume of essays entitled *Il pensiero debole*, which he co-edited with Pier Aldo Rovatti, triggered an acrid public exchange among Italian philosophers and theorists.[3] In addition to his scholarly endeavours, Vattimo is a weekly contributor to *La Stampa*, one of Italy's leading newspapers, and in 1986 hosted a series of nationally televised debates with other philosophers. In the last few years international interest in the problematic of 'weak thought' has increased exponentially; as a result, Vattimo has been invited to teach at a number of universities in the United States, including Yale and New York University, and has lectured widely in Western Europe, as well as in North and South America. While two of his books have previously been translated into French, this is the first to appear anywhere in the English-speaking world.[4]

The End of Modernity must be set against the backdrop of the tradition of European nihilism to which it belongs. This tradition, however, does not have particularly deep roots in Italy, and readers will notice that Vattimo makes relatively few references to the work of other Italian philosophers past or present. A few brief and highly schematic observations on the recent history of philosophy in Italy may help to make clearer the reason for this. Although hardly unaware of the development of philosophy in postwar France and Germany, most philosophers working in Italy in the period between the fall of the fascist regime and the 1970s chose to operate within either the Marxian/Gramscian tradition, or, to a lesser degree, the existential and phenomenological tradition. Haunted by the spectre of irrationalism and fascist totalitarianism, postwar Italian philosophy and the secular intelligentsia in general reacted by placing great value on the powers of reason and rationalist thought.[5] New rational and systematic foundations – and new justifications – had to be discovered by postwar Italian philosophy and social theory for the rest of the new Italian culture. There can be little doubt that this emphasis on rationality eventually contributed to the explosive growth of structuralism and semiotics in Italy, both of which have been exported to other countries with greater success (Umberto Eco's work being the prime example) than any other product of postwar Italian culture prior to 'weak thought'. With the rise of the influential post-structuralist movement in France in the late 1960s, however, the central role assigned by Italian philosophers and social thinkers to reason and to the use of rational procedures in the search for truth began to be displaced, as post-structuralist ideas were absorbed into Italian culture. The innovative ideas of Lacan, Foucault,

Barthes, Deleuze, Derrida, Baudrillard, Lyotard and others (virtually all of whom had been influenced by the work of Nietzsche and, to a lesser extent, Heidegger[6]), caused the debate in Italy over the possibility of new foundations and new truths for contemporary thought – whether conceived in terms of a Marxian-inspired historicism or a universalizing and ahistorical structuralism – to give way over the course of the 1970s to a questioning of the very notions of reason and truth.[7] Vattimo, who had long been working on Nietzsche and Heidegger, began to emerge at this time as a key figure in the development of Italian philosophy. By the end of the decade a crisis in philosophy had produced a philosophy of crisis; and the essays in this volume, the earliest of which dates back to 1979, are evidence of the profound changes in the direction of Italian thought in the 1980s which that new philosophy has generated. This, summarily speaking, is the context in which Vattimo's work on 'weak thought' arises, and he himself has stated that it is inseparable from this context.[8]

The significance of Vattimo's philosophy of post-modernity, at least in the context of contemporary Italian culture, lies primarily in its insistence on taking philosophical nihilism seriously. The term 'European nihilism' comes from the first book of Nietzsche's *The Will to Power*, which has it as its title, and which begins: 'nihilism stands at the door: whence comes this uncanniest of all guests?'[9] What is the meaning of Nietzsche's announcement that 'nihilism stands at the door', and what makes it the 'uncanniest of all guests' for modern Europe? This question lies at the very heart of *The End of Modernity*, and can only be answered after a careful examination of the different phases of the book's argument. European nihilism is chiefly concerned with the resolution and dissolution of truth into value, which takes the form of human belief and opinion, or, as Nietzsche puts it, the form of the will to power.[10] What this means, simply put, is that the philosophy of nihilism aims to dissect and dissolve all of the claims to truth of traditional metaphysical thought, in a process that stops only when it reaches the point where these supposed 'truths' – such as God or the soul – are revealed to be no less subjective values, and no less 'errors', than any other human beliefs or opinions. Nietzsche remarks in this regard that, when analyzed in a nihilistic fashion, metaphysics appears as 'the science . . . which deals with the fundamental errors of mankind – but as if they were fundamental truths.'[11] Nihilistic thought seeks to show that metaphysical 'truths' simply express the subjective values of a given individual or social group, not the immutable, unchanging essence of either the divine, human or natural world. Thus nihilism attacks rationality wherever it is encountered, whether in science, philosophy or art, since the concepts of 'reason' and 'truth' are entirely interdependent in the tradition of Western metaphysical thought. The project of nihilism is to unmask all systems of reason as systems of persuasion, and to show that logic – the very basis of rational metaphysical thought – is in fact only a kind of rhetoric. All thought that pretends to discover truth is but an expression of the will to power – even to domination – of those making the truth-claims over those who are being addressed by them; in particular, the disinterested, scientific, wholly rational search for the objective, neutral truth of a proposition is an illusion produced by metaphysical thought for its own benefit. In the perspective of nihilism, Nietzsche points out, the difference between error and truth is *always* a delusory one; and to do away with one means to do away with the other as well.[12]

The theory of European nihilism is inseparable from what is now usually referred to as the 'philosophy of difference', whose founders are Nietzsche and Heidegger. The philosophy of difference contends that all distinctions between truth and falsehood, essence and appearance, the rational and the irrational must be dissolved, insofar as no ultimate guarantee or unshakable ground of 'difference' (for example, God) exists, outside or prior to our language and the concepts embedded in it, to whose authority we could appeal in order to make these distinctions in a strictly objective way. Once God is dead and the 'foundation' of rational thought is lost, it becomes apparent that difference is essentially a product of the human will to power (which is another way of saying 'the will to interpret', or even 'ideological interest') and can in no logical manner be assigned or attributed to a divine essence or transcendental reason that reaches beyond the limits of the individual human subject. This means that everything we encounter in our experience of the world is no more and no less than an *interpretation* – things in the world are always interpreted into the terms of our own subjective values, and thus *the only world that can ever be known is a world of difference* (that is, a world of interpretations). The concerns of this philosophy are central to the work of many of the French post-structuralists, such as Derrida, Deleuze, Foucault and Lyotard; more importantly, the philosophy of difference supplies one of the key links between nihilism and hermeneutics (or the philosophy of interpretation) upon which Vattimo's argument in *The End of Modernity* depends. The work's subtitle *Nihilism and Hermeneutics in Post-Modern Culture*, openly suggests this. The reduction of truth to value (or to a 'perspective', to use Nietzsche's term for 'belief'), then, cannot in turn lead to the discovery of a new truth or a new foundation for thinking, for the world of difference is the only world there is. The philosophy of difference concentrates on the dismantling or deconstruction of all metaphysical truth-claims and all metaphysical systems of logic, but at the same time denies the possibility of a new truth and a new reason that could take the place of what has been done away with: there is no exit, for twentieth-century humanity, from a world of contrasting and often conflicting interpretations.[13]

Nietzsche's and Heidegger's respective notions of nihilism do diverge as well, and *The End of Modernity* explores this divergence in some detail. Vattimo is first and foremost a Heideggerean thinker, and he follows Heidegger in revising Nietzsche's emphasis on the unchallenged centrality of the will to power in nihilistic thought. For Heidegger, unlike Nietzsche, difference is not simply or solely a product of the will to power. There is, prior to any such difference, an *ontological* difference between Being and beings. By 'beings' Heidegger means all subjects and objects in the world; what he means by 'Being' is more complex, for few terms in all of philosophy are as resistant to definition as 'Being'. Ontology, as the metaphysical science or philosophy of Being, has wrestled with the meaning of the term since Parmenides and Heraclitus. All things in the world *are*, and therefore Being (as the self-identical, unchanging 'is-ness' present in whatever exists in the world) is what is common to all things, but Being itself is like none of them. For this reason Being differs from beings, and cannot be compared to them. Because there is an 'ontological difference' between Being and beings, Heidegger contends, we can never speak about Being as if it were *something*, or, in other words, as if it were some kind of object, entity or being which could be defined in the way we are accustomed to defining things. To try to define Being in logical terms – to say 'Being is X or Y' – is to lapse into tautology, for that would mean to say 'Being is a being'. For Heidegger the question of Being dissolves the subject–object relation upon which traditional philosophy relies, for in the perspective of this question both subject and object equally *are*, and therefore there is no longer any ontological difference between them: the real ontological difference is between Being itself and the realm of subjects and objects – that is, beings. As Ernesto Grassi points out, 'every attempt to say what Being is forces us to define it as a being among other beings, which means that we necessarily fail to say what it is *as* Being.'[14] Nothing logically or rationally definite can ever be said about Being, and this, Heidegger concludes, reveals its primacy over the concern of metaphysics for reason and logic, inasmuch as Being exists in an 'autonomous, independent, and foundational way' and is never in the power of the thinking, reasoning subject (p. 20). The idea of ontological difference, according to Heidegger, has been systematically repressed or 'forgotten' by Western metaphysics, which has since Plato consistently refused to grant priority to the question of Being (since that question places in doubt the thinking, reasoning subject as the basis of philosophy).

Many readers who are not trained in philosophy will invariably think of 'metaphysics' as the opposite of 'rationality'. While it is generally known that metaphysics, as a branch of theoretical philosophy, employs abstract reasoning to examine so-called 'first principles' in the form of concepts such as time, cause, essence and so on, the adjective 'metaphysical' usually serves in everyday English today as a reproach for overly rarefied and abstruse thinking, or to connote a kind of supernatural, mystical thinking that is fundamentally anti-rational. The reader of *The End of Modernity* ought not, however, to be misled by such usages. Metaphysics signifies for Heidegger, as it does for Vattimo, a philosophical system of thought that is 'always led by the question of logical truth' and the use of reason.[15] If twentieth-century technology is the most historically advanced form of Western metaphysics, as Heidegger contends, this is because it represents the most extreme degree of rationalization thus far to be produced by Western thought. To go beyond the procedural logic and rationality of metaphysics is to return to both the question of Being with which Heidegger is constantly concerned, and the philosophy of nihilism. Heidegger argues that in Western metaphysics, instead of the question of Being, 'the starting point is the problem of truth and the primacy of this investigation is upheld throughout the whole history of this tradition of thought. The question of truth stems from a relationship among beings, the subject–object relationship.'[16] Traditional Western philosophy, in other words, from Plato to Nietzsche, has always pursued the question of logical truth in an effort to deduce rationally – to give reasons or grounds for – the relationships between beings in the everyday world. Since, however, this search for the reasons or grounds of the truth of the relationship between beings always presupposes existing beings, that is, subject and object, Heidegger complains that 'it proves from the outset incapable of posing "the question of

Being", let alone of developing and answering it.'[17] The search for truth that constitutes Western metaphysics has thus resulted in the forgetting of the question of Being, and of the basis of existence itself, 'because the questions that man has raised are directed to beings and not to Being, that is, they are directed to nature, man, and all of those things that affect us directly and urge themselves upon us' but which are not prior to Being itself.[18] One of the most compelling aspects of *The End of Modernity* is its effort to recollect and to raise anew the question of Being at the end of modernity, even though the Being whose meaning Vattimo seeks is, as it is for Heidegger, radically different from the traditional metaphysical one. The insights that result from Vattimo's re-examination of this question are many and complex, and, as we will see in the pages that follow, lead to some surprising conclusions about the nature of post-modernity itself.

In his introduction, Vattimo presents a number of the key terms and concepts that figure prominently in *The End of Modernity*. Some of these, such as ontology, Being, and nihilism, have already been discussed above in regard to European nihilism and the philosophy of difference. One group of concepts which plays an important role throughout the book, but is treated most thoroughly in the introduction, centres on the terms 'post-history' and 'secularization'. Vattimo borrows both of these from the work of the German social theorist Arnold Gehlen, whose 1967 essay *Die Säkular-isierung des Fortschritts* (*The Secularization of Progress*) serves as a fundamental reference for Vattimo's own thinking about modernity. The starting point of Vattimo's account is that what characterizes the point of view of modernity itself is '*the idea of history*', with its 'two corollary notions of progress and overcoming'. To help avoid confusion, it should be said at the outset that Vattimo does not have in mind what is called 'modernism' in the arts when he speaks of modernity. For, in the history of the arts in Europe, modernism belongs to the first decades of the twentieth century and to avant-garde movements such as imagism, cubism, and constructivism; at most, the origin of modernism might be traced back to Baudelaire's seminal 1863 essay on 'The Painter of Modern Life'. Vattimo instead uses the term 'modernity' to refer to the period stretching roughly from Descartes to the present day. The distinguishing traits of modernity as he defines them ('the idea of history, with its two corollary notions of progress and overcoming') are particularly those of the positivist and historicist culture of mid-to-late nineteenth-century Europe. Nietzsche fiercely polemizes against this culture in nearly all of his works, perhaps most memorably in the early essay 'On the Uses and Disadvantages of History for Life' (1874) and in *Human, All Too Human* (1878). Nietzsche and Heidegger, Vattimo observes, radically call into question the heritage of European thought and the culture of modernity, but paradoxically 'refuse at the same time to propose a means for a critical "overcoming" of it' (p. 2). Both thinkers are caught in a difficult double bind: while, on the one hand, they reject on principle the system of Western metaphysical thought, on the other hand they are equally cognizant of the fact that the concept of 'overcoming' belongs to that same system, and must therefore also be rejected. Because of this double bind and the conceptual cul-de-sac into which it leads, there can be no clear break with, or dramatic overcoming of, modernity for either Nietzsche or Heidegger. It is impossible, they suggest, for us to think our way out of modernity with the philosophical system of thought and language supplied by modernity; yet no system that has 'overcome' the errors of modernity and 'progressed' beyond them is currently available to us, and there is no choice but to continue to use the existing system. Clearly this leaves Nietzsche and Heidegger in a quandary – but it is a quandary that for Vattimo defines post-modernity itself as a 'peculiar "critical" relationship with Western thought' (p. 3) that works to dissolve the culture of modernity, while prolonging it by continuing to depend upon its philosophical system. Not surprisingly, then, Vattimo locates the emergence of post-modern philosophy in the final quarter of the nineteenth century, with the publication of Nietzsche's mature philosophical writings and his espousal of European nihilism. Although this might seem at first to imply that the philosophy of post-modernity begins *after* the philosophy of modernity has ended, Vattimo's argument is in reality a different one. Post-modernity is an experience of 'the end of history', not the appearance of a different, or newer, stage of history itself. Any attempt to name the precise historical moment when modernity comes to an end is therefore destined to fail, for modernity and post-modernity must coexist in the same conceptual and historical space, bound together in that 'peculiar "critical" relationship' in which the latter does not, and cannot, entirely leave the former behind.

Post-history or *post-histoire* – the experience of 'the end of history' – is taking place today for several fundamental reasons. First of all, Vattimo notes, fewer and fewer historians accept the thesis that history is a unitary, organic process; what was traditionally referred to as 'history' is now perceived as having broken down into an infinity of 'histories' that can no longer be (re)combined into a single narrative governed by a central theme such as 'the march of progress' or 'the triumph of enlightenment'. This is accurately reflected in the explosive growth of 'microhistory' in the past decades (for example, in the work of Emmanuel Ladurie or Carlo Ginzburg, and in much recent feminist historical scholarship). Secondly, the work of such theorists as Michel Foucault, Michel de Certeau and Hayden White on the rhetorical and literary elements present in historical writing has belatedly led to a widespread recognition of the *narrative*, and therefore fictional, basis of a unified image of history. History appears today as a kind of writing, which persuades its readers through the use of carefully chosen rhetorical strategies of the 'truth' of its account of events. Thirdly, the notion of progress, which is at the basis of all traditional Western concepts of history, has entered into crisis because it has been 'secularized'. This means that in the contemporary world progress has, in Gehlen's terms, 'become routine'. Progress today no longer possesses its original sense of destination or of a teleological end-point (such as the 'Kingdom of Heaven' or the 'classless society') toward which it is directed; it has simply become a part of the routine of consumer society, which depends upon the constant production of 'new' items of consumption – whether clothes, cars, or ideas – and therefore upon constant progress 'for the system simply to survive' (p. 7). Advertisements proclaim a given automobile as the 'ultimate driving experience' marking the culmination and conclusion of all progress in automotive technology – a claim which is quickly belied by the appearance of next year's 'newer' and 'better' model. Seen in this light, progress no longer seems to lead anywhere except to the creation of 'conditions in which [more] progress . . . is always possible in an always new guise' (p. 7). This circular process, where progress leads only to more progress, dissolves the very meaning of progress as a *forward* movement in history and of the new as something qualitatively different from what precedes it, thus producing an experience of the 'end of history'. Vattimo finds the experience of post-history to be anticipated in the works of Nietzsche and Heidegger, and to figure more and more prominently in contemporary life. The secularization of progress and the subsequent emergence of post-history are, however, not to be understood as negative events in the development of Western culture and society. On the contrary, although he offers only a very broad theoretical sketch, and nothing like a programme for putting his theory into practice, Vattimo sees the experience of the loss of history and historicity – and, together with them, the category of the new and the concept of overcoming – as a 'positive opportunity' and a 'field of possibility' for late twentieth-century humanity. The end of history, then, is the beginning of something else; but to understand what this beginning might signify we need to look more closely at the philosophical basis of post-modernity.

The End of Modernity is divided into three sections – *Nihilism as Destiny, The Truth of Art*, and *The End of Modernity* – comprising essays on related philosophical topics. A certain

number of key terms, such as *Verwindung* (pp. 11 ff.) recur
throughout and help to join together the different essays and
sections into an organic discourse. The first, and briefest,
section of the book introduces the question of nihilism in
contemporary philosophy. This question, as we have already
seen, looms large for both Nietzsche and Heidegger, although
in somewhat different ways. Vattimo's positive assessment of
post-modernity is inseparable from his consideration of the
question of nihilism. Taking his cue from Nietzsche and
Heidegger, he defines a non-metaphysical conception of truth
and of Being as a fundamental step in exploring the experience
of the end of history and modernity. In Western philosophy
since Plato, Being and truth (that is, the truth of Being) have
been conceived as stable, autonomous entities possessed of
both permanence and grandeur (such as, for instance, the
soul). Vattimo's 'non-metaphysical' notion of truth and Being
instead understands both truth and Being as *events* – as, in
other words, what is constantly being reinterpreted, rewritten,
and remade – rather than as objects endowed with permanence
and stability. This means that while truth can certainly be
experienced by us (in an encounter with a work of art, for
example), it can never be appropriated and transmitted to
others as a kind of rational knowledge. To treat truth as
rational knowledge means to transform it into an object
(something that can be handed from one person to another),
rather than to preserve its eventual character as something that
occurs in the unique circumstances of each interpretive
encounter. How is it possible to say, Vattimo wonders, that
metaphysical Being and truth are now being annihilated? And
what does the disappearance of metaphysical Being and
truth signify for philosophical thought today? The necessary
first step in this inquiry is to recognize that Being has been
reduced to 'exchange-value' in modernity, and that nihilism
itself is in fact none other than the 'reduction of Being to
exchange-value' (p. 22). The implications of this are more far-
reaching than simply the reduction of the traditionally 'strong'
Being to value (that is, belief) through nihilistic analysis.

Insofar as there is no longer a highest value, such as God, to which all other values may refer as their foundation, then all values must be said to stand in a relationship of universal equivalence where each value is equal to all other values and can be converted into, or exchanged for, any other given value. When deprived of the hierarchical order established by the highest value, in other words, the system of values itself becomes an infinite process of transformation, in which no value can appear to be 'higher' or more 'authentic' than any other. After Nietzsche's announcement of the death of God, Vattimo infers, it may legitimately be said that the 'true nature' of all value is exchange-value; and it is into this flux of values that the traditional metaphysical Being has today begun to dissolve and disappear. In the era of philosophical nihilism nothing can stand outside the realm of universal equivalence or lay claim to 'authenticity'; for every aspect of the world – even Being itself – is forever subject to further revaluation or, to put it another way, to the interpretive process though which the value that has previously been assigned to something is exchanged for another equivalent value.

Vattimo insists that the generalization of exchange-value manifest in the disappearance of the highest value and of the foundations for metaphysical thought which the highest value formerly supplied is by no means a catastrophic event for humanity. On the contrary, the loss of the conditions which made authenticity and genuinity possible prefigures 'a possible new human experience' (p. 26) rather than nothingness and alienation. This experience, which may be called post-modern, has its origin in the reduction of everything – including Being – to exchange-value, and may be broadly defined as the *infinite interpretability* of reality. In a situation such as the contemporary one, in which all values are exchangeable for others, and in which no one value can legitimately be privileged over any other and considered 'true', every human subject engages in an endless labour of interpretation of every aspect of existence. Without a highest or absolute value, humanity is left with a world that can only be interpreted or, in other words, assigned value by human subjects; but this process, once begun, cannot be expected to lead to the discovery of a new foundation (such as another God) which would put an end to the need for further interpretation. After the arrival of philosophical nihilism, each human subject is faced with a world in which there are always only further interpretive choices, rather than absolute values, awaiting him or her. The infinite interpretability of reality is what allows us to speak today of the 'weakening' of metaphysical Being and truth. In making his apology for nihilism's dissolution of foundational thought (that is, for the process of thinking that leads to the death of God), Vattimo contends that the experience of infinite interpretability has led to 'the weakening of the cogent force of reality' because it has made 'all that is given [by metaphysics] as real, necessary, peremptory and true' into simply another interpretive possibility among a plethora of such possibilities (p. 27). If every experience is reduced to an interpretation in contemporary existence, from the effects of science and technology to the 'true' and the 'real' themselves, then the formerly 'strong' categories of thought – such as truth, Being and logic – have indeed consequently been 'weakened', for they have been turned into a potentially *fictional* experience, that is, an experience about which we can never unequivocally say, 'it is true'. Vattimo believes that we should open ourselves up to precisely such 'a fictionalized experience of reality which is also our only possibility for freedom' (p. 29) at the end of modernity. The metaphor of 'weak thought' serves to describe the philosophy of post-modernity that is concerned with this fictionalized experience of reality, namely *hermeneutic ontology*. For hermeneutic ontology, whose definition will be examined in greater depth shortly, 'is nothing other than the interpretation of our condition or situation, since Being is nothing outside of its "event", which occurs when it historicizes itself and when we historicize ourselves' (p. 3).

The philosophy of hermeneutic ontology or 'weak thought' primarily relies upon a strategy of 'destructuration'. This strategy requires that the governing discursive forms of Western culture, and all their claims to possessing the truth or to operating according to a scientific logic, be revealed – through a nihilistic analysis that 'destructures' or 'deconstructs' them – to be only interpretations. Vattimo is clearly indebted to Heidegger for this strategy, which is presented in chapter 2: 'The Crisis of Humanism'. Vattimo begins by defining humanism in generally accepted terms, as 'a perspective that places humanity at the centre of the universe and makes it the master of Being' (p. 32). Following closely Heidegger's argument in his 1946 'Letter on Humanism', Vattimo contends that today humanism is in crisis *because* of the death of God and the concomitant decline of metaphysics; paradoxically enough, the crisis of humanism has come about because humanity has replaced God at the centre of the universe. Humanism is in crisis, in other words, because of the arrival of the era of nihilism first announced by Nietzsche. However unlikely this might seem at first, Vattimo notes:

there is no humanism without the bringing into play of a metaphysics in which humanity determines a role for itself which is necessarily central or exclusive. On the other hand, as Heidegger shows in his constantly renewed efforts to reconstruct the history of metaphysics, metaphysics may survive only insofar as its 'humanistic' nature (meaning its reduction of everything to the human subject itself) remains hidden from view. When the reductive nature of metaphysics instead makes itself explicit . . . metaphysics has arrived at the moment of its decline, and with it – as we notice every day – humanism has also arrived at the moment of its decline. For this reason the death of God, which is at once the culmination and conclusion of metaphysics, is also the crisis of humanism. (pp. 32–3)

Humanism coincides with metaphysics, then, because it represents the ultimate rationalistic reduction of everything (even Being) to the measure of the human subject itself, thus forgetting the original ontological difference. Vattimo's strategy of destructuration, as displayed in the above passage, brings into a relation of identity (where a = a) two terms, 'humanism' and 'metaphysics', which are normally understood to stand in direct opposition to each other, so that they finally become freely interchangeable: humanism *is* metaphysics.

How, though, is the identification of humanism and metaphysics specifically linked to the crisis of humanism? To answer this question, Vattimo turns to the nature of technology today. As we have seen, Heidegger defines technological civilization as the most advanced phase of Western metaphysics because in technology 'objectivizing thought', or rationalism, has been taken to the most extreme degree experienced thus far by humanity. The global project of technology is to link 'all entities into predictable and controllable causal relationships' (p. 40), namely to rationalize the world; but this is for Heidegger and for Vattimo simply the logical outcome of the same process to which rational metaphysics itself belongs. Furthermore, once this bond between technology and metaphysics is recognized and accepted, humanism cannot 'convince us that its values offer an alternative to technological ones' (p. 40), since its own defining traits also belong to metaphysics. Humanism is in crisis today because technological civilization has, in its open and often brutal manipulation of human beings as objects, *disclosed* the nature of humanism's dependency on Western metaphysics; the crisis is occurring not because technology threatens the values of humanism, but rather because technology has revealed the outcome to which these values must of necessity lead. According to Vattimo, the only way to exit from the domination of technology – and the rational, objectivizing thought that underpins it – is to insist, together with Heidegger, that 'the essence of technology is not something technological'. That is to say, by insistently returning to the Heideggerean proposition that the essence of technology is metaphysics itself, and by thus placing technology in a tradition of Western thought that dates back to Plato, we may dispute the technological world's claim to its *own* inescapable and unique reality, its cogency and necessity for contemporary existence. Technology is effectively reconnected to the history of philosophy in this way, and its laws are made subject to the same kind of scrutiny as the laws of the kind of rationalist metaphysical thought from which it derives. By leading technology back to the philosophical tradition that prepared the way for it, 'weak thought' undermines the efforts of technological civilization to impose its own version of the world as the sole possible reality. Any such claim to possess the only possible reality contradicts the nihilistic principle of the infinite interpretability of the world, and must be refuted. For post-modern thought, technological 'reality' is weakened because it is stripped of its claims to cogency; but post-modern thought is at the same time free of all nostalgia for humanism and its vision of a universe with the human subject standing at the centre, controlling and dominating a world of objects. What we are left with, when there is no longer either an authentic metaphysical, humanistic, or technological reality in which to believe, is the subject of the rest of *The End of Modernity*.

In the second section of *The End of Modernity*, which begins with an essay on 'The Death or Decline of Art' and includes three other essays on art, Vattimo develops at length his notion of the aesthetic character of the experience of truth in post-modern thought. Here he discusses theories of the avant-garde, poetic language, decorative art, artistic genius, and the evolution of artistic style and taste over the course of Western history, while engaging, or at least skirmishing with, the works of Kant, Hegel, Adorno, Benjamin, Bloch, Heidegger, Gadamer, Gombrich, Kuhn, Gehlen and others. As noted earlier, Vattimo's is a theoretical philosophy, and his approach to the aesthetic character of the experience of truth typifies this. Throughout these essays he is more concerned with other works of theory than with concrete analysis of works of art, as the lengthy list of theorists and philosophers given above indicates. But this ought not to be seen as a shortcoming in Vattimo's procedure; on the contrary, it exemplifies his efforts to think philosophically in a post-modern fashion. By engaging

with the modern philosophical tradition of aesthetics –
roughly speaking, from Kant to Adorno – his aim is to
perform an act of what Heidegger calls *Andenken*, or 'recollection' of the tradition. To remember and recollect the tradition,
to think of it and to traverse it once again, does not mean to
return uncritically to it. Rather, Vattimo turns back to the
tradition of aesthetic theory in order to try to distort and
dissolve that tradition from the inside, erasing the vestiges of
metaphysical thought still present in it, while at the same time
– inevitably, but with self-conscious irony – prolonging it as
well. This recollecting or rethinking (*Andenken*) is thus always
accompanied by an act of *Verwindung*, a term that for Vattimo
designates the definitive mode of post-modern philosophy.

In his own writings, Heidegger sets the concept of
Verwindung in opposition to the concept of *Überwindung*, or
'overcoming', which implies a transition from one phase or
moment to another, 'higher' one in a given process (as in
Hegel's famous dialectical *Aufhebung*, or synthesis, of two
contraries). The term *Verwindung* indicates, as Heidegger told
his French translators, a 'going-beyond that is both an
acceptance [or 'resignation'] and a deepening', while also
suggesting both a 'convalescence', 'cure' or 'healing' and a
'distorting' or 'twisting' (p. 172). To *verwinden* the era of
metaphysics means to 'overcome' it, but not in the commonly
accepted sense of a 'leaving behind' and 'going beyond';
rather, it means to go beyond metaphysics by accepting it and
being resigned to it, while seeking at the same time to be cured
of metaphysics by twisting it in a different direction in order to
drain it of its strength. 'Weak thought' performs a *Verwindung*
of the era of metaphysics in an attempt to abandon it and to
enter fully into the era of post-modernity, while knowing,
however, that this attempt can only succeed in returning to
and distorting, diluting, deforming and prolonging the former.
The *Verwindung* of the metaphysical tradition is at once a
recovery from *and* a resignation to metaphysics and its strong
notion of Being: contemporary philosophy can, Vattimo
contends, go beyond the latter only through a slow 'weakening'

of it that brings it along with us – and repeats it (with a difference) – as we convalesce from its era and its errors. 'Weak thought' does not and cannot claim to do away altogether with what has gone before, any more than Western culture can be said to have broken fully with its religious and mythical past and to have arrived at a truly secular basis for culture, freed from all residual traces of magical or mythical thought. (In much the same manner, as will be evident to readers of *The End of Modernity*, Vattimo prolongs and 'destructures' Heidegger's own thought and terminology, remaining within the orbit of Heidegger's project, rather than replacing it with something else. Nor are traditional terms such as 'Being' and 'truth' discarded and replaced with new ones; they remain, but their meaning is no longer exactly what it was for metaphysics.) What came before can only be remembered, and distorted, as a part of an ongoing decline and as a part of the *asthenia* of Being – its lack of vitality and energy, its depleted and debilitated form – for this is the way in which it occurs in the contemporary world. The one real freedom in this post-modern situation is to interpret all given structures of thought as 'events', and in so doing to discover *Verwindung* as a possible law of history.

In 'The Death or Decline of Art', Vattimo remarks that 'the death of art is a phrase that . . . constitutes the epoch at the end of metaphysics'. The advent of the death of art distinguishes the era at the end of modernity; yet, paradoxically, this same era is that in which truth appears precisely *as an experience of art*. How can Vattimo speak both of the death of art and the truth of art? One part of the answer lies in the fact that the death of art is a complex phenomenon, and takes at least three different forms. First of all, at the end of modernity the work of art ceases to be a specific fact; there is no longer an autonomous realm of Art, isolated from all other modes of discourse, as idealist aesthetics (from Shaftesbury to Croce) maintains, and as bourgeois institutions such as the museum, the theatre, and the concert hall generally take for granted. In the era of the death of art, the work instead calls into question its own status and traditional institutional framework, a gesture manifest in the emergence of body art, street theatre, and earth-works such as James Terrell's gigantic Roden Crater project in Arizona. Art opens up its borders to the plurality of discourses in contemporary culture, and its own distinctive 'essence', or 'originality', gradually vanishes as it absorbs these other discourses and is no longer isolated within certain institutions. Secondly, the new technologies of mass reproduction in twentieth-century Western culture, such as photography, also contribute significantly to the death of art (here Vattimo is, as he acknowledges, deeply indebted to Walter Benjamin's ground-breaking 1936 essay on 'The Work of Art in the Age of Mechanical Reproduction'). The loss of what Benjamin calls the 'aura' of the work of art – namely its uniqueness and authenticity – in the age of mass reproduction, where a potentially infinite number of identically reproduced images may coexist, subverts the notion sustained by Western aesthetics since at least the seventeenth century that art exists in a domain apart from the rest of existence. At the same time, twentieth-century Western mass culture has produced a general aestheticization of experience itself, principally through the diffusion of the print and electronic media, which play an ever greater and more decisive role in everyday life. This aestheticization of experience at a mass level (through television, advertisements, etc.) has also helped to break down the notion that the domain of art is sealed off from the rest of mass culture, since mass culture itself, including mass politics, has undergone a profound aestheticization. Finally, Vattimo notes, high art has regularly sought to commit suicide in the twentieth century, and this is the third form of the death of art. Rejecting the *Kitsch* of mass culture, many artists (Adorno gives the example of Samuel Beckett) have sought refuge in an aesthetics of silence or in the negation of the traditional traits of aesthetic experience, such as the 'pleasure of the beautiful' or the 'sublime'.

What has become the basis for the experience of truth for post-modernity is a world of 'artistic products', such as

painting, poetry and sculpture, which are linked to the various
forms of the death of art. We must, Vattimo argues, abandon
all preconceptions about artistic 'genius' or 'individual great-
ness' inherited from romanticism and modernism before
beginning to consider these artifacts, for they 'have meaning
only if situated in regard to the world of images of the mass
media or the language of this same world' (p. 58). These
'artistic products' are no longer works of art in the traditional
sense, for they deliberately distort the traditional definition of
art, enmeshing it with the image-saturated world of mass
culture and the mass media in a post-modern gesture of
Verwindung. The Pop Art of the 1960s, whose chief icon is
Andy Warhol's Campbell's Soup Can, exemplifies this contamination of high art by mass culture, while Michael Clarke's
choreography offers another, more recent example. Thus it is
more accurate to talk of the 'decline' of art today – meaning its
dissolution into a world of hybrid, contaminated 'artistic
products' – than of its complete disappearance. Despite the
different forms of its death in the twentieth century, art
survives, but only in 'artistic products' which have undermined
the traditional definition of art as a unique product of
individual genius. The experience of art which is at the basis
of the post-modern conception of truth refers to this latter
kind of 'art', in which the originality and authenticity of the
artist's vision have been weakened and drained by contact
with the world of mass culture. Vattimo points out that
Western aesthetic philosophy, in turn, must come to see that
the difficulties it 'encounters in accounting for the experience
of the decline of art . . . derive from the fact that it continues
to think of the work as a necessarily eternal form, and, at a
deeper level, in terms of Being as permanence, grandeur, and
force' (p. 63). The decline of art calls, in other words, for an
'ontology of decline' to accompany it: both the 'artistic
product' and Being, at the end of modernity, share the same
ephemeral traits of a fleeting, weakened existence, like the
flickering image on a video screen. Traversed by the endless
messages of the mass media, and stripped of all claims to

represent the 'real' and the 'eternal', the post-modern work of art, like the weak Being that accompanies it, reveals the truth of the age in which we live.

Originally presented at a symposium on 'Ontology and Reference in Contemporary Italian Poetry' held at New York University in March 1979, chapter 4 (entitled 'The Shattering of the Poetic Word') is the earliest of the essays in *The End of Modernity*. In its intricate revision of Heidegger's theory of poetry, it is also one of the most technically demanding for the general reader. Heidegger's 1936 essay on 'The Origin of the Work of Art' provides the basis for Vattimo's reflections here on the art of poetry and, more particularly, on poetic language; as always, his procedure is to interpret texts from the philosophical tradition, working through them to arrive at a philosophical position of his own. The question that concerns Vattimo in 'The Shattering of the Poetic Word' is: what does Heidegger mean when he says that a work of art founds, or inaugurates, a world? This question leads back to the observation made in the previous essay on 'The Death or Decline of Art' that the work of art is not an eternal form, but rather one which registers the effects of 'the passage of time', like the stone façade of a Greek temple or the faded figures of a Renaissance fresco. No matter what its theme may be, the work of art is for Heidegger always concerned with the effects of temporality, or, more specifically, with the *mortality* of all things that are subject to the ravages of time. The poetic work, in particular, is able to found or inaugurate a world of meaning precisely by allowing us 'to experience the connection between language and mortality' (p. 69). It can do this because the poetic work itself has, in what Heidegger calls its 'earthly' dimension, the character of a monument. That is to say, the poetic work is 'built to bear the traces and the memory of someone across time, but *for others*' (p. 73), as a monument is intended to do, and is thus constitutively bound to the effects of temporality and to mortality. It always speaks to its listeners from across time, from the past crowded with the voices of the dead and from the tradition that belongs to that past. In its function as a bearer of memories and traces, of linguistic messages from the past, the poetic work most closely resembles a funerary monument or tombstone, constructed not to defeat time but to endure *in* time, like the great pyramids in Egypt, in order to communicate a trace and a memory to future generations. This link to mortality defines the weak and essentially nihilistic nature of the poetic word for us; it endures only as something which can shatter and die, not as an eternal expression of genius ('the poetic word shatters insofar as it is prepared to endure only in the figure of death' (p. 74)). This in turn is what Heidegger terms the 'setting-into-work' of truth in the work of art. For the monumentality and the shattering of the poetic word show us that, despite the claims of science and technology, the experience of truth today is an essentially poetic and artistic experience. This is because the only possible contemporary experience of truth, once it has been denied the attributes assigned to it by metaphysics, is as the arising of a trace or a memory that comes to us across time – like a monument or a funerary inscription – from the tradition. When deprived of all foundations, neither truth nor Being can ever be made completely present; they can only occur as that which *has been*, and can return only in the form of a trace or a recollection of the past. 'The truth of Being itself . . . can . . . only arise in the form of a recollection' (p. 86), notes Vattimo, in a statement highly reminiscent of Proust's *Remembrance of Things Past*. The model for the post-modern, post-metaphysical experience of truth is therefore the one provided by the poets, who set truth 'into work' through the monumentality of poetic language. In the era of philosophical nihilism, truth appears in the same light as myth, which rational metaphysics has always understood instead as 'inferior' to truth. Myth once functioned as a kind of knowledge for primitive humanity, but for rational thought it appears to possess a fundamentally *poetic* meaning; now, during the decline of modernity, the same may be said for metaphysical truth as well. In the experience of poetry, we may 'recollect' metaphysical truth, but we encounter it only as something which has lost its former grandeur, and is characterized, like all traces, myths, and memories, by its ability to die. The world of meaning that poetry founds is thus also a world of *ungrounding*, or of the loss of foundations in the experience of mortality – the mortality of truth – offered by poetic language.

Chapter 5, 'Ornament/Monument', was originally presented at a colloquium on contemporary aesthetics and the theory of decorative art held in Urbino, Italy in July 1982. Like the preceding chapter, it too is largely an interpretation of Heidegger's philosophical writings on art and aesthetics (in this case, a little-known 1969 essay on 'Art and Space'). Here Vattimo turns his attention to the traditional opposition between the 'essence' of the work of art and what are considered its 'ornamental' or 'decorative' features. The latter are usually seen as a kind of artistic surplus or excess – like the architectural details in a Louis Sullivan skyscraper, or the magnificent oriental carpets draped over the altars and chairs in Carlo Crivelli's religious paintings – whose elimination would not detract from the overall effect of the work of art. Ornament and décor are generally thought to serve as a backdrop to the work of art, and thus to lack any foundation in what is truly *proper* to the work (that is, its real essence), in the same way, for instance, that the picture frame is usually considered inessential to the painting it encloses. Vattimo takes strong exception to this notion of the peripheral, marginal nature of ornament and decoration, and to the allied notion of an 'essence' of the work of art. Turning to the same Heideggerian thesis of the work of art as a 'setting-into-work' of truth which he explored in chapter 4, he observes that 'the definition of the work of art as the setting-into-work of truth does not just concern the work of art, but also and above all the notion of truth' (p. 83). As we have already seen, the work of art is the place, or site, where truth occurs in the post-modern, post-metaphysical era. This post-metaphysical truth can never be thought of in terms of a stable, objective, verifiable kind of knowledge; rather, as is argued in 'The Shattering of the Poetic Word', it always arises as a trace or a recollection. The so-called ornamental and decorative elements of the work of art have in point of fact been pushed to the periphery and devalued, in traditional thinking about art, precisely on the basis of a strong metaphysical notion of Being as that which 'truly is' (or, in other words, on the basis of a theory of artistic essences). Hermeneutic ontology, however, maintains that there is no longer any fixed difference between essence and appearance, subject and object, or centre and periphery, and that therefore 'the occurrence of Being is . . . an unnoticed and marginal event which takes place in the background' (p. 86) in the post-modern era. And the same, Vattimo infers, must be the case for art as the setting-into-work of truth: if the truth which occurs in the work of art is a weak and de-centred one, and takes the form of a 'marginal event', then we may legitimately speak of the 'decorative nature of *all art*' (my italics). Everything in the work of art is ornament or décor, insofar as the post-modern work of art, like post-modern Being itself, has no essence or centre which could then be used to distinguish what is proper to the work from what is inessential or marginal to it. This distinction between centre and periphery, which has its basis in meta-physical thought, has lost all validity today. Chapter 5 concludes with the provocative statement that, in the philos-ophy of post-modernity, ornament 'becomes the central element of aesthetics and, in the last analysis, of ontological meditation itself'. Here, more than anywhere else in *The End of Modernity*, we may see the generic resemblance between Vattimo's strategy of 'destructuration' and Derrida's strategy of 'deconstruction'. Both Vattimo and Derrida radicalize Heidegger's own philosophy of difference by taking an apparent binary opposition, such as 'centre/periphery', 'fore-ground/background', or 'essence/ornament', and analysing the paired terms of the opposition in such a way that the hierarchical difference between the two eventually collapses, and the terms become indistinguishable from – or, in other words, identical with – one another.[19] The figure of thought known as a 'paradox', produced when the two terms of an antithesis which cannot both be true at the same time (such as 'on' and 'off') are joined together, is for both philosophers generally the result of this exercise. Vattimo's destructuring analysis of the opposition 'artistic essence/ornament' does indeed lead him to the paradoxical conclusion that 'art in general has . . . a decorative and "marginal" essence' (p. 85). Unlike some of Derrida's epigones, however, Vattimo is never content to rest his analysis at this point. He instead sees 'destructuration' as a necessary step in the search for a positive philosophy of post-modernity, just as Heidegger's proposed 'destruction of ontology' was intended as only one part of a far larger philosophical project.

Thus it is that in the final essay in *The Truth of Art*, entitled 'The Structure of Artistic Revolutions', Vattimo returns once again to the task of defining a positive philosophy of post-modernity. Here he takes up his task in terms of the question of how 'change' in the arts may be measured in historical and aesthetic terms. The essay takes as its starting-point Thomas Kuhn's famous 1962 work on the theory of paradigms of scientific change, *The Structure of Scientific Revolutions*, but quickly shifts its argument to other ground. Vattimo borrows the notion of 'paradigm' from Kuhn because it can help us see how artistic revolutions or paradigm-shifts, like scientific ones, succeed one another in history in a fundamentally discontinuous fashion. The history of art, like the history of science, appears as a series of sudden leaps and ruptures between one generally accepted way of thinking, or paradigm, and another, such as the transition from Renaissance science to early modern science, or from romanticism to modernism. In this perspective, there is no slow process of cumulative development of the truth of art, but only a series of dramatic substitutions of one paradigmatic 'code' of representation (a system of artistic techniques, themes and procedures) for another. The choice made between two contrasting paradigms, whether in art or in science, cannot be attributed exclusively either, on the one hand, to external forces, such as invasions, economic upheavals, or political revolutions, or, on the other hand, to the universal recognition that a given paradigm, such as Newtonian physics or expressionism, offers us 'better' scientific or artistic truths. Kuhn's key discovery is that this choice is instead ultimately made on the basis of the *persuasive* power, and hence the rhetorical efficacy, of a given paradigm: a paradigm imposes itself on a given society or social group through its powers of conviction rather than of scientific demonstration. When seen as a series of paradigm shifts, then, both the history of science and the history of art display the same essentially rhetorical traits. This in turn, Vattimo infers, can only mean that there is an 'aesthetic model of historical transformation' underlying our understanding of the past *as a whole*, for rhetoric has since classical antiquity been considered an 'art' (the 'art of persuasion') rather than a 'science'.[20] Thus it is that 'the aesthetic as a domain of experience and as a dimension of existence . . . assumes exemplary value as a model for thinking about historicity in general' (p. 95).

The connection between the aesthetic and the historical offers a valuable clue to understanding post-modernity precisely because the aesthetic/rhetorical model of historicity diverges radically from the modern Western view of history as a process of cumulative development or progress. Modernity is the era of faith in progress, which is equivalent to faith in the value of the new (since what is new is granted greater value than what is not new). This faith is, as Vattimo first noted in his introduction, the result of the secularization of the Judeo–Christian vision of history; when history is fully secularized, the end-point of the teleological movement of history is no longer any kind of 'paradise', but rather the new – or, in other words, permanent progress – itself. Vattimo observes in this regard that 'modernity is that era in which being modern becomes a value, or rather, it becomes *the* fundamental value to which all other values refer' (p. 100). This defining trait of modernity, however, can only become apparent to us when we are already at a distance from modernity ('the definition of modernity as the era in which being modern is the base-value is not a definition which modernity could give of itself'

xxxvi   *Translator's Introduction*

(p. 103)). Our very awareness of the philosophical meaning of modernity would seem to suggest that we have gone beyond it, and are able now to look back on modernity with a certain degree of detachment. What is it, though, that has distanced contemporary thought from modernity, and pushed it towards the post-modern era? Not surprisingly, what is responsible for this change is precisely the dissolution of progress and of the value of the new, and in Vattimo's view this is a key component of the meaning of the post-modern. The philosophy of post-modernity seeks to shake off the 'logic of overcoming, development and innovation' that has been elaborated and sustained by modernity, although the meaning of this effort is not altogether clear, for it leaves us uncertain as to what the shape of history or even the nature of time itself would be without such a familiar and reassuring logic. Nevertheless, the aesthetic model of a discontinuous historicity outlined above suggests that there are indeed possible ways of experiencing history and time other than those supplied by modernity. The domain of the arts, in particular, has seen an intensive search in our century for a means by which to break free of linearity in representing temporal and historical processes (Vattimo notes that Proust, Musil and Joyce all focus their work on the problem of time itself). And what are now called 'post-modern' architecture and fine art display, although in different ways, the same basic tendency to dissolve and do away with the value of the new (one example is the Italian architect Aldo Rossi's 'Theatre of Memory' in Venice, a 'post-modern' reconstruction of Giulio Camillo's lost Renaissance building of the same name). The arts thus correspond ' . . . to Heidegger's attempt to prepare a post-metaphysical kind of thought which would stand not in a relation to metaphysics of *Überwindung*, but rather of *Verwindung*' (p. 31), and represent, together with philosophical nihilism, the most advanced phase of post-modernity to appear in Western culture thus far. With this last point Vattimo draws to a close his lengthy discussion of aesthetics in post-modernity, making a major claim for the art-world as a domain which has advanced further beyond metaphysics towards the experience of truth than have science and technology. It is only fitting, then, that he should turn in the concluding section of his book to the task of an apology for aesthetic consciousness itself.

The final section of this volume, entitled *The End of Modernity*, begins with an essay on 'Hermeneutics and Nihilism' which was first presented as a talk at Yale University in early 1981. Here Vattimo outlines, in the form of an apology for aesthetic consciousness, the profound identity of these two branches of contemporary philosophy. Hermeneutics (literally, 'the science of interpretation') attempts to discover – or, better still, recover – the truth of a text or a work of art through an act of interpretation. For this reason, hermeneutic theory is usually oriented towards the reconstruction of meaning in discourse, and, more broadly still, towards the question of how understanding between human beings – that is, between writers or artists and their audience – can occur. On the other hand, aesthetic consciousness, which Kant first defined as the 'awareness of beauty', could be considered 'the aesthetic *attitude* to a work of art', in which we consider and judge the work in light of our conception of art itself (as the 'beautiful', the 'true', etc.).[21] This awareness of the status of the work of art as an aesthetic object or product distinguishes the modern approach to art from the basically religious one of the Middle Ages and Renaissance, which appreciated the work of art primarily in terms of its representation of the divine. Gadamer, in the first section of his 1960 *magnum opus*, *Truth and Method*, criticizes aesthetic consciousness as overly 'abstract' – or, to put it another way, idealistic – and insufficiently concerned with the *historical* nature of our experience of the work of art. For Gadamer, as Vattimo notes, the work of art is principally 'a historical event, and our encounter with it is also a historical event in that in it we are changed' (p. 124) by our efforts to interpret it and to recover its truth. Both the work of art and its interpreters therefore belong, in Gadamer's perspective, to the same continuous cultural/historical tradition, a view that leads him to place great emphasis in his theory of hermeneutics on the significance of the 'classic' work of art. Vattimo, who instead considers aesthetic consciousness and hermeneutics to be closely allied, objects to Gadamer's critique on the grounds that any attempt to link hermeneutics with a historicizing humanism of this sort ignores the fundamentally nihilistic implications of Heidegger's philosophy. Aesthetic consciousness is for Vattimo 'an experience of truth precisely insofar as this experience is substantially nihilistic' (p. 114) rather than historical in nature (and here let us recall the fundamental connection between art and truth proposed in the previous section on *The Truth of Art*). Thus his apology for aesthetic consciousness, and for the experience of truth it offers today, takes the form of an exploration of the link between hermeneutics as a 'science of interpretation' and nihilism as a philosophy of difference and as the will to interpret the world.

Vattimo's argument in chapter 7 is often quite technical, and resists any brief paraphrase because of its use of many complex Heideggerean terms and concepts. The gist of his discussion concerns Heidegger's hermeneutic ontology, whose basis is a profound ' . . . connection between Being and language'. How can the identification of Being with language, he asks, be defined as nihilistic in nature? We have already seen that Being occurs in the post-metaphysical era only as a memory, or, in other words, through an act of what Heidegger calls *Andenken*. This term signifies a 'keeping in mind' of the tradition of Western philosophy and culture, like Heidegger's project of rereading and reinterpreting the great works of Western philosophy and poetry from Parmenides to Rilke. Vattimo remarks that, in the perspective of hermeneutic ontology, 'recollection as a retracing of the decisive moments of the history of metaphysics is . . . the *definitive* form of the thought of being that we are to carry out' (p. 119). The philosophy of post-modernity returns to the tradition in order to 'recall' the original metaphysical Being, but because the act of *Andenken* summons only the memory of a strong Being that has now vanished, or that now returns only as another text in the tradition, we may say that the Being which occurs as a memory is a profoundly weakened and depleted Being. Metaphysical Being can only be remembered as something which no longer is, and this is the sole conceivable way of thinking or speaking about Being after the end of metaphysics. To put it another way, 'Being can never really be thought of as a presence, and the thought that does not forget it is only that which remembers it or, in other words, always already thinks of Being as absent, vanished, or gone away' (p. 119) because the metaphysical categories which supported the claims of Being to presence and cogency have themselves begun to be dissolved by the philosophy of nihilism. Thus recollection (*Andenken*) is inseparable from the philosophy of nihilism, because for both one and the other there is now virtually nothing left of Being as such.

Being survives in the form of the messages and traces transmitted to the contemporary world from the tradition of philosophy and art: Being today *is* language, or rather, as Gadamer puts it, 'the Being that can be understood is language'. This meaning of Being as what is handed down through 'linguistic messages from one generation to another', as a series of texts and traces from the tradition that must always be interpreted once again, is in Vattimo's view 'the opposite of the metaphysical conception of Being as stability'. Post-metaphysical Being is inseparably linked to the cycle of the generations and the passage from birth to death; the meaning of the messages (that is, the texts of the tradition) that constitute Being are always altered anew in the act of *Andenken*, and in the new interpretations formulated by each successive generation. Thus the weakness of Being at the end of modernity is defined by the fact that the meaning of Being for a given generation is not eternal, but perishes with the disappearance of that generation from the historical scene. Hermeneutics and nihilism converge precisely because both are concerned with a Being that ' . . . tends to identify itself with nothingness, with the fleeting traits of an existence

enclosed between the boundaries of birth and death' (p. 121).
This ground of convergence between hermeneutics and
nihilism, in turn, leads back at last to the question of aesthetic
consciousness with which the essay began. For the experience
of the truth of art, Vattimo contends, is a deeply discontinuous
one, in spite of Gadamer's claim that great contemporary art is
historically continuous with the tradition. The experience of
the truth of art is a *momentary* experience which arises, like
Being itself in the post-metaphysical era, as an interpretation
and an event rather than as a stable structure of meaning. In
its eventual nature the work of art openly displays its own
mortality; for the very fact that it is always open to further
interpretation (that is, that its meaning is not forever fixed)
means that it too, like its audience, is bound to the laws of
temporality, and therefore takes 'its being subject to the action
of time – like, for instance, the patina on a painting, or the
growing corpus of interpretations . . . – as a positively
constitutive aspect of its meaning' (p. 126). In this manner the
work of art reveals the same lack of foundation – the same
mortal and eventual nature – that nihilism has shown to be
destined to belong to Being in the post-metaphysical era. In
the permanent instability of the meaning of the work of art
'there is an element of ungrounding which is inseparable from
founding itself', Vattimo notes, and this is what gives value to
aesthetic consciousness in Western culture today. Since the
work of art is subject to the disruptive effects of the passage of
time, 'in the form of birth, aging, and death', and expresses no
lasting, permanent knowledge, or even a wisdom based on
historical continuity with the tradition, aesthetic consciousness
offers us a weak experience of truth that can only be called
nihilistic, and that serves as a model for all areas of post-
modern thought.

  Chapter 8, entitled 'Truth and Rhetoric in Hermeneutic
Ontology', expands upon the link between language and truth
in hermeneutic ontology. Vattimo here considers this link as it
appears in the work of Gadamer, for whom language is always
characterized in *ethical* rather than in purely linguistic or

semiotic terms (for instance, the 'signifier/signified' relation). The basis of Gadamer's theory of the ethical nature of language is that all language is 'a locus of total mediation of every experience of the world and every occurrence of Being' (p. 131). This means that no experience, and no occurrence of Being, can ever be isolated from language; each and every experience is, like Being today, essentially linguistic. Vattimo observes, however, that this ' . . . is not so much, or not principally, a matter of showing that every experience of the world is made possible for the individual by the possession of language' (p. 132). Rather, the real importance of language as a mediator of humanity's experience of the world lies in its *centrality* for all those who speak it. Language unifies social life by uniting all speakers within its web of words, and so expresses the collective ethos, or character, of a given society. It is 'this shared world that is articulated in language', and that reveals the specific ethos of a given social order, which serves as the means of total mediation of our experience, for all speakers of a language always refer to it in addressing each other. The point of Gadamer's argument is that this central locus of social life also offers an experience of the true, precisely because the true is 'an experience of our belonging . . . to that horizon of collective consciousness that is represented by language itself and the tradition that is continued by it' (p. 135). Truth, when defined in this way, can only be transmitted rhetorically. Tradition, and the collective ethos, do not demonstrate their validity in a scientific or logical manner; they seek instead to persuade us of the common sense and the truth of their contents. One does not belong to, or subscribe to, a given tradition, such as the Western or Eastern one, on the basis of its scientifically demonstrated superiority, but rather on the basis of belief. This essentially persuasive quality of tradition and collective consciousness can only be understood in rhetorical terms. When language is understood in the light of what has been said above, the public and rhetorical nature of truth – as an experience of belonging to a language and a collective tradition –

diverges from the metaphysical understanding of truth as either an 'interior vision' of the thinking subject or as the product of logical and rational procedures. (Vattimo points out in this regard that Gadamer's argument implicitly displaces all scientific discourse into the realm of rhetoric as well; or rather, it represents 'a radicalization of the essentially rhetorical nature of science itself'.) Such a notion of truth is free of any 'special emphasis on consciousness', and thus takes its distance from the metaphysical subject who discovers truth through the use of reason. In assigning to truth a public and rhetorical (that is, non-logical) origin which is 'outside' the individual mind and the rational procedures of metaphysical thought, Gadamer's analysis weakens one of the fundamental categories of modern metaphysics.

But how does any of this differ, Vattimo wonders, from 'an apology for what already exists'? Does not Gadamer, in privileging the tradition and the collective ethos as the primary locus of the experience of truth today, also privilege the social, political, and cultural status quo? For his hermeneutic theory of the rhetorical nature of truth as 'an experience of our belonging . . . to that horizon of collective consciousness that is represented by language itself and the tradition that is continued by it' (p. 135) does not allow for criticism of this tradition, only for a constant reconstruction and reconstitution of it. The deeply conservative implications of this, insofar as his theory upholds the value of a restored, revitalized tradition as the basis for contemporary life, make Gadamer's notion of truth difficult to accept. Objecting that for Gadamer collective consciousness 'seems . . . to be [already] fundamentally in order', and that in his work the contemporary world stands in 'a relation of fundamental continuity' with the tradition, Vattimo proposes a return to Heidegger's thought in order to establish a more critical philosophical stance towards 'what already exists'. Heidegger, as we have already seen, assumes a relation of fundamental discontinuity between contemporary thought and the tradition, and condemns science and technology in no uncertain terms for their links with metaphysics.

For this reason Vattimo takes up once again Heidegger's meditations on poetry and art as the most advanced form of philosophical reflection on the end of modernity. Because works of art are the densest known 'zones' of language for Heidegger, where the event of Being is most recognizable because its weakness is so openly displayed, 'these zones . . . also become the points of greatest strength for a critique' of metaphysics and technology. By returning to Heidegger's definition of the experience of the truth of art as a fundamentally nihilistic and anti-humanistic experience (cf. chapters 1 and 2), Vattimo insists, 'we may be able to lead hermeneutics beyond a simple acceptance of collective consciousness and beyond the risk of being reduced to an apology for what already exists' (p. 142). In other words, the effort to break with the metaphysical tradition that post-modernity represents – namely the *Verwindung* of metaphysics – must be foregrounded in hermeneutic ontology; in the era of nihilism the relation with the tradition can no longer be conceived in terms of a fundamental or unproblematic continuity, but rather in terms of a search for a radical discontinuity. Gadamer's valuable insight into the ethical nature of language needs to be qualified by what is implicit in the nihilistic experience of the work of art, namely the weakening of 'what already exists' in the form of the founding categories of metaphysics and the scientific–technological world.

In chapter 9, entitled 'Hermeneutics and Anthropology', the contemporary experience of anthropologists and ethnologists in encountering primitive cultures is interpreted as another possible symptom of the weakness of Being for post-modernity. Vattimo's reflections here on anthropology and ethnology have their source in an observation in the final chapter of Richard Rorty's *Philosophy and the Mirror of Nature* (1979): ' . . . cultural anthropology (in a large sense which includes intellectual history) is all we need.'[22] Rorty takes the term 'cultural anthropology' from the work of Jürgen Habermas, but uses it to argue that philosophy today has to free itself 'from the notion that philosophy must center around the discovery of a permanent framework for inquiry'.[23] In other words, he suggests, contemporary philosophy ought to become a kind of cultural anthropology or a cultural hermeneutics whose framework shifts according to the particular conditions of the inquiry being undertaken; it ought to be a kind of flexible 'conversation' between minds, texts, or cultures that differ from one another, a conversation which is always contingent on a given set of circumstances and always open to change, rather than a search for the absolute and immutable nature of truth, objectivity, and reason (which is the task of metaphysics).[24] Rorty is the preeminent American philosopher to have taken up the issues of contemporary Continental thought; over the past decade he has engaged Vattimo, Derrida, and many others in debates on hermeneutics, deconstruction and so on.[25] His theory of philosophy as a kind of hermeneutics – as an ongoing 'conversation' between different points of view – appears considerably more congenial to Vattimo's argument in *The End of Modernity* than, say, the textualism of Derrida or the rationalism of Habermas. However, Rorty's assertion that 'cultural anthropology . . . is all we need' implies that philosophy could somehow be dissolved into cultural anthropology (that is, 'the science of humanity'), and this provokes a critical response from Vattimo. While agreeing with Rorty that cultural anthropology is particularly important today because of its hermeneutical vocation for interpreting cultures that are *other*, Vattimo objects that to define anthropology and hermeneutics exclusively in this fashion – as a discourse seeking an understanding of cultures, texts, etc. which are other, and therefore alien to us – assumes the *alterity* of a given culture as the basic precondition for an analysis of it. For Rorty, the 'conversational' function of hermeneutics/anthropology is to assimilate discourses that are not (yet) commensurate with – and must therefore be presupposed to stand in a relation of alterity – to one another. For Vattimo, though, this assessment needs to be revised in the face of contemporary events. In particular, the notion of 'alterity' at the basis of cultural anthropology/cultural hermeneutics does not sufficiently take into account the current international domination of Western science and technology. Heidegger pointed out over thirty years ago that 'the very possibility of such a dialogue with cultures that are truly other is . . . menaced by the "complete Europeanization of earth and of humanity'' (p. 151); and the world-wide process of 'Europeanization' has accelerated dramatically since then. It is impossible, Vattimo argues, for philosophy to ignore the evidence of contemporary events, which reveals that cultural differences are being rapidly and definitively undermined by the spread of the electronic 'global village' described by McCluhan, and by the successes of imperialistic capitalism, which acts like an invisible solvent on local traditions and indigenous social formations. With this situation the authentic 'alterity' of primitive cultures becomes a less and less viable notion for post-modern thought.

The process of Westernization of the planet therefore signals for Vattimo more than merely the disappearance of cultures that are radically other from our own, or even the fact that anthropology, in its searching out and conversing with cultures that are other, now appears as but 'an internal aspect of the general process of Westernization and homologation' of the earth. Vattimo contends that the global condition of cultural contamination and Westernization in the so-called primitive societies existing at the margins of the contemporary industrialized world represents a vast 'construction site' of traces and residues, and ought not to be viewed simplistically (and nostalgically) as the tragic loss of an archaic authenticity – as if primitive cultures were somehow closer to the original 'essence' of humanity than contemporary Western culture. It is in this situation of generalized cultural contamination, perhaps best exemplified by the South Seas cargo cult, that 'the hermeneutic – but also anthropological – illusion of encountering the other . . . finds itself faced with a mixed reality in which alterity is entirely exhausted' (p. 159). The historical reality of Westernization thus calls into question the established definition of both anthropology and hermeneutics as the locus of 'a possible dialogue or interplay between different cultures' or of 'an authentic encounter with the other'. This in turn has profound implications for the philosophy of post-modernity. For the disappearance of alterity across the face of the planet indicates that the metaphysical categories of Being upon which both traditional anthropology and hermeneutics depend (such as the dialogue with otherness) are themselves well on the way towards dissolution. In the era of the planetary domination of science and technology, only an oscillating, impoverished, marginal Being remains, just as the primitive 'other' today is found in a form that is always already at the margins of (and therefore not wholly alien to) Western culture, but that is also a 'construction site' of surviving traces of the archaic past. Vattimo infers from this that neither cultural anthropology nor hermeneutics can be described, as was formerly the case, as a dialogue with otherness that results in a new unity and hence a 'strong' truth. By the same token, however, 'in the process of homologation and contamination, the texts belonging to our [Western] tradition, which have always served as the measure of our humanity (that is, the 'classics' in the literal sense of the term), progressively lose their cogency as models and become part of the [same] vast construction site of traces and residues' as well (p. 160). The contemporary world is one single immense 'construction site' of traces wherever we look, and no qualitative distinction can be drawn between the 'classics' of Western culture and the lingering hybrid forms of archaic culture. Both represent what remains of a tradition of thought that has been, but is now lost (in the case of the former, metaphysics; in the case of the latter, myth). When seen in this light, the destiny of the West itself, Vattimo contends, appears as an experience of the decline of being in the form of a generalized cultural contamination in a world which no longer offers a sharp split between subject and object, sameness and otherness, or fiction and truth. Across the planet, then, 'the disappearance of alterity occurs not as a part of a dreamed-for total organization of the world, but rather as a condition of widespread contamination' (p. 159) in which all cultures, Western or not, tend to become marginal and hybrid. In the last analysis, this summons us once again to an active nihilism, in terms of which the weakening of Being described above appears as the very meaning of the process of history itself in our century.[26]

The concluding chapter, 'Nihilism and the Post-Modern in Philosophy', is the most recent of the essays in *The End of Modernity*, dating from 1984–5. Vattimo here reviews, and offers fresh insights into, the philosophy of post-modernity he has elaborated in the book as a whole. He returns once again to the works of Nietzsche and Heidegger as the fundamental point of departure for any attempt to think about post-modernity in a rigorously philosophical fashion. In particular, his inquiry centres upon the importance of Heidegger's concept of *Verwindung* for the question of the post-modern in philosophy. How is it that we may now say that we are at a later point than modernity, or that modernity is now coming to an end, while having at the same time rejected the possibility of a critical overcoming and leaving behind of modernity? Vattimo's answer to this question is that only by taking up and reflecting on the notion of *Verwindung* can the peculiar critical relationship between post-modernity and modernity possibly be given philosophical rigour. We have already seen that the notion of *Verwindung* contains the essence of the post-modern in philosophy, and is indeed 'the sole possible form of metaphysical thought' available today because it is, paradoxically, opposed to metaphysics. Perhaps, however, it would be more accurate to say instead that the notion of *Verwindung* is the sole *legitimate* form of metaphysical thought that survives today, but only because it weakens and drains metaphysics, acknowledging that the latter can only arise today as what has, along with modernity itself, reached its end and become virtually exhausted.

Vattimo locates the beginning of philosophical post-modernity in the work of Nietzsche, specifically in the years between the writing of the second of the *Untimely Meditations* ('On the

Uses and Disadvantages of History for Life' (1874)) and the completion of *The Gay Science* (1882).[27] In a detailed discussion of these and other texts of the same period, he shows how Nietzsche first attempts to formulate an alternative to the notion of a critical overcoming of the past through progress and to initiate 'a true dissolution of modernity'. In Nietzsche's 1874 essay he 'already very clearly sees that overcoming is a typically modern category, and therefore will not enable us to use it as a way out of modernity'; but it is only in later works such as *Human All Too Human* (1878) that he discovers that the way out of this impasse is 'to dissolve modernity through a radicalization of its own innate tendencies'. Truth, when its claims are carefully analyzed in their own terms, reveals itself to be 'a value which dissolves into itself', or, in other words, no more and no less than a belief without foundation. The dissolution of truth into value is a key component of what Nietzsche calls his 'philosophy of morning', and his discovery of it is the moment of emergence of philosophical post-modernity. It is worth repeating here that the post-modern cannot be confined to a specific historical era *after* the end of modernity; it is rather an experience of the end of metaphysics and the end of history which accompanies the most advanced phases of modernity itself, up to and inlcuding the end of modernity. Nietzsche conceives 'the task of thought in the epoch where both the foundation and the idea of truth have been dissolved', which is the epoch of the experience of the end of metaphysics, to be that of *deconstruction* rather than *critique*. Speaking in very general terms, the practitioner of critique, which Vattimo often refers to as 'critical overcoming', seeks to discover, unmask, and liquidate philosophical error. Yet Nietzsche argues that error may be exposed and demystified as something fundamentally false only in the name of a truth that is understood as more 'authentic' and more 'legitimate' than error. This is the primary mode of philosophical modernity, and one that is still pervasive in Western thought today (for instance, in the 'critique of ideology' or dialectical materialism). Nietzsche's 'deconstructive intent' is to show, on the contrary, that since the death of God means there is no longer any absolute foundation for thought (what Plato calls the *ontos on*) that could be used to contradict the non-true and to guarantee the discovery of the true, then a critical overcoming of error is no longer thinkable. Consequently, thought is left with the task of dissolving the strong categories of modernity and metaphysics from *within*, by uncovering the errors embedded in every assertion of truth. Unlike critique, deconstruction cannot call on some other, supposedly superior form of truth to take the place of what has been dissolved, for this would be to remain in the mode of critical overcoming and thus in the mode of modernity itself. Nietzsche's deconstruction can only seek to rediscover, over and over again, that error constitutes the very 'essence' of all truth, all reality, and all of the metaphysical thought of modernity; with the invention of deconstruction the experience of post-modernity is thus first made possible in Western culture.

Despite the advent of the era of nihilism announced by Nietzsche, however, there is no need to be resigned to a world of unreality and to the impossibility of knowledge. Vattimo takes up once again the by now familiar concept of *Verwindung*, which he sees as already present in embryonic form in Nietzsche's work, in order to reiterate this point. The term *Verwindung* ' . . . defines Heidegger's basic position and understanding of the task of thought at the moment in which we find ourselves today, namely at the end of philosophy in the form of metaphysics' (p. 173), and Heidegger's understanding of the task of philosophy today can be traced back to Nietzsche's initial insights into the end of metaphysics and modernity. What makes *Verwindung* such a crucial concept for any philosophical nihilism that is not resigned to a world of illusion and the paralysis of all understanding is precisely its denial of the possibility of a complete and total freedom from the past that nevertheless, as Marx once said, 'weighs like a nightmare on the brain of the living'. If post-modernity is a *Verwindung* of modernity, then we may say that post-

modernity is a *repetition* of modernity which yet does not
accept modernity as it is or fully acknowledge its legitimacy.
The philosophy of post-modernity is resigned to the impossi-
bility of breaking with the philosophy of modernity once and
for all, but at the same time it deconstructs or destructures the
metaphysical categories belonging to that philosophy. It is a
repetition with an ironic difference, then, for although post-
modernity inevitably prolongs the categories of modernity and
must resign itself to them, it also tries to twist them in another
direction and to turn them against themselves. Metaphysics
cannot simply be shed like a tattered, worn-out garment, or
left behind like a doctrine in which we no longer believe; post-
modern thought acknowledges this, and does not pretend to
represent the revolutionary overthrow or reversal of the
heritage of modern thought. The *Verwindung* of modernity is a
fundamentally ironic gesture that rejects any heroic or
romantic posture vis-à-vis the Western tradition. The decline
of modernity, however, also opens up the opportunity for a
new, – but weakly new – beginning for thought, and this
is what permits us to consider philosophical nihilism a
responsible, rather than a despairing, response to the crisis
of the contemporary world.

The function of *Verwindung* closely resembles that of
recollection, or *Andenken*; indeed, these two terms together
define for Vattimo the nature of hermeneutic ontology as the
fundamental post-modern mode of philosophizing. Being
occurs today 'as that from which we have always already taken
our leave'. For the post-metaphysical philosophy of post-
modernity, Being is but a fading signal of what has been
(*gewesen*), and can never be grasped 'as an object which is
given before us' in the same way that the rational subject
perceives and apprehends an object. It comes to us as a
message from the tradition, an overture from the past to be
interpeted ever anew. This is turn means that 'the experience
of Being is always [both] an *Andenken* and a *Verwindung*,
inasmuch as it is an experience of the reception of, and
response to, these transmissions' and signals that come

flickering across the ruins of time (p. 176). Vattimo employs the Latin term *pietas* ('piety') to define the post-modern attitude toward this experience of Being as an ever-changing inter-pretation of tradition. *Pietas* describes a dutifully respectful approach to the past and to everything that is transmitted to us from the past, in which ontology (or the 'science' of Being) effectively becomes hermeneutics (or the 'science' of inter-pretation). The past may well be, as Nietzsche's deconstruction shows, no more than the 'history of errors', but we are summoned to traverse that past – that is, to recollect and interpret it – over and over again by the voices that call out from it, for this history of errors is none other than Being itself. Vattimo repeatedly reminds his readers that in the experience of the post-modern there is almost nothing left of Being as such; there is only a welter of fragmentary messages and enigmatic traces of what no longer exists – traces that together constitute the weakness of contemporary Being. In approaching the contemporary experience of Being with an attitude of *pietas*, we seek to recollect and interpret – and therefore always also distort – what is handed down from the tradition, for this is the way to begin thinking without using the customary categories of metaphysical thought (such as the 'permanence' of Being and the 'self-evident nature' of truth).

It would be tempting to conclude that the hidden agenda of Vattimo's philosophy of post-modernity is to eliminate the possibility of radical or revolutionary social, political or cultural change, since his philosophy insists upon the impossi-bility of overcoming and calls into question the value of the new. The call for an ironic return to the tradition would seem to lead thought towards a profound immobility, fixated only on what has already occurred. Yet this is not the case, as the final few paragraphs of chapter 10 indicate. Here it is argued that the experience of Being as an experience of the reception of, and response to, messages from the past must also serve as the occasion to interpret the 'messages' of science and technology, which are the 'languages that tend to dominate

our society' today. How does 'weak thought' relate our
experience of the tradition of Western art and philosophy to
our experience of the contemporary technological world?
Vattimo's answer to this question wholly depends upon
Heidegger's connection of science and technology to the
Western tradition of rational metaphysical thought. In the
Heideggerean perspective, as we have seen, science and technology, which have so rapidly and profoundly transformed the
face of the planet, have also realized one of the deepest desires
of Western metaphysics, namely the rational domination of a
world of objects. The era of the scientific and technological
domination of the earth therefore represents the most advanced
phase of the metaphysical tradition; Vattimo (and Heidegger
before him) would in this way dissolve the shallow and
misleading opposition between 'science' and 'culture', and
identify the global triumph of science and technology as the
logical outcome of the tradition of rational metaphysical
thought. What does it mean, though, to distort the languages
of science and technology today through a *Verwindung* of
them? The answer is not altogether clear at present, Vattimo
admits, and it would be reasonable to expect that in his future
work he will attempt to respond to this question more
satisfactorily. What is already clear, however, is that hermeneutics is not possessed of an exclusively humanistic orientation,
and is not simply directed toward the Western tradition of art
and philosophy. The philosophy of post-modernity, or hermeneutic ontology, has to reconnect science and technology to
the Western tradition through a *contamination* of the languages
of science and technology. Gadamer has argued that science
and technology should be placed 'under the control of the
moral imperatives related to our cultural heritage' in order to
keep them from growing more and more alien to that heritage,
but Vattimo objects that this would run the risk of canonizing
the tradition and its supposed coherence and stability.
Instead, he states, 'what philosophy, in its present form, can
do is perhaps only to propose a "rhetorically persuasive" view
of the world, which includes in itself traces, residues, or

isolated elements of scientific knowledge' By renouncing any claim to produce a logical and verifiable 'view of the world', post-modern philosophy may freely reflect upon the different dimensions of contemporary knowledge, including science and technology, and may exploit all of these dimensions in forming a non-scientific, non-metaphysical (that is, 'rhetorically persuasive') theory of the *unity* of this knowledge. The practice of 'weak thought' would consist in contaminating the rational languages of science and technology by insisting on their connection to, and unity with, the other languages of contemporary culture (such as those of the arts and the mass media). It would then be possible to see the entire field of post-modern discourse in an 'oscillating setting, which can be imagined as the world of a reality that has been made "lighter" for us because it is less sharply split between truth, on the one hand, and fiction, information, and images on the other.'[28] This description of the 'contaminating' function of the philosophy of post-modernity and the unity of discourse to which it aspires is, admittedly, rather abstract, but Vattimo offers no concrete example of how the messages of science and technology could be effectively contaminated and weakened. It would therefore be useless to speculate further on the matter at this time, except to say that the purpose of such a contamination is not, as might wrongly be supposed, solely to aestheticize the languages of science and technology. Rather, the philosophy of post-modernity seeks to collapse the difference between technological and aesthetic culture, and, together with it, the fundamental difference between rationalism and irrationalism that has long sustained what we now call 'modernity'.

Writing in 1979, Rorty comments that 'I do not know whether we are in fact at the end of an era. This will depend, I suspect, on whether Dewey, Wittgenstein, and Heidegger are taken to heart.'[29] *The End of Modernity* takes Heidegger's work very much to heart, and dares to suggest that the end of modernity is close at hand. While other contemporary philosophers (such as Lyotard and Habermas) have explored in depth the question of post-modernity prior to Vattimo, his originality lies in his insistence on a return to ontology and the question of Being as the key to understanding the end of modernity. Although his theory as a whole remains within the orbit of Nietzsche's and Heidegger's influence, Vattimo's synthesis of nihilism, hermeneutics, ontology and the problematic of post-modernity is unlike anything else in the panorama of contemporary philosophy. It is worth insisting here that his work cannot be dismissed as merely eclectic or derivative, despite its assimilation of a number of different conceptual 'sets' taken from other thinkers. 'Weak thought' may be best understood as a *style* of thought rather than as a fully developed and self-consistent philosophical system.[30] Vattimo is not interested in producing a systematic theory of post-modernity, for that would mean reaffirming, ironically and inevitably, the 'modern' notion of systematic reason. Nor is he particularly interested in proving his own originality as a thinker. In an era where the 'new' has lost its value, the notion of philosophical originality itself can no longer be of overriding concern to philosophers. Rather, in combining many familiar elements of twentieth-century thought and twisting them in a different direction, Vattimo formulates a consistently nihilistic approach to the question of Being as it emerges in a number of different fields of contemporary discourse. Yet the disappearance of philosophical systematicity, and the emergence of the philosophical style of *Verwindung*, does not signal the death of philosophy itself. Even if twentieth-century post-metaphysical, post-modern philosophy seems no more than 'a state of awkward transitional backing and filling (as sixteenth-century philosophy now seems to us)', as Rorty suggests, 'there will still be something called "philosophy" on the other side of the transition.'[31]

Western thought today is immersed in the twilight of a world where both Being and illusion are in decline, but have not yet disappeared altogether. 'Weak thought' proposes that we travel along an itinerary that leads away from the history of

metaphysics as the history of Being, although not toward any
fixed point of arrival: it indicates a direction rather than a
destination. Vattimo refers to this itinerary, as we have seen,
as an 'ontology of decline'. The West is indeed the *Abendland*,
Nietzsche's 'evening land'; but this evening is not that of a
decadent, failing Western culture and society. The West today
is instead the site of the decline – the twilight or the evening
(Vattimo freely intermixes the terms *declino* and *tramonto*) – of
metaphysical Being and of the rational thought that accompanies it from classical Greece to the end of modernity. This
announcement of the 'decline' and 'twilight' of the metaphysical episode ought not to be confused with the apocalyptic
overtones of a work such as Oswald Spengler's *The Decline of
the West*. Vattimo instead depicts the 'decline' of Being (and,
together with it, of truth, the Platonic *ontos on*, and the *logos*)
as an opportunity for a philosophical reconstruction, rather
than as a symptom and declaration of decadence, even though
contemporary thought can no longer claim to possess a
privileged position or genuinely critical function in regard to
political and social praxis.[32] This reconstruction takes the
form of an 'accomplished' nihilism, namely a philosophy
which recognizes that, while the highest values are bankrupt
and God has departed from the scene, we must constantly guard
against any metaphysical attempt to discover another foundation to take his place. For Vattimo, the truly 'accomplished'
nihilist ('*il nichilista compiuto*') is the one who recognizes that
there are no longer any foundations available for thought, but
who at the same time ackowledges that neither can anything
be made foundational through an act of will, not even the will
to power itself.[33] Habermas denounces the 'homelessness'
of nihilism in this regard, but this would seem to miss the
point altogether.[34] What makes this version of nihilism
'accomplished' is that it cannot be reduced to a mere apology
for what already exists, as nihilism in general is so often
accused of being. On the contrary, an accomplished nihilism
' . . . does not just duplicate what already exists, but claims to
be able to criticize it' as well (p. 13), in order to lay the

groundwork for a fully *secular* philosophy, one that reaches beyond the realm of metaphysics and its deluded dreams of reason. The philosophy of nihilism tries to hold open the door to the future that must follow the long episode in Western thought extending from classical antiquity to present-day technological civilization. The value of Vattimo's nihilism consists precisely in this overture toward a possible secular philosophy and culture for the West, where at last all forms of foundation, from theology to dialectics, would definitively be cast aside, even if no one can now say exactly when or in what guise that philosophy and that culture will finally appear.

NOTES

1 See, for instance, Charles Jencks, *What is Post-Modernism?* (London: Academy Editions; New York: St. Martin's Press, 1986); Hal Foster, Ed., *The Anti-Aesthetic: Essays on Postmodern Culture* (Port Townsend, WA.: Bay Press, 1983); Jean-François Lyotard, *The Postmodern Condition: A Report on Knowledge*, trans. Geoff Bennington and Brian Massumi (Minneapolis: University of Minnesota Press, 1984); Jonathan Arac, ed., *Postmodernism and Politics* (Minneapolis: University of Minnesota Press, 1986); and Jürgen Habermas, *The Philosophical Discourse of Modernity*, trans. Frederick Lawrence (Cambridge: MIT Press, 1987).

2 Besides *La fine della modernità*, Vattimo has published the following books in Italy: *Il concetto di fare in Aristotele* (1961); *Essere, storia, e linguaggio in Heidegger* (1963); *Poesia e ontologia* (1967); *Schleiermacher, filosofo dell'interpretazione* (1968); *Introduzione a Heidegger* (1971); *Il soggetto e la maschera* (1974); *Le avventure della differenza* (1980); *Al di là del soggetto: Nietzsche, Heidegger, e l'ermeneutica* (1981); *Introduzione a Nietzsche* (1985). He has also translated Hans-Georg Gadamer's *Wahrheit und Methode* into Italian (*Verità e metodo*, 1972). In addition, he has edited or co-edited many other books, and has produced a prodigious number of research articles.

3 See, for instance, the rubric 'Debole/forte' which appeared in *Alfabeta* in 1984 and 1985 (nos 60, 62–70).

4 The author has made a number of minor revisions to the original Italian text on the occasion of its publication in English. The only truly major alteration, however, is a revised concluding section to chapter 10.

5 Cf. Pier Aldo Rovatti and Gianni Vattimo, 'Premessa', in *Il pensiero debole*, ed G. Vattimo and P. A. Rovatti (Milan: Feltrinelli, 1983). p. 8.

6 Thomas McCarthy notes, in his introduction to Habermas's *The Philosophical Discourse of Modernity*, p. vii, that 'for French post-structuralism . . . it is above all Nietzsche and Heidegger who furnish the inspiration and set the agenda.'

7 Habermas's work vigorously defends the values of modernity and rationality, and thus is diametrically opposed to Vattimo's (which rejects outright any such defence); it is chiefly for this reason that Habermas is barely mentioned in *The End of Modernity*. Cf. Martin Jay, in an unpublished paper on 'Habermas and Postmodernism', who notes that no one involved in the debate over post-modernism ' . . . has been as forthright and unflinching a defender of the still uncompleted project of modernity as Jürgen Habermas'.

8 Gianni Vattimo, 'Le deboli certezze', *Alfabeta* 67 (Dec. 1984), p. 8.

9 Friedrich Nietzsche, *The Will to Power*, trans. Walter Kaufmann and R. J. Hollingdale (New York: Vintage, 1968), p. 7.

10 Maurizio Ferraris, *Tracce: nichilismo, moderno, postmoderno* (Milan: Multhipla, 1983), p. 5.

11 Friedrich Nietzsche, *Human All Too Human: A Book for Free Spirits*, trans. R. J. Hollingdale (Cambridge: Cambridge UP, 1986), p. 22 (translation slightly altered).

12 Nietzsche, *Twilight of the Idols*, trans. R. J. Hollingdale (Harmondsworth: Penguin, 1968), p. 41: 'We have abolished the real world: what world is left? Perhaps the apparent world? . . . But no! *with the real world we have also abolished the apparent world!*'

13 It goes without saying that Nietzsche's philosophy is far more complex than this brief account suggests, and includes such concepts as the 'eternal return of the Same', the 'overman', and so on.

14 Ernesto Grassi, *Heidegger and the Question of Renaissance Humanism: Four Studies* (Binghamton: MRTS, 1983), p. 33.

15   Ibid., p. 79.
16   Ibid., p. 78.
17   Ibid., p. 35.
18   Ibid., p. 34.
19   Jacques Derrida puts forward a very similar argument in his *The Truth in Painting*, trans. Geoff Bennington and Ian McLeod (Chicago: University of Chicago Press, 1987), which analyzes the *parergon* as the marginal aspect of the artwork (like the frame of a painting).
20   Aristotle, *The 'Art' of Rhetoric*, trans. J. H. Freese (London: William Heinemann; Cambridge, Mass.: Harvard University Press, 1926), p. 15: 'rhetoric then may be defined as the faculty of discovering the possible means of persuasion in reference to any subject whatever.'
21   Hans-Georg Gadamer, *Truth and Method*, translation edited by Garrett Barden and John Cumming (New York: Crossroad, 1984), p. 72.
22   Richard Rorty, *Philosophy and the Mirror of Nature* (Princeton: Princeton UP, 1979), p. 381.
23   Ibid., p. 380.
24   Ibid., p. 389.
25   Cf. Richard Rorty, *The Consequences of Pragmatism: Essays 1972–1980* (Minneapolis: University of Minnesota Press, 1982), which contains essays on Heidegger, Derrida, et al.
26   Vattimo, 'Le deboli certezze', p. 8.
27   This is also Habermas's thesis in his *The Philosophical Discourse of Modernity*. See 'The Entry into Postmodernity: Nietzsche as a Turning Point', pp. 83–105.
28   Vattimo, *La fine della modernità* (Milan: Garzanti, 1985), p. 189. This passage is not found in the English-language edition.
29   Rorty, *Philosophy and the Mirror of Nature*, p. 393.
30   Pier Aldo Rovatti, 'Una metafora necessaria?', *Alfabeta* 60 (May 1984), p. 11.
31   Rorty, *Philosophy and the Mirror of Nature*, p. 394.
32   Vattimo, 'Dialettica, differenza, pensiero debole', in *Il pensiero debole*, p. 26.
33   Ferraris, *Tracce: nichilismo, moderno, postmoderno*, p. 38.
34   Habermas, *The Philosophical Discourse of Modernity*, p. 161.

Translator's Note

The original versions of many of the texts discussed in *The End of Modernity* are in German, French, or Italian. Wherever possible, the notes refer the reader to a published English-language translation of a given text, and the page number and edition are duly indicated. Unfortunately, in a number of cases it has not been possible to do this because no published translation exists. In each of these cases the note refers the reader to the original edition, and the translation in the main body of the text is my own.

Introduction

This book is a study of the relationship that links the conclusions reached by Nietzsche and Heidegger in their respective works (to which I shall constantly refer) to more recent discourses on the end of the modern era and on post-modernity. I shall argue that to place these two fields of thought in direct contact with each other, as some have begun to do,[1] means to discover in them both new and richer aspects of truth. Indeed, the scattered and often incoherent theories of post-modernity only acquire rigour and philosophical credibility when seen in relation to the Nietzschean problematic of the eternal return and the Heideggerian problematic of the overcoming of metaphysics. At the same time, if Nietzsche's and Heidegger's philosophical intuitions are to appear once and for all irreducible to the kind of *Kulturkritik* that permeates all early twentieth-century philosophy and culture, they may do so only in relation to those things that are revealed by post-modern reflection on the new conditions of existence in the late industrial world. It is possible to take Heidegger's critique of humanism or Nietzsche's announcement of an accomplished nihilism as 'positive' moments for a philosophical reconstruction, and not merely as symptoms and declarations of decadence. The first two chapters of *The End of Modernity* do precisely this. Such an interpretation is possible, however, only if we have the courage (and not, hopefully, just the imprudence) to listen attentively to the various discourses concerning post-

modernity and its specific traits that are at present being
developed in the arts, literary criticism, and sociology.

The first decisive step in making the connection between
Nietzsche, Heidegger, and 'post-modernism' consists in discovering why the latter term employs the prefix 'post-' – for
'post-' signifies precisely that attitude which, in different
but deeply related terms (at least according to my own
interpretation), Nietzsche and Heidegger have tried to establish
in regard to the heritage of European thought. Both philosophers
call this heritage into question in a radical manner, but at the
same time refuse to propose a means for a critical 'overcoming'
of it. For both philosophers, the reason for this refusal is that
any call for an 'overcoming' would involve remaining captive
to the logic of development inscribed in the tradition of
European thought. From the point of view of Nietzsche and
Heidegger, which we may consider to be a mutually held one
in spite of the considerable differences between the two
philosophers, modernity is in fact dominated by the idea that
the history of thought is a progressive 'enlightenment' which
develops through an ever more complete appropriation and
reappropriation of its own 'foundations'. These are often also
understood to be 'origins', so that the theoretical and practical
revolutions of Western history are presented and legitimated
for the most part as 'recoveries', rebirths, or returns. The idea
of 'overcoming', which is so important in all modern
philosophy, understands the course of thought as being a
progressive development in which the new is identified with
value through the mediation of the recovery and appropriation
of the foundation-origin. However, precisely the notion of
foundation, and of thought both as foundation and means of
access to a foundation, is radically interrogated by Nietzsche
and Heidegger. Both philosophers find themselves obliged, on
the one hand, to take up a critical distance from Western
thought insofar as it is foundational; on the other hand,
however, they find themselves unable to criticize Western
thought in the name of another, and truer, foundation. It is
this that rightly allows us to consider them to be the

philosophers of post-modernity. The 'post-' in the term 'post-modern' indicates in fact a taking leave of modernity. In its search to free itself from the logic of development inherent in modernity – namely the idea of a critical 'overcoming' directed toward a new foundation – post-modernity seeks exactly what Nietzsche and Heidegger seek in their own peculiar 'critical' relationship with Western thought.

Does this effort to 'position' these different currents of thought, though, really make any sense?[2] Why should it be important for philosophy (since I intend here to remain within its confines) to establish whether we are living in a modern or a post-modern era, or, more generally speaking, to define our place in history? A first attempt to answer this question involves one of the most typical concerns of philosophy, especially of much of the nineteenth- and twentieth-century philosophy which represents the most recent part of our philosophical heritage. It involves, in other words, the negation of stable structures of Being, to which thought must necessarily have recourse if it is to 'found' itself upon solid certainties. This dissolution of the stability of Being can only be said to take place partially within the great systems of nineteenth-century metaphysical historicism. Being is not understood by them to 'be' but rather to become, yet this occurs according to necessary and recognizable rhythms which nevertheless maintain a certain ideal stability. Instead, Nietzsche and Heidegger radically conceive of Being as an *event*; for both of them it is vitally important, in order to be able to speak of Being, to understand at 'what point' we are, and at 'what point' Being itself is. Ontology is nothing other than the interpretation of our condition or situation, since Being is nothing apart from its 'event', which occurs when it historicizes itself and when we historicize ourselves.

All this, some will say, is typically modern. One of the most widely held and altogether typical visions of modernity, in point of fact, involves seeing modernity as an 'era of history' which is opposed to the ancient way of thinking governed by a cyclical and naturalistic vision of the course of events in the

world.[3] Only modernity, in developing and elaborating in
strictly worldly and secular terms the Judaeo-Christian heritage
– i.e., the idea of history as the history of salvation, articulated
in terms of creation, sin, redemption, and waiting for the Last
Judgement – gives ontological weight to history and a
determining sense to our position within it. If this is so,
though, then it would appear that every discourse on post-
modernity is a contradictory one: and this is indeed one of the
most widespread objections today to the very notion of the
post-modern. For if we say that we are at a later point than
modernity, and if we treat this fact as in some way decisively
important, then this presupposes an acceptance of what more
specifically characterizes the point of view of modernity itself,
namely the idea of history with its two corollary notions of
progress and overcoming. Even though it in many ways has
the typical emptiness and inconclusiveness of purely formal
arguments (such as the all-too-typical argument against
scepticism, which asserts that 'if one says that everything is
false one still claims to be telling the truth, therefore . . .'), this
objection to the notion of post-modernity points to a very real
difficulty, for it emphasizes the difficulty of individuating an
authentic turning-point in the conditions of existence and
thought that can be called 'post-modern' in relation to the
general traits of modernity. If it were simply a question of an
awareness – or assumption – of representing an historical
novelty which constitutes a new and different figure in the
phenomenology of the spirit, then the post-modern would be
positioned along the lines of modernity itself, since the latter is
governed by the categories of the 'new' and of 'overcoming'.
Things change, however, if we see the post-modern not only
as something new in relation to the modern, but also as a
dissolution of the category of the new – in other words, as an
experience of 'the end of history' – rather than as the
appearance of a different stage of history itself (whether it
appears as a more or less advanced stage is in this regard
unimportant).

An experience of 'the end of history' seems to be widespread in twentieth-century culture. We can find, in many different forms, the continually recurring expectation of a 'decline of the West', which most recently appears particularly impending in the form of an atomic catastrophe.[4] The end of history is, in this catastrophic sense, the end of human life on earth. Since such an end is a real possibility for us, the sense of catastrophe so widespread in contemporary culture is anything but an unmotivated one. Contemporary philosophical positions which call for a return to the origins of European thought, sometimes even by citing Nietzsche and Heidegger, can also be traced back to it.[5] These philosophical positions call for a vision of Being which has not yet been subverted by the nihilism implicit in any acceptance of the idea of becoming, upon which the rise and development of modern technology – with its destructive implications that threaten us all – in turn depends. The basic flaw of such positions consists not only in the illusion that it is possible to return to these origins (although they do not, however, formulate this project in such ingenuous terms), but especially in the conviction that there might not *have* to come out of these same origins what has in fact come out of them. This is far more serious, for probably a 'return' to Parmenides would mean only to start again from the beginning, unless we were rather nihilistically to assert an absolute randomness in the process that has led from Parmenides to modern science and technology, and, of course, to the atomic bomb.

This book does not treat post-modernity as the 'end of history' in this catastrophic sense. Rather, even the sense of an impending atomic catastrophe (which is certainly quite possible today) will be treated as a characteristic element of this 'new' way of living our experience, which may be called the 'end of history'. It would help, perhaps, if we were to speak of the 'end of historicity' instead, but this might permit a misunderstanding to remain: for we might lose sight of the distinction between history as an objective process within which we are located, and historicity as a certain way of being aware of this fact. Now, the end of history in post-modern experience is characterized by the fact that, while the notion of historicity has become ever more problematic for theory,[6] at the same time for historiography and its own methodological self-awareness the idea of history as a unitary process is rapidly dissolving. Furthermore, in concrete existence there appear effective conditions which grant it a kind of truly non-historical immobility, not only in the form of an impending atomic catastrophe, but above all in technology and information systems. Nietzsche and Heidegger, along with all those philosophers who refer to the themes of hermeneutic ontology, are taken here to be the thinkers who have established the basis for constructing an image of existence in these new conditions of non-historicity, or, better still, of post-historicity. It is the theoretical elaboration of this image – which for now, granted, is only in its initial phase – which may confer weight and meaning to the discourse on the post-modern. Only in this way may many objections to the notion of the post-modern be removed, as well as the suspicion that we are dealing with yet another 'modern' fashion and another overcoming which tries to legitimate itself solely on the grounds that it is more up-to-date, newer, and thus more valid in relation to a vision of history as progress. Yet this would be, of course, merely an appropriation of the same mechanisms of legitimation which typify modernity itself.

There is a risk involved in describing our current experience in terms of post-historicity, for it appears to indulge in the kind of oversimplifying sociology that philosophers are often guilty of using. Yet any philosophy that wishes to remain faithful to experience cannot but argue on the basis of some sort of approximation of general experiential traits that must be assumed to be apparent to all. This is what the philosophy of the past has done, as have Husserlian phenomenology, Heidegger in *Sein und Zeit*, and Wittgenstein in his analysis of language-games. Even our references here to other authors, whether philosophers or sociologists or anthropologists, always presuppose a choice that may be considered justified (without preliminary demonstration) in reference to what are estimated to be general traits of our common experience. Looking at our own experience in contemporary Western societies, the discourse on post-modernity acquires legitimacy precisely insofar as the most adequate notion for describing this experience would appear to be *post-histoire* (or 'post-history'), a term first introduced by Arnold Gehlen.[7] Many of the theoretical elements mentioned thus far can be usefully placed in this category. Gehlen argues that *post-histoire* designates the condition in which 'progress becomes routine': human capability to order nature through technology has increased and will continue to increase to such a point that, even while ever-newer achievements have become possible, the increased capability to order and arrange simultaneously makes them ever less 'new'. In a consumer society continual renewal (of clothes, tools, buildings) is already required physiologically for the system simply to survive. What is new is not in the least 'revolutionary' or subversive; it is what allows things to stay the same. There is a kind of profound 'immobility' in the technological world which science fiction writers have often portrayed as the reduction of every experience of reality to an experience of images (no one ever really meets anyone else; instead, everyone watches everything on a television screen while alone at home). This same phenomenon can already be sensed in the air-conditioned, muffled silence in which computers work.

The condition that Gehlen calls 'post-historical' does not only reflect, however, an extreme phase of the development of technology, one at which we have not yet arrived but at which it seems reasonable to expect to arrive; progress also becomes routine because, in theoretical terms, the development of technology has been prepared and accompanied by the 'secularization' of the very notion of progress: the history of ideas thus leads – through a process which could also be described as the logical development of a line of reasoning – to its voiding. For Christianity, history appears as the history of salvation; it then becomes the search for a worldly condition of perfection, before turning, little by little, into the history of progress. But the ideal of progress is finally revealed to be a hollow one, since its ultimate value is to create conditions in which further progress is possible in a guise that is always new. By depriving progress of a final destination, secularization dissolves the very notion of progress itself, as happens in nineteenth- and twentieth-century culture.

Heidegger's arguments regarding the non-historicity of the technological world offer, in different terms, a similar description of this process. Gehlen, in making his own argument, not only echoes the catastrophic tones of early twentieth-century *Kulturkritik* (later to be taken up again, in another philosophical context, by the Frankfurt school of critical theory), but also the changing notion of history in contemporary culture. The fact that, in contemporary thought, there is no 'philosophy of history' is probably not totally unrelated to the situation that Gehlen describes: even Marxist discourse in our culture can be found to be most rigorous wherever it has broken away from the philosophy of history (as in Althusser's 'structuralist' version of Marxism). Moreover, the absence of a philosophy of history is accompanied by what can be termed a true dissolution of history in the current practice and methodological awareness of historiography.[8]

This dissolution of history means, first and foremost, the breakdown of its unity, and not that it has simply come to an end. The history of events – whether political, military, or theoretical – is but one history among many. The history of everyday life, for instance, which has a much slower rhythm of change, and almost takes the form of a 'natural history' of human affairs, differs sharply from the history of events. In an even more radical fashion, the application of the techniques of rhetorical analysis to historiography has shown that our image of history is completely conditioned by the rules of a literary genre; in other words, history is much more of a 'story' or narrative than we are generally inclined to admit. This awareness of rhetorical mechanisms in the text is accompanied by an awareness – coming from another theoretical matrix – of the ideological nature of history. Walter Benjamin, in his 'Theses on the Philosophy of History',[9] discusses the 'history of the victors'; only from their point of view does the historical process appear to be a unitary one which can be described as rational and consequential. The vanquished cannot see it in the same light, primarily because their own affairs and struggles have been violently cancelled from the collective memory. The victors are the ones who control history, preserving in it only what fits the image of history that they have created in order to legitimate their own power. Even the idea that underneath these different images of history and the different temporal rhythms which characterize them there lies a unitary, strong 'time' (as Ernst Bloch argues[10]) belonging to the class that is a non-class – that is, the proletariat, which alone expresses the true essence of humanity – now appears as a last metaphysical illusion. If there is no unitary and privileged history, though, but only different histories or different levels and ways of reconstructing the past in the collective consciousness and imagination, then it is difficult to see to just what extent the dissolution of history – in the form of a dissemination of 'histories' – does not also constitute an end to history as such. This dissolution marks an end to historiography as the image, albeit a constantly varied one, of a unitary process of events, a process which itself loses all recognizable consistency when deprived of the unity of the discourse that formerly defined it.

The 'dissolution' of history (in the different senses that can be attributed to this phrase) is probably the one characteristic that most clearly distinguishes contemporary history from 'modern' history. By 'contemporary history' I do not mean the history that begins with the French Revolution, as is often held to be the case. Contemporaneity is the era in which, despite the perfecting of instruments for the collecting and transmitting of information which now at last make possible a 'universal history', the task of constructing a 'universal history' has paradoxically become impossible. As Nicola Tranfaglia points out,[11] this is a result of the fact that the world of the mass media – which is spread out far and wide across the face of the earth – is also the world in which the 'centres' of history have multiplied. By 'centres' Tranfaglia means the powers capable of collecting and transmitting information on the basis of a unitary vision which is always the result of specific political choices. Perhaps even this, though, does not simply indicate that a 'universal history' is not possible as historiography or as *historia rerum*; rather, it shows that the very conditions necessary for a universal history as a unitary process of events (or as *res*) have ceased to exist.

It ought, perhaps, to be said that living in history and feeling oneself as a moment that has been conditioned and sustained by a unitary process of events is an experience that is possible only for modern man: reading the newspapers is, in this sense, the morning prayer of the truly *modern* man. Only with the advent of modernity – or the Gutenberg era, as McLuhan has called it – are the necessary conditions created for the construction and transmission of a global image of human affairs. However, such an experience once again becomes problematical – and, in the last analysis, impossible – in what McLuhan terms the television era, given the greater sophistication of the instruments available for collecting and transmitting information. From this point of view, contemporary history is not only the history of those years which are, chronologically speaking, closest to ourselves. It is, more rigorously speaking, the history of that era in which, thanks to the use of new means of communication (especially television), everything tends to flatten out at the level of contemporaneity and simultaneity, thus producing a de-historicization of experience.[12]

With the idea of post-history we can hope to obtain (whether or not Gehlen ever intended the term to be used in this fashion) a more concrete point of reference for the discourses on the modern and the post-modern. What legitimates post-modernist theories and makes them worthy of discussion is the fact that their claim of a radical 'break' with modernity does not seem unfounded as long as these observations on the post-historical character of contemporary existence are valid. These observations are supported not only by recent theoretical work, but also by more empirical data provided by the new social order based on the diffusion of information systems, by historiographical practice, by the arts, and by a widespread social self-awareness. These all indicate that late modernity is the place where, perhaps, a different possibility of existence for man emerges. When seen in this light, the prophetic overtones of philosophies like those of Nietzsche and Heidegger appear less apocalyptic and more in line with our own experience. The central theoretical role played by Nietzsche and Heidegger in this book will be supplemented by references to other, only seemingly heterogeneous theories, such as the most recent developments in hermeneutics or the revival of rhetoric and pragmatism in recent philosophy. But the ideas of Nietzsche and Heidegger, more than any others, offer us the chance to pass from a purely critical and negative description of the post-modern condition, typical of early twentieth-century *Kulturkritik* and its more recent offshoots,[13] to an approach that treats it as a positive possibility and opportunity. Nietzsche mentions all of this – although not altogether clearly – in his theory of a possibly active, or positive, nihilism. Heidegger alludes to the same thing with his idea of a *Verwindung* of metaphysics which is not a critical overcoming in the 'modern' sense of the term (for more on this idea, see the final chapter of this book). In both Nietzsche and Heidegger, what I have elsewhere called the 'weakening' of Being allows thought to situate itself in a constructive manner within the post-modern condition.[14] For only if we take seriously the outcome of the 'destruction of ontology'[15] undertaken by Heidegger, and before him by Nietzsche, is it possible to gain access to the positive opportunities for the very essence of man that are found in post-modern conditions of existence. It will not be possible for thought to live positively in that truly post-metaphysical era that is post-modernity as long as man and Being are conceived of – metaphysically, Platonically, etc. – in terms of stable structures. Such conceptions require thought and existence to 'ground' themselves, or in other words to stabilize themselves (with logic or with ethics), in the domain of non-becoming, and are reflected in a whole-scale mythization of strong structures in every field of experience. This is not to say that everything in such an era will be accepted as equally beneficial for humanity; but the capacity to choose and discriminate between the possibilities that the post-modern condition offers us can be developed only on the basis of an analysis of post-modernity that captures its own innate characteristics, and that recognizes post-modernity as a field of possibility and not simply as a hellish negation of all that is human.

Therefore, one of the constant themes of this book is the need to open up a non-metaphysical conception of truth which would interpret truth not so much on the basis of a positivistic model of scientific knowledge as, for instance (in accordance with the typical procedure of hermeneutics), on the basis of either an experience of art or the model of rhetoric instead. In very general terms, and referring to a number of different concepts that we can only begin to explore here, it may probably be said that the post-modern – in Heideggerian terms, post-metaphysical – experience of truth is an aesthetic and rhetorical experience. As we shall see in the pages to come, this has nothing to do with reducing the experience of truth to 'subjective' emotions and feelings. On the contrary, it is a first step toward recognizing the link between truth on the one hand and what may on the other hand be called the monument, the social contract, or the very 'substantiality' (in the Hegelian sense of the objective spirit) of historical transmission. My allusion to the aesthetic character of the experience of truth, however, has another sense which is inseparable from this first one. For it also intends to call attention to the fact that the occurrence of truth cannot be reduced to the simple recognition and reinforcement of 'common sense', even though we must acknowledge the decisive significance of the latter for any possible experience of truth that is not purely subjective (as Gadamer's analyses – to

which I shall return later on – of the concept of *kalon*
demonstrate[16]). The passage to the domain of the true,
however, is not a simple passage to 'common sense', even
though the 'substantial' significance of the latter may be great
indeed. To identify in aesthetic experience the model of the
experience of truth means also to accept that it has to do with
something more than simply common sense. That is to say, it
deals with more intensely concentrated nuclei of meaning, for
these constitute the only possible point of departure for any
discourse that does not just duplicate what already exists, but
rather claims to be able to criticize it.

As we shall see, all these problems are raised and explored
rather than resolved in this book, which makes no claim
to be systematic and definitive. Although this very trait is
traditional in philosophical discourse (whose argumentative
procedures I shall seek to follow in the pages to come), it is
also perhaps something more: it is a way, however 'weak', of
experiencing truth, not as an object which can be appropriated
and transmitted, but as a horizon and a background upon
which we may move with care.

NOTES

1 See, for example, R. Schürmann, 'Anti-humanism: Reflections
   on the Turn towards the Post-modern Epoch', *Man and World*,
   2 (1979), pp. 160–77. See also the collection of texts published
   in *Postmoderno e letteratura*, ed. Peter Carravetta and Paolo
   Spedicato (Milan: Bompiani, 1984).
2 I place this term between quotation marks because I want to use
   it in the same sense in which Martin Heidegger, in his works,
   uses the term *Er-örterung*, which must be translated as 'position'
   (the emphasis is on the etymon rather than on its lexical sense,
   which is instead akin to 'discussion'). Cf. Gianni Vattimo,
   Essere, storia e linguaggio in Heidegger (Turin: Ed. di 'Filosofia',
   1963).
3 This juxtaposition is delineated in more precise and more
   sweeping terms in a deservedly famous book by Karl Löwith,

Meaning in History (1949; English trans. Chicago: Chicago UP, 1957). Another work by Löwith, *Nietzsches Philosophie der ewigen Wiederkehr des Gleichens* (*Nietzsche's Philosophy of the Eternal Return of the Same*) (1934; repr. Stuttgart: Kohlhammer, 1956), also refers to this same issue.

4   Cf. a recent book by G. Sasso, *Tramonto di un mito. L'idea di 'progresso' fra Ottocento e Novecento* (Bologna: Il Mulino, 1984).

5   'To Return to Parmenides' is the title of an essay by E. Severino that constitutes the first part of the volume *Essenza del nichilismo* (1972; Milan: Adelphi, 1982).

6   On this point cf., once again, Sasso, *Tramonto di un mito*, chapters 4 and 5.

7   See chapter 6 below.

8   I have discussed these ideas in detail in 'Il tempo nella filosofia del Novecento', an essay written for *Il mondo contemporaneo*, vol. X: *Gli strumenti della ricerca*, part 2 (Florence: La Nuova Italia, 1983). Cf. also my introduction to the bibliography of the human sciences in vol. XII of the *Enciclopedia Europea* (Milan: Garzanti, 1984).

9   Walter Benjamin, *Illuminations*, trans. Harry Zohn (New York: Schocken Books, 1969), pp. 253–64.

10 Cf. Ernst Bloch, 'Differenzierungen im Begriff Fortschritt' ('Differentiations in the Concept of Progress') (1956), now in *Tübinger Einleitung in die Philosophie* (Frankfurt: Suhrkamp, 1964), vol. I, pp. 160–202. On Bloch's philosophy of history, see R. Bodei, *Multiversum. Tempo e storia in Ernst Bloch* (Naples: Bibliopolis, 1979).

11 Cf. Nicola Tranfaglia's introduction to *Il mondo contemporaneo*, vol. X, part 2, pp. 535–6.

12 Even if we agree that modernity is characterized by the 'primacy of scientific knowledge', as C. A. Viano claims in 'La crisi del concetto di "modernità"', in *Intersezioni*, 1 (1984), pp. 25–39, it should be said that today this primacy takes the form of the primacy of technology. (Viano misses this point, arguing instead that the theories of the end of modernity are an attempt to exorcize the primacy of science.) The post-modern primacy of technology should be understood, more specifically, as that of information systems technology. The difference between the developed and underdeveloped countries in the world today is measured by the degree to which computer technology has

penetrated into their respective economies. This is probably where the difference between the 'modern' and the 'post-modern' is to be found.

13 The 'critical theory' of the Frankfurt school appears more and more – at least in certain aspects – as one of these offshoots. Habermas's polemic attack on the notion of the post-modern may be taken as a confirmation of this. Habermas defends the idea of a return to modernity's own programme of emancipation, which has not been 'dissolved', but only betrayed, by the new conditions of existence in late-industrial society. See now Jürgen Habermas, *The Philosophical Discourse of Modernity*, trans. Frederick G. Lawrence (Cambridge, Mass.: MIT, 1987).

14 Cf., besides my *Le avventure della differenza* (Milan: Garzanti, 1979) and *Al di là del soggetto* (Milan: Feltrinelli, 1981), my contribution to *Il pensiero debole*, ed. G. Vattimo and P. A. Rovatti (Milan: Feltrinelli, 1983).

15 Heidegger uses this expression in paragraph 6 of *Being and Time*, trans. John Macquarrie and Edward Robinson (1927; English trans. New York: Harper, 1962), where he defines it as a task for his own thought. He undertakes this same task in the works that follow *Being and Time*, although in them the very sense of the term 'destruction' undergoes profound transformations.

16 See chapter 8 below.

PART I

Nihilism as Destiny

1

An Apology for Nihilism

The question of nihilism is not principally a historiographical problem. If anything, it is a *geschichtlich* problem in the sense of the connection made by Heidegger between *Geschichte* (History) and *Geschick* (Destiny). Nihilism is still developing, and it is impossible to draw any definitive conclusions about it. We can and we must, however, try to understand at what point it stands, in what way it concerns us, and what the choices and attitudes are that it asks us to decide upon. I believe that our position in regard to nihilism (which is to say, our location in the process of nihilism) can be defined by making recourse to a phrase that often appears in Nietzsche's work, namely that of an 'accomplished nihilism'. The accomplished nihilist has understood that nihilism is his or her sole opportunity. What is happening to us in regard to nihilism, today, is this: we begin to be, or to be able to be, accomplished nihilists.

Nihilism signifies here what it means for Nietzsche in the note found at the beginning of the first edition of the *Will to Power*: the situation in which 'man rolls from the centre toward X.' But nihilism in this sense is also identical to the kind of nihilism defined by Heidegger, namely the process in which, at the end, 'there is nothing left' of Being as such. This Heideggerian definition addresses the forgetting of Being by humanity [*l'uomo*] but not as though nihilism were only a matter of a mis-taking, of a deception or self-deception of knowledge against which one could take refuge in the always current and present solidity of Being itself, 'forgotten' but neither dissolved nor vanished.

Neither the Nietzschean nor the Heideggerian definition concerns the human subject alone at the psychological or sociological level. On the contrary, if we roll 'from the centre toward X', this is possible only because 'there is nothing left of Being as such.' Nihilism concerns first of all Being itself, even if this point should not be taken to mean that nihilism is a matter of considerably more and different things than 'simply' humanity.

Over and above the differences in their theoretical approaches to the question, Nietzsche's and Heidegger's respective arguments are also in agreement in regard to the contents – that is, the ways of manifesting itself – of nihilism. For Nietzsche the entire process of nihilism can be summarized by the death of God, or by the 'devaluation of the highest values'. For Heidegger, Being is annihilated insofar as it is transformed completely into value. This characterization of nihilism is constructed by Heidegger in such a way as to include that accomplished nihilist Nietzsche, even if, for Heidegger, it seems possible and desirable to go beyond nihilism, while for Nietzsche the accomplishment of nihilism is all that we should wait and hope for. Heidegger himself – from a more Nietzschean than Heideggerian point of view – is also a part of the history of the accomplishment of nihilism, for nihilism seems to be precisely that mode of thought beyond metaphysics for which he is looking. All this, though, is the significance of the thesis according to which an accomplished nihilism is today our only chance . . .

In the meantime, however, what does it mean to say that the Nietzschean and Heideggerian definitions of nihilism coincide? For the one, the death of God and the devaluation of the highest values; for the other, the reduction of Being to value. This coincidence would seem difficult for us to admit as long as the fact is emphasized that, for Heidegger, the reduction of Being to value places Being in the power of the subject who 'recognizes' values (somewhat as the principle of sufficient reason is a *principium reddendae rationis*: the cause functions as such only inasmuch as it is recognized by the Cartesian subject). Nihilism would therefore be, in the Heideggerian sense, the illegitimate claim that Being, instead of existing in an autonomous, independent, and foundational way, is in the power of the subject.

But this is probably not the ultimate meaning of the Heideggerian definition of nihilism that, when isolated in these terms, would lead us in the end to conclude that Heidegger simply wants to reverse the subject–object relationship in favour of the object (which is how Adorno reads him in his *Negative Dialectics*[1]). In order to understand adequately Heidegger's definition of nihilism and to see in it an affinity with Nietzsche's, we must attribute to the term 'value' – which reduces Being to itself – the rigorous sense of 'exchange-value'. Nihilism is thus the reduction of Being to exchange-value.

How does this definition coincide with Nietzsche's arguments regarding the death of God and the devaluation of the highest values? The answer lies in the fact that for Nietzsche also values have not disappeared *tout court*: only the highest values – which are in essence expressed by that highest of all values, that is, God – have vanished. This, however, far from stripping all sense from the notion of value (as Heidegger correctly sees), instead liberates that notion in all its vertiginous potentiality: only where there is no terminal or interrupting instance of the highest value (God) to block the process may values be displayed in their true nature, namely as possessing the capacity for convertibility and an indefinite transformability or processuality.

Let us not forget that Nietzsche elaborates a theory of culture in which 'the insignificance of the origin increases with the full knowledge of the origin.'[2] That is to say, in Nietzsche's theory culture is transformation (supported by the laws of displacement, condensation, and sublimation in general) or, to put it another way, it is where rhetoric completely replaces logic. If we follow the main thread

supplied by the nexus nihilism/value, we may say that – in
Nietzsche's and Heidegger's use of the term – nihilism is the
consumption of use-value in exchange-value. Nihilism does
not mean that Being is in the power of the subject; rather, it
means that Being is completely dissolved in the discoursing
of value, in the indefinite transformations of universal
equivalence.

What has twentieth-century culture opposed to, or how has
twentieth-century culture answered, the advent of nihilism?
At a philosophical level, some examples seem particularly
emblematic: Marxism, in its various theoretical forms (with
perhaps the exception of Althusser's structuralist Marxism),
has dreamed about the recovery at a practical/political level,
prior to a theoretical one, of use-value and its norms.

Socialist society was originally conceived as a society in
which work would be freed from its alienating characteristics
because its products, once removed from the perverse cycle of
commerce, would retain a relationship of fundamental identity
with their producer. However, the harder that this de-
alienation of work tries to escape from the idealization of
artisanal and 'artistic' production, the more it must define
itself in terms of complex political mediations that end up
rendering it problematic and that in the last analysis expose its
mythic nature.

Outside the dialectical – and hence totalizing – perspective
of Marxism, twentieth-century philosophy has been distinguished by the great debate over the opposition between the
'sciences of the spirit' and the 'natural sciences'. This
discussion also seems to reveal a defensive attitude in regard to
an area where use-value still applies, or in any case where it
distinguishes itself from the purely quantitative logic of
exchange-value which is operative for the natural sciences,
which ignore the qualitative individuality of historical and
cultural facts. The need to go beyond exchange-value, in the
direction of a kind of use-value that can be kept free of the
logic of permutability, is a dominant one for phenomenology
(at least from the point of view that concerns us here) and

for early existentialism as well, including *Sein und Zeit*. Phenomenology and early existentialism, together with humanistic Marxism and the theorization of the 'sciences of the spirit', all belong to the same strand of thought that unifies a large sector of European culture. This could be defined as being characterized by a 'pathos of authenticity', or, in Nietzschean terms, as a resistance to the accomplishment of nihilism. To this same strand has recently been annexed a tradition that until now, in many of its forms, had appeared as an alternative. This tradition begins with Wittgenstein and Viennese culture in the period of the *Tractatus* and leads up to the development of Anglo-Saxon analytic philosophy. Even here, at least to the extent to which emphasis may be placed on Wittgenstein's notion of the 'mystical', we confront an effort to isolate and defend an ideal zone of use-value, namely a place where the dissolution of Being into value does not occur.

The rediscovery of Wittgenstein's notion of the 'mystical' has had a decisive cultural importance – in different ways – for Italian culture (in the debate over the 'crisis of reason') and for Anglo-Saxon culture (in the discovery of the historical nature of logic). But from the point of view of the accomplishment of nihilism, this rediscovery is in reality a rearguard skirmish. The struggle to show that *even* Wittgenstein defines – as a kind of non-foundational fundamental – a zone of 'silence', in the belief that we can recognize in this an affinity with Heidegger and, in other ways, with Nietzsche, overlooks the fact that what happens instead (where? – in philosophical consciousness, in the giving-forth of Being, in the planetary event of the Heideggerian *Ge-stell*[3]) is that nihilism arrives at the phase of its accomplishment, that it reaches its extreme form, by consuming Being in value. This is the event that finally makes it possible, and necessary, for philosophy today to recognize that nihilism is our (only) chance.

From the point of view of nihilism, and in terms of a generalization that might seem somewhat exaggerated, it appears that twentieth-century culture has witnessed the dissolution of every project of 'reappropriation'. In this process figure not only theoretical developments, such as for example the Lacanian elaboration of Freudianism, but also (and perhaps more fundamentally) the political developments of Marxism, revolutions and socialism. Whether we understand reappropriation in the form of the defence of a zone free of exchange-value or in the more ambitious form (which unites Marxism and phenomenology at a theoretical level) of a 'refoundation' of existence in a horizon focused on use-value and beyond the reach of exchange-value, the perspective of reappropriation has been used up – and not only in terms of practical check-mates and failures, which would still take nothing away from its ideal and normative significance.

In fact, the perspective of reappropriation has lost its meaning as an ideal norm; like Nietzsche's God, such a perspective reveals itself in the end to be superfluous. In Nietzsche's philosophy, God dies precisely because knowledge no longer needs to arrive at ultimate causes, humanity no longer needs to believe in an immortal soul, etc. Even if God dies because he must be negated in the name of the same imperative demand for truth that was always considered one of his own laws, the meaning of an imperative demand for truth itself is lost together with him. Ultimately this is because the conditions of existence are by now less violent and, at the same time, less prone to pathos. It is here, in this emphasis on the superfluity of the highest values, that the roots of an accomplished nihilism may be found.

For the accomplished nihilist, even the liquidation of the highest values does not signify the establishment or re-establishment of a situation of 'value' in the strong sense of the term. It is not a reappropriation, because what has become superfluous is whatever is 'proper' in the first place (even in the semantic sense of the term). 'The world has become a fable,' writes Nietzsche in *Twilight of the Idols*[4] and he means not just the 'supposedly' real world, but the world *tout court*. And even if Nietzsche adds that, by the same token, the fable is not a 'fable' as such because there is no truth that would unveil it to us as appearance and illusion, the notion of 'fable' does not for that reason lose all meaning; instead it forbids us to attribute to the appearances that constitute it the cogent force that once belonged to the metaphysical *ontos on*.

This is a risk that seems to be present in contemporary nihilism (in thought that refers back to Nietzsche and that follows his initiative): one may think, for instance, of certain passages in Deleuze's *Différence et répétition* on the 'glorification' of simulacra.[5] Among the many snares and pitfalls in Nietzsche's text there is also this one: once the real world has been recognized as possessing the structure of a fable, the fable could then be said to acquire the ancient metaphysical dignity (the 'glory') of the real world. The experience that opens up for an accomplished nihilism is not, however, an experience of fullness, glory, or *ontos on*, which has only been detached from any claim to the supposedly highest values and attached instead – in an emancipated fashion – to the values that the metaphysical tradition has always considered base and ignoble, values which in this way may be restored to their true dignity. Examples are easily found to show that, in the face of devaluation of the highest values and the death of God, the usual reaction is one which makes a grandiose metaphysical appeal to other, 'truer' values (for example, the values of subcultures or popular cultures as opposed to dominant cultures, the rejection of literary or artistic canons, etc.).

Like the term 'fable', the term 'nihilism' – even when it refers to an accomplished nihilism, not a passive or reactive nihilism – maintains in Nietzsche's philosophical vocabulary some of the same traits that it has in everyday language. The world in which the truth has become a fable is in fact that place of an experience that is no 'more authentic' than that offered by metaphysics. This experience is no *more* authentic because authenticity – understood as what is 'proper', or as reappropriation – has itself vanished with the death of God.

When read in the light of Nietzsche, Heidegger, and the accomplishment of nihilism, this occurrence can be understood in terms of the generalization of exchange-value in our society: it is that same occurrence which appeared to Marx to be still definable strictly in the moralistic terms of 'generalized prostitution' and the desacralization of what is human. Could not the resistance to this desacralization, for example in the kind of critique of mass culture that has its origins in the Frankfurt school, still be described as a nostalgia for reappropriation, for God, for the *ontos on*; and, in psychoanalytic terms, as a nostalgia for an imaginary self that refuses to yield to the peculiar mobility, uncertainty, and permutability of the symbolic?

The distinguishing traits of existence in late capitalist society, ranging from commercialization in the form of a totalized 'simulacrization' to the consequent collapse of the 'critique of ideology' or the Lacanian 'discovery' of the symbolic, are all fully understandable as a part of what Heidegger calls the *Ge-Stell*. They do not represent solely the apocalyptic moments of a *Menscheitsdämmerung* or dehumanization, but instead gesture toward a possible new human experience.

Heidegger has seemed to many to be the philosopher of a nostalgia for Being, even in its metaphysical characteristics of *Geborgenheit*. Yet he has written that the *Ge-Stell* – the universal imposition and challenge of the technological world – is also a 'first flashing up of the *Ereignis*',[6] or of the advent of Being in which every appropriation (every giving-forth of something *qua* something) occurs only as a trans-propriation. This process of dizzying circularity strips both humanity and Being of every metaphysical characteristic. The transpropriation in which the *Ereignis* of Being is realized is, in the end, the dissolution of Being in exchange-value, that is, in language and in the tradition constituted by the transmission and interpretation of messages.

The effort to overcome alienation defined in terms of reification or a fading from view of subjectivity has always been developed in the twentieth century in the direction of reappropriation. But generalized reification, as the reduction of everything to exchange-value, is precisely that world which has become a fable. To try to re-establish something 'proper' in the face of this dissolution is still always a reactive nihilism; for this effort to reverse the rule of the object by setting up a dominion of the subject in its place is still configured reactively with the same characteristic cogent force which belongs to objectivity.

The process described so well by Sartre in *The Critique of Dialectical Reason*[7] as a relapse into counter-finality and the practical-inert unequivocally shows us the destiny of these kinds of reappropriation. Nihilism appears as our opportunity precisely in this sense, somewhat as – in *Sein und Zeit* – being-towards-death and the anticipatory decision that it assumes both appear as the one possibility truly able to make possible all the other possibilities that constitute existence. They represent, therefore, a suspension of the world's cogency as well, which places at the level of the possible all that claims to be real, necessary, peremptory, and true.

The consumption of Being in exchange-value, that is, the transformation of the real world into a fable, is nihilistic even insofar as it leads to a weakening of the cogent force of 'reality'. In the world of generalized exchange-value all is given – as it always was, but now in a more evident and exaggerated fashion – as narration or *récit*. Essentially, this narration is articulated by the mass media, which are inextricably intertwined with the tradition of messages that language brings to us from the past and from other cultures: the mass media thus represent not just an ideological perversion, but rather a vertiginous form of this same tradition.

We often speak, in this connection, of a social 'imaginary'; but the world of exchange-value is not only, and necessarily, the Imaginary in the Lacanian sense of the term – for it is not only an alienated rigidity, but may assume the peculiar mobility of the symbolic (though this indeed still depends upon an individual or social decision).

The various kinds of relapse into the practical-inert, into counter-finality, etc., or the elements of permanent alienation which – in the form of the additional repression defined by

Marcuse – characterize our society (a society which is nevertheless technologically capable of freedom), could all be interpreted as a permanent transcription, in terms of the imaginary, of the new possibilities of the symbolic that have been opened up by technology, by secularization, and by the 'weakening' of reality that are typical of late-modern society.

The *Ereignis* of Being that flashes up through the im-positive structure of the Heideggerian *Ge-Stell* is precisely the announcement of an era of the 'weakness' of Being, in which the 'propriation' of entities is explicitly given as a trans-propriation. Nihilism offers us an opportunity, from this point of view, in two senses. The first of these is a performative and political one; the mass culture and mass media – as the process of secularization, loss of roots, etc. – which constitute late-modern existence are not necessarily an accentuation of alienation or an expropriation in the direction of a wholly administered and regulated society. The process of making the world ever less real may not only take us towards the rigidity of the imaginary, and toward the establishment of new 'highest values', but also toward the mobility of the symbolic.

This chance, however, depends upon the way in which we discover how to live it individually and collectively. Here we arrive at the second sense of the term 'nihilism'. The relapse into counter-finality is linked to the permanent tendency to live the process in which the world becomes ever less real in terms of a reappropriation. The emancipation of humanity certainly also consists, as Sartre states, in the reappropriation of the meaning of history on the part of those who actually make it. But this reappropriation is a 'dissolution': Sartre writes that the meaning of history must 'disperse' itself in the individuals who together create it.[8] This dissolution is to be understood in a much more literal sense than the one that Sartre believes it to have. A meaning for history can be reappropriated only insofar as we accept that it has no metaphysical and theological weight and 'essential' value.

Nietzsche's accomplished nihilism also fundamentally possesses this meaning, for the call that comes to us from the world of late modernity is a call for a *taking leave*. This call echoes in the work of Heidegger, who is too often and too simplistically considered the philosopher of (the return of) Being. Yet it is Heidegger who speaks of the necessity of 'forgetting about Being as foundation'[9] if we are to 'leap' into its 'abyss'. Inasmuch as this abyss calls to us from the generalization of exchange-value, and from the *Ge-Stell* of modern technology, however, it cannot be identified with any deeper meaning with overtones of a negative theology.

To listen to the call of the essence of technology, though, does not mean giving oneself up entirely to its laws and its games. It is for this reason that Heidegger insists on the fact that the essence of technology is not something technological, and it is to this essence that we must pay particular attention. This essence sends out a call that is inextricably linked to the messages that the *Über-lieferung* ('trans-mission') sends us; modern technology also belongs to the same *Über-lieferung*, and is the coherent accomplishment for the metaphysics that began with Parmenides.

Even technology is a fable or *Sage*, a transmitted message: when seen in this light it is stripped of all its (imaginary) claims to be able to constitute a new 'strong' reality that could be taken as self-evident, or glorified as what Plato calls the *ontos on*. The myth of a dehumanizing technology, as well as the 'reality' of this myth in a wholly administered and regulated society, are metaphysical accretions which lead us to continue to read the fable as a 'truth'. An accomplished nihilism, like the Heideggerian *Ab-grund*, calls us to a fictionalized experience of reality which is also our only possibility for freedom.

NOTES

1   Cf. Theodor Adorno, *Negative Dialectics*, trans. F. B. Ashton (New York: Seabury, 1973), in particular chapter 1 of the first part (where 'ontological need' is discussed).

2 Friedrich Nietzsche, *Daybreak*, trans. R. J. Hollingdale (Cambridge: Cambridge UP, 1982), aphorism 44.

3 On this interpretation of the Heideggerian *Ge-Stell*, see my *Le avventure della differenza* (Milan: Garzanti, 1979), chapters 5 and 7.

4 This is the title of a chapter of Nietzsche's *Twilight of the Idols*, trans. R.J. Hollingdale (Harmondsworth: Penguin, 1968).

5 For this concept in the work of Gilles Deleuze, see esp. *Différence et répétition* (Paris: PUF, 1968).

6 Cf. Martin Heidegger, *Identity and Difference*, trans. Joan Stambaugh (1969; New York: Harper and Row, 1974).

7 Cf. Jean-Paul Sartre, *Critique of Dialectical Reason* (1960), trans. Alan Sheridan-Smith, ed. Jonathan Rée (London: New Left Books, 1976).

8 Ibid., vol. I, pp. 53–64.

9 Cf. Heidegger, *On Time and Being*, trans. Joan Stambaugh (1962; English trans. New York: Harper and Row, 1972), p.6. Stambaugh's translation reads: 'To think Being itself explicitly requires disregarding Being to the extent that it is only grounded and interpreted in terms of beings and for beings as their ground, as in all metaphysics. To think Being explicitly requires us to relinquish Being as the ground of beings . . .'

2

The Crisis of Humanism

We might begin this discussion of humanism by paraphrasing a joke that went around some time ago, pointing out that in the contemporary world 'God is dead, but man isn't doing so well himself.' Although in one sense this is just a joke, it is also something more than that, inasmuch as it captures and conveys the difference between contemporary atheism and the more classic kind of atheism represented by Feuerbach. Such a difference consists precisely in the macroscopic fact that the negation of God, or the realization of his death, cannot lead today to any 'reappropriation' by man of some alienated essence of his through the fetish of the divine. Many apologists continue to find in this point – either implicitly or explicitly – an argument against atheism, which they accuse of being a necessary prelude to a general destruction of all that is human. Atheism appears in this light as another catastrophic Tower of Babel which will lead to the downfall of a humanity in rebellion against the very metaphysical dependency which constitutes it. Although this sort of crude apologetics ought to be rejected out of hand, it is undeniable that a connection exists between the crisis of humanism and the death of God. In the first place, this characterizes contemporary atheism in a peculiar way, since it can no longer be a 'reappropriative' atheism. In the second place, and more importantly, it marks in a determining manner the crisis of humanism, which finds itself in difficulty because it can no longer resolve matters through an appeal to a transcendental foundation. In this second perspective, we might also acknowledge the hypothesis that humanism is in crisis *because* God is dead: that is to say, the true substance of the crisis of humanism is the death of God. It is no coincidence that this should be announced by Nietzsche, the first radically non-humanistic thinker of our age.

The connection between the crisis of humanism and the death of God, moreover, seems paradoxical only if one insists that humanism must necessarily be a perspective that places man at the centre of the universe and makes him the master of Being. Yet the text that first opens up a contemporary awareness of the crisis of humanism, Heidegger's letter *Über den Humanismus* (1946), describes humanism in far different terms, demonstrating the extremely close relationship that it has with the onto-theology characteristic of all Western metaphysics. In Heidegger's text, humanism is in fact synonymous with metaphysics, inasmuch as it is only in the perspective provided by metaphysics as a general theory of the Being of entities – which is thought of in 'objective' terms, thus forgetting ontological difference – that humanity can discover a definition on the basis of which it can 'construct' and educate itself through a *Bildung*. This applies equally to the *humanae litterae* that define Humanism as a moment in the history of European culture. There is no humanism without the bringing into play of a metaphysics in which the human subject determines a role for itself which is necessarily central or exclusive. On the other hand, as Heidegger shows in his constantly renewed efforts to reconstruct the history of metaphysics, metaphysics may survive as such only insofar as its 'humanistic' nature (meaning its reduction of everything to the human subject itself) remains hidden from view. When the reductive nature of metaphysics instead makes itself explicit, as – according to Heidegger – happens in the work of Nietzsche (in the notion of Being as the will to power), metaphysics has arrived at the moment of its decline, and with it – as can be seen every day – humanism has also arrived at the moment of its decline. For this reason the death of God, which is at once the culmination and conclusion of metaphysics, is also the crisis of humanism. To put it another way, humanity maintains its position as the 'centre' of reality, as the current notion of humanism suggests, only through reference to a *Grund* that verifies this role. St Augustine argues that God knows the human subject more intimately than that subject knows itself, but this argument has never been a real threat to humanism; on the contrary, as can be historically demonstrated, it has served rather as a means of support for the latter. *Larvatus prodeo*: this phrase is a familiar one in psychoanalytic thought, but it is the law of metaphysical thought as well, which in this sense is always also ideological. In the history of thought the subject affirms its own centrality only by disguising itself in the 'imaginary' appearance of a foundation. It is likely that there is more than a simple relationship of analogy or superficial proximity between the Heideggerian notion of metaphysics and the Lacanian theory of the interplay of the imaginary and symbolic realms. This is not a matter of formulating a psychologistic interpretation of metaphysics, in the sense that the term has for Heidegger. If anything, it is rather a matter of placing the problematic of the constitution and development of the self within an ontological horizon, according to the line of thought first put forward by Heidegger in *Sein und Zeit*.

In what sense, more precisely, can the connection that Heidegger makes between humanism and metaphysics help us to understand the crisis of humanism more adequately? The answer, it seems, is that it gives an exact philosophical significance to a group of ideas whose connections to each other are often unclear but which together define our awareness of the crisis of humanism in contemporary culture. In Heidegger, in fact, the crisis of humanism – inasmuch as it is linked to the culmination and the end of metaphysics – is related in a far from incidental way to modern technology, for it is exactly in connection with technology that we speak today of the crisis of humanism. Technology appears as the cause of a general process of dehumanization that includes both the displacement of humanistic cultural ideals in favour of a modelling of the human subject based on the sciences and on rationally controlled productive capabilities, and a process of accentuated rationalization at the level of social and political organization that reveals the features of the wholly administered and regulated society that Adorno describes and criticizes. Heidegger provides a decisively important theoretical approach to precisely this connection between the crisis of humanism and the triumph of technological civilization, a connection that is quite customarily made in today's culture.

The existentialist vein that distinguishes European philosophy and culture during the first thirty years of the twentieth century tends to see in the crisis of humanism merely a process of the *practical* decadence of a value – that is, humanity – which nevertheless remains *theoretically* defined by the same traits traditionally assigned to it. From this point of view, the debate that develops between the late nineteenth and early twentieth centuries over the distincton between the 'natural sciences' and the 'sciences of the spirit' is highly significant. The increased importance of the natural sciences is generally perceived as a menace against which a zone or area of peculiarly human values that stand outside the quantitative logic of positive knowledge must be defended. Even if, in the following decades, hermeneutics – with its anti-metaphysical and anti-humanistic implications – is developed from a consideration of the sciences of the spirit themselves (and this is the history of the nexus that links Heidegger to Dilthey), the original significance of the debate is of a 'defensive' kind. If it is true that a form of rigour and precision which satisfies the requirements of methical knowledge must be sought for the field of the human sciences as well, this must be done without failing to acknowledge what is irreducible and specific to man. Yet this is still the nucleus of traditional humanism, which centres around the freedom, choice, and unpredictability of behaviour – that is, around its constitutive historicity. Husserl, in his *Krisis*, frees the humanistic nucleus of the early twentieth-century debate from any appearance of belonging to a 'methodological' debate, and defines it in the effective terms of theoretical content. For Husserl the crisis of humanism is linked to the loss of human subjectivity in the mechanisms of scientific objectivity and, subsequently, technological objectivity. The only way to exit from the general crisis of civilization which develops as a result of this loss is through a recovery of the central function of the subject. Husserl's subject continues to harbour no doubts about its own true nature, which is only externally threatened by an ensemble of mechanisms created by this same subject, but still capable of being reappropriated by it. There is not the shadow of a doubt that, although these dehumanizing mechanisms have been set in motion by the subject, there might be something wrong with the very structure of the latter. Later phenomenologists, especially in France, have stressed in their interpretations of Husserl positions that take a distance from his humanistic stance; they are concerned above all with the reconstruction, in a non-idealistic way, of the relationship between thought and perception, the body and the emotions. It is difficult, though, to say how far this 'naturalistic' phenomenological thematic really strays from a humanistic horizon. If we consider that, through its appeal to these aspects which have traditionally been 'repressed' by metaphysical philosophy, what it seeks is the recomposition of a more complete *humanitas* of the subject – namely a more extensive and more controllable dominion of self-consciousness – that would consolidate its position through a more and more comprehensive awareness of its own full dimensions (in accordance with an understanding of phenomenology that ultimately leads back to Hegel himself), we can begin to see the extent to which this phenomenology is similar to Husserl's original humanism.

If the crisis of humanism is certainly linked, in the experience of twentieth-century philosophy, to the growth of the technological world and of a rationalized society, this link – in all its different possible interpretations – also constitutes a line of demarcation between profoundly different concepts of the meaning of this crisis. The point of view developed in the debate over the human sciences, which finds an exemplary theoretical expression in phenomenology but which in general is linked to the existentialist tendencies present in much early twentieth-century culture (as, for instance, in Marxism), could thus be called a nostalgic and reconstructive reading of the crisis of humanism. The relationship with technology is seen essentially as a threat to which philosophical thought reacts in two ways: first of all, by becoming ever more concerned with the special traits that distinguish the human world from the world of scientific objectivity, and, secondly, by attempting to prepare, in theory or praxis (as with Marxist thought), a reappropriation by the subject of its own centrality. This recuperative notion does not substantially call the traditional kind of humanism into question, for it does not see this crisis as affecting the contents of the humanistic ideal, but only the possibility of its historical survival in the new conditions of existence of the modern world.

Another and more radical attitude makes headway in the same cultural horizon and in the same arc of time, according to which the advent of technology is not so much of a threat as a provocation and a call to action. The classic collection of Expressionist poetry published by Kurt Pinthus in 1919 is entitled *Menscheitsdämmerung* ('The Twilight of Humanity'), but contains a number of texts which are more suggestive of dawn than twilight. The new conditions of life created, above all, by the structure of the modern city are depicted as an uprooting of man from his traditional setting, or, we might say, from his basis in the organic community of the village, the family, and so on. In this process of uprooting, even the well-defined and reassuring horizons of form itself crumble; so that, in a certain sense, the stylistic revolt represented by Expressionism appears as but one aspect of a larger process implicating an entire civilization. This process is not, however, experienced as a loss. The cry that rings out because the uprooting of man by modernity makes the fixed and definite nature of forms collapse is not simply the cry of pain that comes from a 'damaged life' – as the subtitle of Adorno's *Minima moralia* will later suggest; it is also an expression of the 'spiritual' which appears through the ruins of form, and thus through the destruction that constitutes the 'twilight' of humanity, and perhaps – more than anything else – of humanism as well. The Heideggerian notion of the crisis of humanism seems to be the most theoretically rigorous one because it addresses the very nature of humanism, and not just the external questions of the greater or lesser historical possibility of its realization. This notion is broadly related to the stance taken by Expressionism. Bloch's *Geist der Utopie*, for example, subscribes to this stance in its Hegelian tripartite division of the eras of art (Egyptian, classical, Gothic), but in reality this reflects the spirit of Nietzsche's *Geburt der Tragödie* instead, insofar as it understands the uprooting of man by modernity as a utopian promise of liberation. However, characteristic above all else of this radical interpretation of the crisis of humanism – and of its possible errors – are two works ideally situated at the beginning and the end of the period in which the awareness of this crisis comes to maturation: Oswald Spengler's *Der Untergang des Abendlandes* (1918), and Ernst Jünger's *Der Arbeiter* (1932). In both these works – but especially in the former – the historical and social components of the crisis of humanism, which tend to disappear in purely theoretical texts, can be clearly seen. As in Expressionism, but more markedly, in Spengler's work the oncoming crisis is above all a crisis of Eurocentrism (in the figurative arts, for instance, we might think of the importance of the discovery of African art for the birth of an avant-garde movement such as Cubism or for Expressionism itself) and of the 'bourgeois' (broadly speaking) model of *Bildung*. Spengler and, later on, Jünger oppose a sort of 'military' ideal of existence to this bourgeois ideal which, in the wake of the First World War, is undermined by the collapse of the dream of a unitary European civilization. Spengler asserts that, in the final or 'twilight' phase at which our civilization has arrived, the most suitable activities for humanity are no longer those that involve the creation of works of art or of thought, for these are characteristically adolescent and youthful in nature; humanity should instead seek the technological, scientific, and economic organization of the world, culminating in the establishment of an authority of an essentially military kind. For Jünger, the exaltation of the 'war of materials' which gives weight to the 'mechanical' aspects of reality prefigures a new existence that finds its highest ideal, not in the life of the soldier, but in that of the industrial worker – who is no longer an individual, but a moment in an 'organic' process of production. As opposed to the bourgeois, the modern industrial worker is no longer obsessed by the problem of security; he leads a more adventurous and flexible existence which is more 'experimental' precisely because it is more detached from any reference to the self. It is true that even the ideal of military life can be seen as a typical bourgeois ideal (and it functions as such, for example, in the first novel in Hermann Broch's 1932 trilogy *Die Schlafwandler*), representing the triumph of form and discipline and offering the opportunity for a nostalgic and ironic distancing from immediate concerns. But what distinguishes Spengler's and Jünger's militarism – the latter's in particular – is the awareness of its connection with technology. What at first appears as a 'military' ideal opposed to the bourgeois *Bildung* is really, in the last analysis, the ideal of a 'technologification' of existence responding to, or yielding itself up entirely to, the provocative call of modern technology, while running the risks that such a response entails. Spengler, for instance, ultimately succumbs to this danger, as do certain other writers as well; the case of Jünger is different, for he always maintains a political position opposed to Nazism, and believes himself to be a sort of socialist.

To emphasize these mistakes, and the risks linked to these perspectives, does not only serve to exorcize them by warning us about them; it also makes us aware, above all, of the fact that we are confronted here with materials and elements that need a more rigorous and theoretically responsible interpretation and collocation if we are to discover a meaning in them. It is possible that such a theoretical perspective could be found in the utopianism of Ernst Bloch, as would today be maintained by many who belong to the vast vein of Marxist thought which has broken away from Lukácsian orthodoxy. *Geist der Utopie* (1918 and 1923) is certainly one of the twentieth-century philosophical works which has most openly explored the 'positive' possibilities connected to the apparently dehumanizing aspects of the new conditions of existence in the technological world. To what point, though, does the subsequent development of Bloch's thought in the direction of an ever more definite inclusion of elements from the Hegelian and Marxist traditions allow us to place him among the philosophers of the 'radical' crisis of humanism? The awareness of the new possibilities of existence offered by the technological world, so alive in *Geist der Utopie* (in which the 'reappropriated subject' is finally modelled on the clown, and thus appears in a 'deranged' or unbalanced form incompatible with the traditional *homo humanus*) is progressively dissolved in a general reinstitution of the contents of humanism within the utopian image of humanity as it is to be created by revolution. Theodor Adorno's work, so deeply conditioned by Bloch's utopianism, and yet so fiercely critical – in the name of an ideal of humanity which is still substantially within the tradition – of any possibility of reconciliation with technological existence, might be seen to offer confirmation of the still deeply humanistic vocation of Marxism.

What this 'humanistic' tradition might actually be, and why its thematics are in crisis, can only be understood from a point of view which belongs to this tradition and yet is already situated outside it, in the kind of 'overcoming' called a *Verwindung*[1] by Heidegger. This term suggests a number of different meanings: to recover from an illness, to resign oneself to something, or to accept (another's judgement). We cannot coherently speak of a crisis of humanism except from a viewpoint which would systematically summarize and interpret the elements of the radical perspective that appears in the work of authors such as, for instance, Spengler, Jünger, the Expressionists, or the early Bloch. Contrary to all appearances, this theoretical point of view cannot be found in critical or utopian Marxism. It is instead constituted by the very meaning of the whole of Heidegger's thought, which is entirely configured as an interpretation of the crisis of humanism as one aspect of the crisis of metaphysics. Like the crisis or the end of metaphysics, the crisis of humanism, which is a part of the former, may also be described in terms of a *Verwindung*: that is, as an overcoming which is in reality a recognition of belonging, a healing of an illness, and an assumption of responsibility.

This *Verwindung* of metaphysics and humanism can only occur after an opening up to the call of the *Ge-Stell*. In the Heideggerian notion of the *Ge-Stell*, with all that it implies, the theoretical interpretation of the radical vision of the crisis of humanism is found. *Ge-Stell*[2] represents for Heidegger the totality of the technological 'setting', and of the summoning, provoking and ordering that constitutes the historical/*geschicklich* essence of the technological world. This essence does not differ from metaphysics, but is instead its fulfilment: that is because metaphysics has always understood Being as a *Grund* or as a foundation which assures the rule of reason and of which reason always assures itself. But technology, with its global project aimed at linking all entities on the planet into predictable and controllable causal relationships, represents the most advanced development of metaphysics. This fact lies at the basis of the impossibility of opposing the errors inherent in technology's triumph to the metaphysical tradition, for they are but different moments of the same process. Since it is a part of metaphysics, humanism cannot somehow convince us that its values offer an alternative to technological ones. Technology is a threat to metaphysics and to humanism in appearance alone, for it is in the very nature of technology that the defining traits of metaphysics and humanism – which both had previously kept hidden from view – should be brought out into the open. This unveiling and disclosing is at once the final moment, the culmination, and the beginning of the crisis of metaphysics and humanism. Such a culminating moment is not the result of an historical necessity nor of a process guided by some sort of objective dialectic; rather, it is *Gabe*, the giving and the gift of Being, whose destiny exists only as a sending-forth, a mission, and an announcement. For these reasons, in essence, the crisis of humanism is not an overcoming but a *Verwindung*, a call for humanity to heal itself of humanism, to yield itself up and resign itself to humanism as something for which humanity is destined.

The *Ge-Stell* is thus not only the moment in which metaphysics and humanism come to an end, in the sense that they break up and disappear, as the nostalgic and recuperative interpretation of this crisis would have us believe. It is also, as Heidegger writes, 'a first flashing up of the *Ereignis*';[3] it is an announcement of the event of Being as its giving-forth beyond the limits of the forgetfulness of metaphysics. *Ge-Stell* in fact allows for the possibility that in it humanity and Being, who are caught up in a challenge to each other, might lose their metaphysical qualifications, especially the one that sets them against each other as subject and object. Humanism, which is both a part and an aspect of metaphysics, consists in the definition of humanity as *subiectum*. Technology does not represent the crisis of humanism because the triumph of rationalization subverts humanistic values, as superficial analyses have led us to believe; rather, it does so because technology – in representing the fulfilment of metaphysics – calls humanism to an act of overcoming or *Verwindung*. In Nietzsche as well, the crisis of humanism is linked to the establishment of technology's dominion over modernity. Humanity can take leave of its own subjectivity, which is defined in terms of the immortality of the soul, and can instead recognize that the self is a bundle of 'many mortal souls', precisely because existence in a technologically advanced society is no longer characterized by continual danger and consequent acts of violence.

Nietzsche's argument places the *subiectum* in crisis in its etymological sense, as that which is 'placed beneath' and which remains throughout the shifts and changes in accidental configurations, thus assuring the unity of the process. In modern philosophy, at least since the work of Descartes and Leibniz, the unity of the *subiectum* as a *hypokeimenon* – in the sense of being also a substratum of material processes – is only that of *consciousness* itself. Even the twentieth-century passage from the concept of substance to the concept of function, as is suggested by the title of a classic neo-Kantian work by Cassirer, is a step in the direction clearly indicated by Heidegger in his commentary on Leibniz and the *principium reddendae rationis*. In this development, however, the subject – as *substantia*, substratum, *hypokeimenon* – is not only further and further reduced to consciousness alone (following the direction taken by all critics of modern subjectivism) – that is to say, to the kind of self-awareness unique to humanity; this self-awareness is also ever more closely configured as the subject of the object, or as the subject which is the correlative term of the object. This can be seen in the Cartesian *cogito*, in which the self-assuredness of consciousness is entirely a function of the fact that the clear and distinct idea is *evidence*. If this is the case, then the reasons for Heidegger's (and Nietzsche's) anti-humanism become ever clearer: the subject, conceived of by humanism as self-consciousness, is simply the correlative of metaphysical Being which is defined in terms of objectivity, that is, in terms of clarity, stability, and unshakable certainty. Historically speaking, the origins of Heideggerian anti-humanism could probably be sought after in phenomenology's polemic against psychologism. But the fact that Heidegger neither simply limits himself to a return to the Aristotelian or Thomist brand of realism (unlike certain other students of Husserl's), nor follows the path leading back to the *Lebenswelt*, indicates in no uncertain terms the meaning of his anti-humanism. It is, for Heidegger, neither a recovery of the 'objectivity' of essences nor a return to the world of life that stands prior to any possible fixing of categories. His anti-humanism is instead a consequent aspect of his re-proposing of the problem of the meaning of Being outside the metaphysical horizon of what is simply present (in the sense of *Vorhandenheit*). Heidegger's anti-humanism, in short, cannot be formulated as the assertion of 'another principle' which, transcending man and his claims of dominion (the 'will to power' and the nihilism that accompanies it), could supply a stable point of reference. It is therefore out of the question to talk about the possibility of a 'religious' reading of Heidegger. The subject is 'overcome' insofar as it is an aspect of the kind of thought which forgets Being in favour of objectivity and simple presence. This kind of thought, among other things, makes it impossible to understand the life of Dasein (human existence) in its historical specificity, and instead reduces it to the moment of self-certainty and to the kind of evidence of the subject that is a scientific ideal. It eliminates, in other words, what is purely 'subjective' (insofar as it is irreducible to the 'subject of the object') in Dasein. For this reason, the humanism that appears in the metaphysical tradition also has a repressive and ascetic nature, which is intensified in modern thought the more that subjectivity is modelled on scientific objectivity and becomes a pure function of the latter.

Hans-Georg Gadamer, in a conversation, pointed out the importance that the notion of *Erde* (or the 'earth'), which Heidegger first introduced in his 1936 essay entitled 'Der Ursprung des Kunstwerkes' ('The Origin of the Work of Art'), possessed for all who in the 1930s were following the development of Heidegger's thought after *Sein und Zeit*. According to Gadamer, this notion derives its importance precisely in connection with the Heideggerian critique of the self-conscious subject. This is a point worth keeping in mind, because in Heidegger's essay on the work of art it is not at all clear that the notion of *Erde* has anything to do with a critique of self-consciousness (which is not the subject of the essay). We can see the connection between them, though, if we consider the fact that the primacy of the subject in metaphysics is a function of the reduction of Being to presence: humanism is the doctrine that assigns to humanity the role of the subject, that is, of self-consciousness as the locus of evidence, in the framework of Being as *Grund*, or, in other words, as full presence. *Sein und Zeit* poses the problem of the meaning of Being in the name of the 'non-humanistic' traits of the subject, that is, its *Befindlichkeit*, its historicity, and its differences. Heidegger initially shows in this work that the concept of Being based on the model of presence is the result of an act of historical and cultural 'abstraction' which is subsequently more clearly to be seen as an event of destiny (*Geschick*). We could say, in any event, that in *Sein und Zeit* there may already be found a first possible indication of an *Erde* behind the historical and cultural *Welt* of metaphysics. Behind Being as the simple presence of objectness there lies Being as time, as an epochal and *geschicklich* occurrence; and behind the consciousness that understands things as evidence there is something else – the 'thrown-ness' of existence – which challenges the hegemonic claims of consciousness.

This 'recovery' of the *irdisch* or earthly elements, which are also the authentically historical (but not historicist) elements of Dasein, can nevertheless not be understood in terms of a reappropriation. The intensity with which Heidegger explores in his late works the notion of *Ereignis* and the related concepts of *Ver-eignen*, *Ent-eignen*, and *Über-eignen*, can be explained as more than just a concern for the nature of Being as an event which is not simply-present; rather, it is an effort to free his original concept of *Eigentlichkeit*, or 'authenticity', from any suggestion of potential reappropriation, which would still be metaphysical and humanistic.

What Heidegger attempts to understand, in his interrogation of the nature of modern technology, is the meaning of the fact that the crisis of contemporary humanism is defined by the lack of any possible basis for a 'reappropriation', that is, by its being inextricably intertwined with the death of God and the end of metaphysics. The significance of the connection that he establishes between humanism, metaphysics, technology and the 'propriative/expropriative' nature of the *Ereignis* of Being is still far from being understood today. I will try here, in the way of developing a working hypothesis, to isolate some of the key elements of Heidegger's argument.

Heidegger connects the crisis of humanism to the end of metaphysics as the culmination of technology and the moment of passage beyond the world of the subject/object opposition. In this way, he not only confers a systematic dignity on those 'radical' intuitions – exemplified by the work of Spengler and Jünger – concerning the crisis of humanism that we have already examined, but, in a more far-reaching way, constructs the theoretical basis for on the one hand situating the crisis of humanism as it occurs in the institutions of late modern society, and on the other for the taking leave of subjectivity developed in important strands of twentieth-century thought, in a relation which is not simply polemical. Adorno's name has already been mentioned: his work is emblematic of a way of thinking that sees the task of twentieth-century thought as one of resistance to the attacks launched against man's humanity – still defined in terms of subjectivity and self-consciousness – by the rationalization of social labour. Adorno's position is representative not only of a vast number of Hegelian-Marxist thinkers in our culture, but of the various versions of phenomenology and – in another discipline – numerous developments in psychoanalysis that generally tend to position themselves within a reappropriative horizon. Other elements and strands of contemporary thought work against this still profoundly humanistic cultural mode by seeking an over-coming of the notion of the subject. These are the theoretical equivalent of the liquidation of the subject at the level of social existence itself. This is not a case of a pure theoretical reflection of, and apologetic for, what occurs at an institutional level. Neither, however, is the only possibility for thought today that of becoming a defence of subjectivity and of *humanitas* against the dehumanizing assault of rationalization. If the liquidation of the subject at the level of social existence may be given a meaning that is not merely a destructive one, this may be achieved through the 'critique of the subject' that the radical theories of the crisis of humanism – especially Nietzsche's and Heidegger's – have developed. The destiny of human existence in technological society, if it is not viewed through a theoretical critique of the subject, can only appear as – and be – the inferno of a wholly administered and regulated society as it is described by the Frankfurt school. It is not a matter of opposing a providential (or, even less so, fatalistic) view of capitalistic rationalization of social labour to Adorno's view; rather, we need to recognize that – contrary to the essentially unfounded claims of critical theory itself – while this rationalization has created the historical and social conditions for the elimination of the subject, at the same time philosophy, psychology, and artistic and literary experience have autonomously acknowledged that this same subject does not merit a defence. If the Heideggerian analysis of the connection between metaphysics, humanism and technology is a valid one, moreover, then the subject that supposedly has to be defended from technological dehumanization is itself the very root of this dehumanization, since the kind of subjectivity which is defined strictly as the subject of the object is a pure function of the world of objectivity, and inevitably tends to become itself an object of manipulation.

To listen to the call of the *Ge-Stell* as a 'first flashing up of the *Ereignis*' thus means to allow oneself to live radically the crisis of humanism. This does not mean – and Heidegger's work serves to confirm this – that one should yield without reserve to the laws of technology, to the multiplicity of its games, and to the dizzying concatenation of its mechanisms. The end of metaphysics does not grant us the freedom for this sort of abandonment. This is the reason why Heidegger always insists that we must think about the *essence* of technology, and that this essence is not itself in turn something technological. The leaving behind of humanism and metaphysics is not an overcoming, but rather a *Verwindung*; subjectivity is not something that can be simply shed like an old, worn-out garment. In supplying the theoretical conditions both for eliminating any demonizing vision of technology and social rationalization and for understanding the elements of destiny in the latter that speak to us, Heidegger also reconnects technology to metaphysics and to the tradition that links us to metaphysics. To see technology in its relation with this tradition means not to permit it to impose its own version of the world as *the* 'reality', which would possess the same peremptory and still metaphysical nature as that of the Platonic *ontos on*. A subject which can no longer be thought of as a strong subject is indispensable if we are to deny the grandeur of the metaphysical *ontos on* to technology, its productions, its laws, and the world that it creates. The crisis of humanism, in the radical sense that it acquires in the work of philosophers such as Nietzsche and Heidegger, as well as in that of psychoanalysts such as Lacan and perhaps even in writers such as Musil, is most likely to be resolved in terms of a kind of 'crash diet for the subject', one which would allow the subject to listen to the call of a Being that no longer arises in the peremptory tone of the *Grund* or the thought of thought (or absolute spirit), but that dissolves its presence-absence into the network offered by a society increasingly transformed into an extremely sensitive organism of communication.

NOTES

1 Cf. *Vorträge und Aufsätze* (Pfullingen: Neske, 1954; repr. 1978), p. 6.
2 Cf. *Vorträge und Aufsätze*, p. 27, on the *Ge-Stell* and its significance; see also the final essay in my *Le avventure della differenza*.
3 Cf. *Identity and Difference* (1957), trans. Joan Stambaugh (New York: Harper and Row, 1969), p. 38: 'In the frame [*Ge-Stell*], we glimpse a first, oppressing flash of the appropriation [*Ereignis*].' Heidegger's term *Aufblitzen* could also here be translated as a 'flashing (up)'.

PART II

The Truth of Art

3

The Death or Decline of Art

As is the case with many of Hegel's ideas, the notion of the death of art has turned out to be prophetic with regard to the development of advanced industrial society. This is so even though the death of art in the contemporary world does not have quite the same meaning that it does for Hegel, but rather – as Adorno repeatedly shows – a strangely perverted one. Is it not perhaps true that the universalization of the domain of information could be interpreted as a perverted realization of the triumph of absolute spirit? The utopia of the return of the spirit to itself – that is, the coincidence between Being and a completely transparent self-consciousness – occurs in some way in our everyday life as a generalization of the realm of means of communication and of the universe of representations diffused by these same means, which can no longer be distinguished from 'reality'. Naturally, the realm of the mass media is not the Hegelian absolute spirit; it is instead perhaps a caricature of it. In any event, though, the mass media are not simply a perversion of it in the sense of a degeneration, but rather something which contains, as is often the case with perversions, cognitive and practical possibilities which need to be explored, and which probably delineate the shape of things to come.

It should be noted right away, even if our argument will not proceed any further in these very general terms, that when we discuss the death of art we are speaking within the framework of this effective perverted realization of the Hegelian absolute spirit. Or rather, in what amounts to the same thing, we are speaking within the framework of an accomplished metaphysics that has arrived at its end, in the sense in which Heidegger – who sees Nietzsche's work as a philosophical announcement of this – speaks of such an occurrence. To bring into play another Heideggerian term, the fact that we speak from within this framework indicates that what is at stake is not so much an *Überwindung* as a *Verwindung* of metaphysics.[1] It is not an overcoming of the perverted realization of the absolute spirit, or, in the case at hand, of the death of art, but rather a healing of it and a resignation to it. The death of art is a phrase that describes or, better still, constitutes the epoch of the end of metaphysics as prophesied by Hegel, as lived by Nietzsche and as registered by Heidegger. In this epoch thought stands in a position of *Verwindung* in regard to metaphysics. Metaphysics is not abandoned like an old, worn-out garment, for it still constitutes our 'humanity' in *geschicklich* terms; we yield to it, we heal ourselves from it, we are resigned to it as something that is destined to us.

Like the whole of the heritage of metaphysics, the death of art cannot be understood as a 'notion' which could be said to correspond (or fail to correspond) to a certain state of things, or which is more or less logically contradictory and could therefore be replaced by some other 'notion', or whose origin, ideological significance, and so on could be explained. It is instead an event that constitutes the historical and ontological constellation in which we move. This constellation is a network of historical and cultural events and of the words which belong to them, at once describing and co-determining them. The death of art concerns us in this *geschicklich* sense of what is 'destined' for us, and is something which we simply cannot ignore. First of all, it concerns us as the prophecy or utopia of a society in which art no longer exists as a specific phenomenon, but has been suppressed and ablated – in a Hegelian way – through a general aestheticization of existence. The last prominent figure to proclaim loudly the death of art was Herbert Marcuse, or at least the Marcuse who was a guru of the 1968 student revolt. From his point of view, the death of art appears as a readily available possibility for a technologically advanced society – that is to say, in our own terms, in a society with a fully realized metaphysics. Now, such a possibility does not exist only as a theoretical utopia. Starting with the early twentieth-century avant-garde movements, the practice of the arts forms part of a wider phenomenon of the 'explosion' of aesthetics beyond the institutional limits which are traditionally assigned to it. The poetics of the avant-garde reject the limitations which philosophy, especially of the neo-Kantian and neo-idealist sort, had previously imposed upon art. Avant-garde art refuses to be considered as a place of non-theoretical and non-practical experience, and instead claims to be the model for a privileged mode of knowledge of the real, a moment of subversion of the hierarchized structure of the individual and society, and thus an instrument of true social and political action. The heritage of the early avant-garde is maintained by the later avant-garde movements, although at a less totalizing and less metaphysical level, which continue to argue in favour of exploding the traditional confines of aesthetics. This explosion becomes, for instance, a negation of the places which had traditionally been assigned to aesthetic experience, such as the concert hall, the theatre, the gallery, the museum, and the book. A series of developments occur – earth-works, body art, street theatre, and so on – which appear somewhat more limited in regard to the revolutionary metaphysical ambitions of the earlier avant-garde movements, but also more concretely within reach for contemporary artistic experience. No longer is art to be rendered out-of-date and suppressed by a future revolutionary society; rather, the experience of art as an integral aesthetic fact is immediately to be sought out. As a consequence, the status of the work becomes constitutively ambiguous: the work no longer seeks a success which would permit it to position itself within a determinate set of values (the imaginary museum of objects possessed of aesthetic quality), but rather defines its success fundamentally in terms of rendering problematic such a set of values, and in overcoming – at least momentarily – the limits of the latter. In this perspective, one of the criteria for evaluation of the work of art seems to be, first and foremost, the ability of the work to call into question its own status. It may do this either directly (and thus often quite crudely) or indirectly, for instance as an ironization of literary genres, as rewriting, as a poetics of citation, or as a use of photography not for creating certain formal effects but for its most elementary function of duplication. In all these phenomena, which are present in different ways in contemporary artistic experience, it is not merely a matter of the sort of self-reference which, in many aesthetic theories, seems constitutive of all art; rather, it is a question of facts which are specifically linked to the death of art in the sense of an explosion of aesthetics which also occurs in these forms of self-ironization of the artistic operation.

The impact of technology is a decisive fact for the passage from the explosion of aesthetics as it appears in the early avant-garde movements – which conceive of the death of art as the suppression of the limits of aesthetics in order to move toward a metaphysical, or historical and political, meaning of the work – to the explosion which appears in the newer avant-garde movements. Technology is taken here to mean what it does for Walter Benjamin in his 1936 essay on 'The Work of Art in the Age of Mechanical Reproduction'. Art's escape from institutional confines no longer either exclusively or principally appears to be linked, in this perspective, to the utopia of metaphysical or revolutionary reintegration of existence; rather, it seems connected to the advent of new technologies which in fact at once permit and determine a form of generalization of aestheticity. With the advent of the ability to reproduce art by mechanical means, the works of the past lose their aura, that is, the halo that surrounds them and isolates them (and together with them the aesthetic realm of experience as well) from the rest of existence. Forms of art are born for which reproducibility is constitutive, such as film and photography: such works not only have no original, but tend to collapse the difference between producer and user because they rely upon the technological use of machines, thus eliminating any argument about the genius of the artist (which is, in essence, the aura as seen from the artist's point of view).

The idea that aesthetic experience is decisively transformed in the era of mass reproduction, as Benjamin contends, represents the moment of passage from a utopian and revolutionary meaning for the death of art to a technological one instead, which ultimately takes the form of a theory of mass culture. This is so even if, as is well known, Benjamin himself would have never made such a claim: he rather distinguishes between a 'good' (socialist) and a 'bad' (fascist) aestheticization of experience. The death of art is not only what will result from the revolutionary reintegration of existence; it is what we are already living in a mass culture, for such a culture produces a generalized aestheticization of life. This can be said to occur because the mass media – who, to be sure, distribute information, culture, and entertainment, but always according to the general criteria of the 'beautiful', that is, the formal attractiveness of products – have assumed in the life of each individual an infinitely more important role than in any other era of the past. An identification between the domain of the mass media and the aesthetic itself is certainly open to objection. However, such an identification becomes relatively simple to sustain if it is kept in mind that, over and beyond the function of distributing information, the mass media serve to produce a consensus through the establishment and intensification of a common language of social life. The mass media do not provide a means for the masses which is at the service of the masses; it is the means *of* the masses, in the sense in which the masses as such are constituted by the mass media as a public realm of common consensus, taste, and feeling. This function, which is usually called (in a pejorative sense) the organization of consensus, is an exquisitely aesthetic one. This becomes clear if we recall one of the fundamental meanings that has been attributed to the term 'aesthetic' since

the *Critique of Judgement*: aesthetic pleasure is not defined as
that which the subject experiences in relation to the object,
but is rather that pleasure which derives from the recognition
of belonging to a group – which, for Kant, is humanity itself as
an ideal – that shares the same capacity for appreciating the
beautiful.

This point of view may be found to exist in different ways:
in the theoretical return to Hegelian concepts by revolutionary
ideology, in early and 'neo-' avant-garde poetics, and in the
experience of the mass media as the distributor of aesthetic
products which are also the sites upon which a consensus
is organized. In this perspective the death of art signifies two
things: in a strong – and utopian – sense, it indicates the end of
art as a specific fact, separate from the rest of experience,
thanks to the renewal and reintegration of existence; in a weak
– or real – sense, it points to aestheticization as an extension of
the domain of the mass media.

The way in which artists often respond to the death of art at
the hands of the mass media also belongs to the category of
death, for it appears as a suicidal gesture of protest. To protest
against *Kitsch*, a manipulative mass culture, and the aestheticization of existence at a low and weak level, authentic art has
often taken refuge in programmatically aporetic positions
which deny any possibility of immediate enjoyment of
the work (its 'gastronomic' aspect, as it were), refuse to
communicate anything at all, and opt for silence instead.
Adorno finds this to be the crucial lesson of Beckett's work, as
is well known, and in various ways sees the same as holding
true for many artistic avant-garde movements; in a world
where consensus is produced by manipulation, authentic art
speaks only by lapsing into silence, and aesthetic experience
arises only as the negation of all its traditional and canonical
characteristics, starting with the pleasure of the beautiful
itself. Even in Adorno's negative aesthetics, as in the case of
the utopia of a general aestheticization of experience, the chief
criterion for evaluating the work of art is its greater or lesser
capacity for self-negation. If the meaning of art resides in its

production of a reintegration of existence, the work of art will appear valid precisely to the degree that it leads back to such a reintegration and necessarily dissolves into it. If, instead, the meaning of the work is found in its resistance to the omnipotence of *Kitsch*, then once again its validity coincides with its own self-negation. In a sense that needs to be more closely examined, the work of art, in present conditions, displays characteristics analogous to Heidegger's notion of Being: it arises only as that which at the same time withdraws from us.

(Naturally, it should not be forgotten that for Adorno the criterion of evaluation of the work of art is not only and explicitly the self-negation of its own status. There is instead also the technical tradition of each art to consider, as that which assures the possibility of a relation between the history of art and the history of spirit. Through artistic technique, above all, the work of art is realized as a fact of the spirit, that is, as containing a truth or a spiritual significance. Since Adorno is not an optimistic Hegelian and does not believe in progress, he sees the technical aspect of art as in the last analysis only a means for guaranteeing a more perfect impenetrability of the work of art and as a means for reinforcing its screen of silence.)

In this sort of philosophical phenomenology of the contemporary *Wesen* of art (in the Heideggerian sense of the term), more is involved than merely the different forms of the death of art as a utopia of reintegration, as an aestheticization of mass culture, and as authentic art's suicide and silence. Other facts need to be considered here as well, facts which constitute the rather surprising survival of art in the traditional and institutional sense. For there are still, after all, theatres, concert halls, and galleries, and there are artists who produce works which unproblematically fit into these frameworks. At the theoretical level, this means that the evaluation of these works cannot be based especially and exclusively on their capacity for self-negation. In the face of the different manifestations of the death of art, the fact that there are still 'works of art' in the institutional sense of the term appears as an alternative to the former and as something irreducible to it. In other words, such works appear as an ensemble of *objects differentiated from each other not only on the basis* of their greater or lesser degree of negativity in respect to the status of art. The world of effective artistic production cannot be described in an adequate way solely on the basis of this criterion. We are continually faced with differentiations of value that elude such a simplistic classification, and that cannot be said to belong to it even in a mediated way. Theory has to reflect most carefully upon this problem, since the notion of the death of art – which appears so simplificatory and comforting in its metaphysical compactness – could serve theory as a convenient means to avoid confronting it at all.

The survival of a world of artistic products with its own internal order, however, has a constitutive relation to the three different manifestations of the death of art defined above. It would be easy to show that the history of painting – or, better still, of the visual arts – and the history of poetry over the past few decades have meaning only if placed in relation to the world of images of the mass media or the language of this same world. This is a matter, once again, of relations which in general can be said to belong to the Heideggerian category of *Verwindung*, for they are ironical-iconical relations that at once duplicate and break down the images and words produced by mass culture, but not only in order to negate such a culture. The fact that in spite of everything else, vital works of 'art' still are produced today probably depends upon this. For these products are the place in which – in a complex system of relations – the three different aspects of the death of art (as utopia, as *Kitsch*, and as silence) are brought into play and come into contact with each other. The philosophical description of this situation could finally become complete through the recognition that the key element in the persistent life of art and in its products – which nevertheless continue to define themselves from inside the institutional frame of art – is precisely this interplay of the various aspects of its own death.

This is the situation with which aesthetic philosophy must deal. Because it persists in always announcing and always once again deferring the death of art, such a situation could be called the *decline* of art.

Traditional aesthetic philosophy has a difficult time taking the measure of this particular group of phenomena, for traditional concepts appear devoid of any basis in concrete experience. It is always somewhat uncomfortable, for anyone concerned with aesthetics who tries to describe the contemporary experience of art and of the beautiful with the somewhat grandiose conceptual language inherited from earlier philosophy, when the former and the latter come into contact with each other. Do we still really find the work of art to be an exemplary work of genius, a concrete manifestation of an idea, or a 'setting-into-work of truth'? Certainly, such an inflated description of the work of art could be undermined at the level of utopia and social critique: we no longer encounter works of art which can be described in these terms because the world of an integrated and authentic human experience is no longer or not yet real. Alternatively, we could entirely reject the conceptual terminology of traditional aesthetics by having recourse instead to the 'positive' notions of this or that 'human science', whether it be semiotics, psychology, anthropology, sociology, or whatever. Both of these approaches remain deeply – or, as Nietzsche would say, reactively – linked to tradition. They both suppose that the world of aesthetic concepts handed down by tradition is still the only possible one for the construction of a philosophical discourse on art. They thus either maintain it by preserving it in a negative perspective (whether utopian or critical), or by declaring that aesthetic philosophy no longer has any meaning. In both cases (although on different levels) we see that the death of aesthetic philosophy mirrors the death of art in the various senses discussed above. The aesthetics inherited from tradition, however, could be neither the only possible conceptual system nor simply an ensemble of notions which are false because they have no connection to experience itself. Like metaphysics (in Heidegger's sense of the term), traditional aesthetics is a destiny for us: it is something to which we must yield, from which we must heal ourselves, and to which we must resign ourselves. The grandiose nature of the concepts which have come down to us from the aesthetics developed within the metaphysical tradition is linked to the essence of this same metaphysics. Heidegger has described it primarily as objectivizing thought, and in general as that epoch of the history of Being in which Being arises and occurs as presence. We may add that this epoch is also especially characterized by the fact that Being arises in it as *force*, namely as grandeur, evidence, definiteness, and permanence – and also, probably, as domination. With the positioning of the problem of Being and time the *Verwindung* of metaphysics begins, and this positioning cannot be interpreted solely as the strategic manœuvre of any single philosopher. Being now arises, as is already announced in Nietzsche's nihilism, as that which disappears and perishes: from the discourse of *Sein und Zeit* on, Being is not that which remains, but rather that which is born and dies.

⌐ The situation of the death – or, better, of the decline – of art in which we are living today is philosophically interpretable as one aspect of the more general event, concerning Being itself, which is the *Verwindung* of metaphysics. How is this the case? To answer this question, we need to look at it in a way that has only infrequently been considered by previous readers of Heidegger: what we experience in the moment of the decline of art is describable in terms of the Heideggerian notion of the work of art as the 'setting-into-work of truth'.

In the era of mechanical reproduction aesthetic experience grows ever closer to what Benjamin calls 'distracted perception'. This perception no longer encounters the 'work of art', of which the aura was once an integral part. It may therefore be said that the experience of art no longer arises, or has yet to arise, but this admission is still always set in the framework of an acceptance of the concepts of metaphysical aesthetics. It is instead possible, though, that it is precisely in the distracted experience of art that seems to be the only one available to us in our present condition that the *Wesen* of art summons us in a sense that requires us to step beyond metaphysics. The experience of a distracted perception no longer comes into contact with works themselves, but rather operates in an atmosphere of twilight, decline, and disseminated meanings as well. This occurs in the same way in which, for instance, moral experience is no longer forced to choose between the absolute values of good and evil, but only between micrological facts in regard to which traditional notions appear grandiose and empty, as is the case with art. In *Human All Too Human* (vol. I, aphorism 34), Nietzsche describes this situation in terms of an opposition between the resentful individual who lives the loss of the pathos and the metaphysical dimensions of existence as a tragedy and the individual who is instead 'free of emphasis'.

The Heideggerian notion of the 'setting-into-work of truth' can be, from a philosophical point of view, productively applied to this same situation. For Heidegger, the work is an 'exhibition' (*Aufstellung*) of a world and a 'production' (*Herstellung*) of the earth.[2] Heidegger emphasizes the notion of 'exhibition' in the same terms we use for 'putting on' an exhibition in a museum or gallery, for instance; for it implies that the work of art has the function of founding and constituting the outlines which define an historical world. A society or social group – in short, an historical world – recognizes the constitutive traits of its own experience of the world (for instance, the implicit criteria for distinguishing between good and evil, truth and error, etc.) in a work of art. This idea affirms the inaugural nature of the work, which depends upon Kant's thesis of the absolute originality of artistic genius. However, *Aufstellung* also refers us to the notion, developed out of the philosophy of Dilthey, that in the work of art, more than in any other product of the spirit, the truth of any historical epoch is revealed. The essential element here is not so much the inaugurality of the work, or a 'truth' which could be opposed to error, as the constitution of the fundamental outlines of a given historical existence, that is, what is called (in depreciatory terms) the aesthetic function as an organization of consensus. In the work each individual's sense of membership in a historical world may be recognized and intensified. In this way the distinction on the basis of which Adorno rejects the world of mass-media-oriented culture as pure ideology can be eliminated: for this distinction is one of a presumed use-value of the work which could be opposed to its exchange-value, namely to its functioning only as a distinguishing sign of recognition for groups and societies. The work as a 'setting-into-work of truth' – in its exhibition of a world – is the place where a sense of membership in a group is made recognizable and is intensified. This function, which is crucial for Heidegger's notion of the exhibition of a world, may belong not only to the work as a great individual achievement. For it is in fact a function which persists and is even more fully suitable in the situation in which individual works, along with their aura, disappear in a setting of relatively functional products that have, however, an analogous value.

The full implications of the Heideggerian notion of the work of art as a 'setting-into-work of truth' can be understood, however, only by examining its other aspect as a 'production' of the earth. In his 1936 essay, the idea of the work as a *Herstellung* of the earth is associated with both the materiality of the work and, especially, the fact that by virtue of this materiality (which is never to be understood as 'physical') the work occurs as something which is always kept in reserve. In the work, the earth is not, strictly speaking, matter; it is the presence of the work as such, namely its concrete appearance as something which always calls attention to itself. Even here, as in the case of the notion of 'world', we need to disentangle the meaning of Heidegger's argument (more than forty years later) from the metaphysical misunderstandings that threaten to compromise it. For the earth is the *hic et nunc* of the work, to which each new interpretation always returns and which always leads to new readings and therefore new possible 'worlds'. If we look carefully at Heidegger's text – for example where he speaks of the earth in the Greek temple as being in relation to the seasons, to the natural decay of matter, etc., or where he speaks of the conflict between world and earth as that in which truth opens up as *aletheia* – we discover that the earth is the dimension which in the work connects the world as a system of discrete and unfolded meanings to its 'other', the *physis*, which sets in motion the tendentially immobile structures of historical/social worlds through its rhythms. In short, the work of art is the 'setting-into-work of truth' because in it the opening up of a world as a context of referrals – like a language – is permanently connected to the earth as the 'other' of the world; and the earth has for Heidegger the features of *physis* (not in his 1936 essay, but in his writings on Hölderlin), which is defined by the fact of birth and growth and death. Earth and *physis* are that which *zeitigt* – or, literally, that which develops as a living being; they are also, however, that which is 'temporalized', in the etymological sense of the verb that Heidegger explores in *Sein und Zeit*. As the 'other' of the world, the earth is that which does not endure. On the contrary, it is that which appears always to withdraw into a 'naturality' that entails *Zeitigen*, namely birth and growth, and bears on its face the traces of the passage of time. The work of art is the one kind of artifact which registers ageing as a positive event that actively contributes to determine new possibilities of meaning.

This second aspect of Heidegger's notion of the work as a 'setting-into-work of truth' seems significant precisely because it points us in the direction of the temporality of the work of art, in a sense that has always eluded traditional meta-physical aesthetics. All the difficulties that aesthetic philosophy encounters in accounting for the experience of the decline of art, distracted perception, and mass culture, derive from the fact that it continues to think in terms of the work as a necessarily eternal form, and, at a deeper level, in terms of Being as permanence, grandeur, and force. The decline of art is instead an aspect of the more general situation of the end of metaphysics, in which thought is called upon to perform a *Verwindung* of metaphysics, in all the various senses of the term that have been discussed above. Aesthetics can fulfil its task as a philosophical aesthetics, from this point of view, if it is able to recognize in the various elements which are assumed to signal the death of art the announcement of an epoch of Being in which – in the perspective of an 'ontology of decline' – thought may open itself up to the only partially negative and 'fallen' meaning (in the sense of *Verfallenheit*) which the experience of aestheticity has acquired in the era of mechanical reproduction and mass culture.

NOTES

1 Martin Heidegger, *Vorträge und Aufsätze* (Pfullingen: Neske, 1954; repr. 1978), pp. 71 ff.
2 Cf. Heidegger, 'The Origin of the Work of Art' (1936), in *Poetry, Language, Thought*, trans. Albert Hofstadter (1971; repr. New York: Harper and Row, 1975), pp. 15–87.

4

The Shattering of the Poetic Word

At the end of his long essay on 'The Nature of Language' (published in *Unterwegs zur Sprache*[1]), Heidegger 'rewrites' the line of Stefan George's poem upon which he has already commented at length in the preceding pages (and upon which he will comment again, together with the rest of the poem to which it belongs, in the essay on 'The Word' that follows in the same collection). George's line goes as follows: '*Kein Ding sei wo das Wort gebricht*' ('where the word breaks off no thing may be'); Heidegger transforms it in a way that only seemingly reverses its meaning: '*Ein "ist" ergibt sich wo das Wort zerbricht*' ('an "is" arises where the word breaks up'). Hence it no longer means 'no thing is where there is no word', but rather 'an "is" occurs where the word fails.'

It is clear from the context that Heidegger, thinking of the poetic word,[2] makes no claim here for an occurrence of Being 'in person', outside or beyond the mediation of language, as if the shattering of the word that occurs in poetry were able to lead us 'to things themselves'. What occurs in originary language – in the language of poetry, which is (at least to a certain extent) the same thing – is a positioning of the thing in the game of *Geviert*, in the framework of earth and sky, mortals and divinities, which occurs only as a 'resounding of silence' or 'ringing of stillness' (*Geläut der Stille*) and possesses none of the objective evidence of essences defined by phenomenology. If this is quite clear, the shattering of the word which lets the 'is' appear in poetic language is nevertheless difficult to reconcile with the Heideggerian doctrine of poetry as the 'setting-into-work of truth'. For this doctrine seems to be completely dominated by an inaugural and foundational notion of art and poetry, namely the one emblematically expressed by Hölderlin's lines which Heidegger repeats and comments upon so often: '*Was bleibet aber/Stiften die Dichter*' ('But that which remains/Is established by the poets').[3] Starting with the essay on 'The Essence of Truth' (1930),[4] and more specifically with the essay on 'The Origin of the Work of Art' (1936),[5] the work of art appears as a 'setting-into-work of truth' insofar as truth is the opening of the historical/*geschicklich* horizon in which every verification of a proposition becomes possible, prior to and more fundamentally than the correspondence of the proposition to the thing. That is to say, it is the act by which a certain historical and cultural world is instituted, in which a specific historical 'humanity' sees the characteristic traits of its own experience of the world defined in an originary way. As we know, for Heidegger inaugural events are events of language, for – already upon the basis of *Sein und Zeit* – it is primarily in language that the originary familiarity with the world unfolds, which constitutes the non-transcendental, always historically finite and 'situated' condition of the possibility of experience. The pre-comprehension of the world into which Dasein has always already been thrown is a horizon of language. This horizon is not, however, the always identical transcendental screen of Kantian reason. It is instead historical and finite, and this is precisely what permits us to speak of an 'occurrence' of truth. What we call poetry are the inaugural events in which the historical/*geschicklich* horizons of experience of particular historical human beings are instituted. It is nevertheless difficult to articulate the question of the relationship between these 'different' inaugural events. Heidegger always speaks of the 'event of Being' only in the singular, and he speaks of the *epoch* of Being also in the singular. In fact, this aspect of Heideggerian thought is probably the one upon which the hermeneutic ontology that takes its lead from him has most fruitfully meditated. We must still not forget, in any event, that in the essay on 'The Origin of the Work of Art', what in *Sein und Zeit* was *the* world instead becomes *a* world, and this at least indicates that the unfolding of truth cannot be conceived of as a stable structure, but rather always as (an) event.

The meaning of the inaugurality of the work of art can be granted greater or lesser importance according to whether one thinks of poetry in the same way as one thinks of the Bible, the great national epics, or the ground-breaking works of our civilization (the Greek tragedians, Dante, Shakespeare, Hölderlin, and so on), or whether one tries instead to test the definition even on 'minor' works of art – in which case this inaugurality might be understood above all as the originality or as the irreducibility of the work to whatever has already been. In any event, placing importance on the inaugural nature of the work as the essence of the truth of poetry is widely popular in contemporary aesthetics, even if it goes under a number of different names. The irreducibility of the work of art to what is already in existence can be seen as the 'quasi-subjectivity' of the work,[6] insofar as it does not let itself be experienced as a thing in the world, but rather presents itself as a new global perspective on the world. It can also be seen as a truly prophetic and utopian figuration of an alternative world or of a harmonized existence with regard to which the existing order is revealed in its injustice and inauthenticity (here I am thinking of theorists like Bloch, Adorno, and Marcuse). It may even be seen as the presentation of various possibilities of existence which, while not claiming to stand as a utopian *telos* or criterion for judgement upon that which already exists, still function by making it fluid and suspending its exclusivity and cogency.[7] In each of these – and other – possible variations, the inaugurality of poetry and art is always conceived in terms of 'founding', that is to say, of figuring *possible* historical worlds which offer an alternative to the existing world, even if the alternative is recognized as a pure utopia which nevertheless preserves its value as a criterion of judgement or as an ideal yardstick. In such a perspective, the shattering and failing of the poetic word, which Heidegger's rewriting of George's line of verse expresses, can be interpreted only in a sense that reinstates the representational relation between words and things. The poetic word is destined to shatter just as the prophetic word does at the moment in which the prophecy is 'realized'. If the inaugural significance of poetry generally consists in the founding of historical worlds (whether real or possible, for even in the latter case they are still historical worlds), poetic language has the same inessential characteristics that representational language does. It is consumed and shattered in referring to the thing, when the thing is (now) made present. The fact that the future to which poetry alludes is always yet to come, like Bloch's, Adorno's and Marcuse's utopia, does not significantly change this inessential structure of its language.

In the same place where he discusses the shattering of the word, Heidegger suggests a meaning of *Zeigen* ('showing') that is radically irreducible to a representational and referential concept of language. It is precisely this representational concept of the relation between language and things which is 'subverted' (Heidegger uses the verb '*umwerfen*') by the *Zeigen* of the originary word that occurs in poetry. The shattering of the word, at which reflection on the nature of language arrives, is indeed to be understood as a *Zeigen* or showing; but rather than fall back into a metaphysical concept of language as a sign *for* something, this *Zeigen* subverts both our usual referential way of understanding the word–thing relation and our own relation to language itself. To experience language as *Zeigen* or, in what amounts to the same thing, as *Sage* ('originary saying')[8] means that 'language is not a mere faculty of man.' It 'ceases to be something with which we, speaking men, have a relationship'; instead, it becomes clear that it is 'the relation of all relations'.[9] Language is *Zeigen* not by being an instrument for showing things; rather, *Zeigen* means *Erscheinen lassen* – that is, to 'make appear', particularly in the sense of making each thing be reflected in the mirror-game of the *Geviert*.[10]

This is why *Nahnis*, meaning 'nearness' or 'proximity', plays such a large part in the definition of *Zeigen*: 'to say means to show, to make appear, the lighting-concealing-releasing offer of world. Now, nearness manifests itself as the motion in which the world's regions face each other . . . . Quiet consideration makes possible an insight into how nearness and Saying, being of the persisting nature of language, are the Same.' The regions of the world of which Heidegger speaks here are the four regions of the *Geviert*: earth and sky, mortals and divinities. The showing in which the word shatters is not a reference back to the thing, but rather a positioning of it in proximity to or in the framework of the regions of the world to which it belongs. Yet man belongs to the *Geviert* insofar as he is mortal: 'mortals are they who can experience death as death. Animals cannot do so. But animals cannot speak either. The essential relation between death and language flashes up before us, but remains still unthought.'[11] Here the shattering of the word in the *Zeigen* of originary saying finds a precise point of reference in one of the constitutive dimensions of Heidegger's existential thought, the being-towards-death which has a central function in his analysis in *Sein und Zeit*. It is not merely a matter of 'poetically evoking' the halo of the world's regions around the thing, which would remain imprecise and leave 'poeticity' with all the vagueness of meaning that it has always had in the metaphysical tradition. The connection between language and mortality, which here 'flashes up before us' but still remains unthematized, as Heidegger himself admits, suggests that the shattering of the word in originary saying and in poetry – if it is not to be seen in terms of referential (or even prophetic) provisionality – must instead be understood as being defined by its relation to the constitutive mortality of Dasein. Although Heidegger changes his terminology, he remains to the end faithful to the premises of *Sein und Zeit*: the authenticity of existence is still always defined by its explicit projection toward death. But whereas in *Sein und Zeit* the *existentiell* significance of the anticipation of death is left undefined, the connection between originary saying and mortality now seems to supply some elements for thinking through the meaning of authentic existence and its decision for death in a more articulate way. For the Heidegger of *Unterwegs zur Sprache* the anticipation of death – upon which the possibility of authentic existence depends – is the experience of the connection between language and mortality, that is, the shattering of the word in the originary saying of poetry.[12] In turn, this shattering is not to be understood as a referential gesture which makes the sign disappear in the presence of the thing signified, but rather as a particular relation between poetic language and mortality.

But how can we understand this constitutive relation between poetic language and mortality in the light of the inaugural concept of poetry which Heidegger develops in his essay on 'The Origin of the Work of Art'? To do so requires an interpretation of the foundational and inaugural significance of poetry which does not exclusively stress the 'setting-into-work of truth' as the institution and opening up of historical worlds. If it is to be a way of experiencing mortality in language, poetry cannot be merely a foundation in the sense of an inauguration, a beginning, or an institution of new horizons of experience in which the lives of historical men unfold. 'That which remains is established by the poets,' Heidegger says, following Hölderlin. But is 'that which remains' no more than a 'world', a historical and cultural setting defined by a lexis, a syntax, a complex of rules for distinguishing between truth and falsehood? The world, understood in this way – that is, the historical world which might seem to be the 'meaning' of poetic discourse, which the word of the poet announces and allows to exist – is not something which 'remains', but is rather precisely that which passes away and changes constantly. It is well known that in the essay on 'The Origin of the Work of Art' Heidegger defines the work as the 'setting up of the world' and the 'setting forth of the earth'. Now, what remains and endures of that which the poets found is probably to be understood as being linked to the *earthly* dimension of the work rather than to its worldly dimension. An exclusive emphasis on the inaugural and prophetic nature of the work of art renders the shattering of the poetic word incomprehensible, reduces the work to the dimension of the world, and ignores its earthly character. The meaning of the formula 'an "is" arises where the word shatters' is to be sought precisely in the dimension of the *Erde*. While the world is the system of meanings which are read as they unfold in the work, the earth is that element of the work which comes forth as ever concealing itself anew, like a sort of nucleus that is never used up by interpretations and never exhausted by meanings. Like *Zeigen*, the earth too sends us back to mortality. *Erde* is in fact a relatively uncommon word in Heidegger's work. It first appears in the 1936 essay on 'The Origin of the Work of Art', and later figures as one of the 'four' of the 'four fold' – earth and sky, mortals and divinities – in the essays in which he speaks of the *Geviert*. If on the basis of Heidegger's texts we try to clarify that obscure element which opposes the world in the work of art, we encounter the earth of the fourfold, to which Dasein belongs as something mortal. Poetry can be defined as that language in which a world (of unfolded meanings) opens up, and in which our terrestrial essence as mortals reverberates.

It is possible to discern here at least three meanings which are distinct and yet closely tied to each other by multiple connections which in part still need to be explored. First of all, it is true that to some extent the shattering of the word lets Being appear as the thing arising 'in person'; but this occurs only paradoxically, since Being does not occur as something beyond the word or as something which was already there independently of it; rather, it occurs as an 'effect of silence'.[13] Heidegger does not lose sight of what phenomenology conceives to be an encounter with the thing itself, but he rethinks it as an effect of silence. To gain access to things themselves does not mean dealing with them as objects, but encountering them in a game of language-wrecking in which Dasein experiences primarily its own death. To accept the force of evidence – as gnoseological realism has always tended to do – always means to experience finitude. This is clearly visible in Kant, for whom the *receptivity* of intuition testifies irrefutably to the finitude of our constitution. To tie the *Zerbrechen* of the word, through which alone an 'is' occurs, to the earthliness and mortality of Dasein might also be a way to rethink in genuinely Heideggerian terms the phenomenological notion of a vision of essences, and the notion of evidence in general, which from the Heideggerian perspective can no longer adopt the model of an *obiectum* imposing itself upon a *subiectum*.[14] Here too the idea of poetry as the site of the 'setting-into-work of truth' finds suggestive confirmation: if it is indeed true that the occurrence of an 'is', even of what we ascertain in experiencing evidence, is an effect of silence linked to the earthliness and mortality of Dasein, then poetry could be singled out as a privileged site in regard to common experience, even from the point of view of truth as the encounter with evidence, for it is precisely in poetry, more than anywhere else, that language arises as that which *zerbricht*, or as what shatters and breaks up.

More specifically, however, where is the *Zerbrechen* of the word – that is, its earthliness and mortality – recognizable in poetry? The poetic attribute which sets forth the earth as self-concealing and as alluding to mortality is, first of all, its *monumentality*. In the realm of Heideggerian hermeneutic ontology, Gadamer was the first to call attention to the status of 'la poésie pure' as an example or model for understanding the essence of poetic works,[15] insofar as language in pure poetry (from symbolism to the various hermetic experiments of the twentieth-century avant-garde artistic movements) attains an essential condition, thus recovering that originary function of *naming* which is precisely the essence of poetry. Apart from its particular concerns, Gadamer's argument can be likened to what has been said about poetic language in formalist circles (Jakobson) or semiotic ones (Morris). Twentieth-century theories have emphasized various types of self-reference, intransitivity, and so on, as constitutive of poetic language, which calls attention to itself as a 'sign' that does not become transparent in the act of reference.

If we do not wish to consider, even if only implicitly, this self-referentiality of poetic language within the framework of a philosophy of self-consciousness (according to which the self-reference of poetic language would be the condition for a more authentic freedom for the subject in the use of language, outside the bonds and practical constraints within which language functions in ordinary life), then we must make recourse to the concept of monumentality. For a monument is not a function of subjective self-reference. It is primarily – perhaps even from the point of view of cultural anthropology – a funerary monument built to bear the traces and the memory of someone across time, but *for others*. The formal rules of poetry, from rhythm and rhyme to the refined techniques through which twentieth-century avant-garde movements have tried to make poetry into an 'essential' language, are the ways in which poetry pursues monumentality. Consonant with the Heideggerian vision of the work as the 'struggle' between world and earth, these cannot be seen as classical but only as neoclassical. In fact the monument is not, as Hegel would have it, a work in which form and content, inside and outside, idea and manifestation are fully identified with each other, and which accordingly represents an eminent example of an accomplished actualization of freedom itself – for example, the beautiful and harmonious humanity of the Greeks that Winckelmann thought to be fully embodied in their sculpture. The monument is rather that which endures in the form, already projected as such, of a funerary mask. The monument – and, historically speaking, neoclassical art is also this – is not the artistic casting of a full life, but rather a *formula* which is already constituted in such a way as to transmit itself, and is therefore already marked by its destiny of radical alienation: it is marked definitively, in so many words, by mortality. The monument-formula is not constructed so as to 'defeat' time, imposing itself on and regardless of time, but so as to endure in time instead. In speaking of the work as the 'setting forth of the earth', Heidegger evokes the example of the Greek temple, which carries its meanings (and hence opens its world) only by virtue of the fact that it allows the signs of time to be inscribed on its stone surface: from the changing light of day to the winds and seasons, and finally to the 'destructive' traces of the passage of the years and centuries. All such exposure to earthliness and mortality, which functions for a thing-instrument of daily life in a limiting and destructive sense, has instead a positive sense for the work of art. In the same positive sense, the critical fortune of a given work of art, which is constituted by a chain of changing interpretations, is linked to the succession of generations and thus to dying as well.[16]

The presence of the earth in the work, that is, the shattering of the word and the experience of mortality, first of all points in the direction not of a classical but a neoclassical reading of the Heideggerian theory of art. We can assign to the shattering of the word the meaning of becoming a monument and a formula. It is not a means of intensifying the fullness of the word, but a weakening and an approximation to the figure of death, or even to some extent a return to the state of the 'natural thing', as can be seen in the example of the Greek temple. But a second meaning of the shattering of the poetic work is also announced in its becoming a formula and a monument. If, in becoming a monument, the poetic word shatters insofar as it is prepared to endure only in the figure of death, then monumentality also alludes to the modality of the occurrence of truth which is explicitly characterized by the two elements of unconcealment and concealment. In fact, the very definition of the work as the 'setting-into-work of truth' which is produced in the conflict between world and earth alludes to these two characteristic elements. In the work of art truth occurs because the unconcealment (world) does not forget the concealment (earth) in which it originates. Heidegger's concept of truth is usually seen as refuting the metaphysical idea of truth as a stable structure (Plato's eternal and immutable *ontos on*); truth is instead understood as an event or, that is to say, as the ever new and different determination of regulative structures of experience, written in the mutable languages of man. But the fact that truth, as the opening through which the world always presents itself to historical men, is an event and not a stable structure (unlike Kant's transcendental Reason, for instance) profoundly alters the essence of truth. The horizon which opens up in the event does not have the qualities of fully unfolded luminosity (evidence) which are proper to metaphysical truth. The evidence of that 'is' which occurs only as an effect of silence is not the same as the evidence of metaphysical principles from which only eternity has been eliminated and eventuality added. When the true occurs – as it does primarily in art, prior to and more fundamentally than in science, where it is precisely the metaphysical principle of evidence that reigns – it appears in a 'faint light', and Heidegger's use of the term *Lichtung* alludes precisely to this.[17] Poetry is also a formula in the sense in which a 'formula' is a linguistic expression that has been worn out and emptied of its content. The effort with which a poet works over the poem, sculpts it, writes it and rewrites it, is not directed toward perfecting the coincidence of form and content, that is, towards that fully transparent *energheia* of the classical work; it is, rather, an anticipation of the essentializing erosion that time exerts upon the work, *reducing it to a monument*. What follows upon the poetic operation is the occurrence of a *Lichtung*, that faint light in which truth no longer arises with the impositive traits of metaphysical evidence. We can find a model for this kind of poetic monumentality in myth and in the manner of its constitution and reconstitution, as described by Lévi-Strauss (up to the similarity between mythopoiesis and *bricolage*). This similarity, not coincidentally, is explicitly negated by those formalistic theories which define poetic self-reference in terms of a game between various levels of language, a game at whose centre the self-conscious subject is still to be found.

Here the shattering of the poetic word finally leads us back to the Heideggerian notion of truth. The work of art can be a 'setting-into-work of truth' because truth is not a metaphysically stable structure but an event. Yet precisely because it is an event, truth can occur only in that shattering of the word which is monumentality, formula, and the faint light of the *Lichtung*: 'That which remains is established by the poets', not so much as 'that which endures' but primarily as 'that which remains' as a trace, a memory, or a monument. Every other experience of truth, even such as is displayed in the procedures of verification of the positive sciences, refers to this truth, which has been stripped of the authoritarian traits of metaphysical evidence. This is the same truth which is capable of that essential relationship with freedom which Heidegger outlines for the first time in his 1930 lecture, 'On the Essence of Truth', and which still demands of us a further effort to arrive at a full understanding of it, even on the basis of the experience of listening to poetry.

NOTES

Translator's note. I wish to acknowledge the influence of Thomas Harrison's translation of 'L'infrangersi della parola poetica', published in *The Favorite Malice: Ontology and Reference in Contemporary Italian Poetry* (New York: Out of London Press, 1983), pp. 221–35, on my own translation of Vattimo's text.

1 Martin Heidegger, 'The Nature of Language', in *On the Way to Language*, trans. Peter D. Hertz (New York: Harper and Row, 1971), pp. 57–108.

2 As is apparent from the final lines of the essay 'The Nature of Language', ibid., p. 108.

3 These lines of Hölderlin's come from the poem *Andenken*, and serve as one of the *Leitworte* of Heidegger's lecture on 'Hölderlin and the Essence of Poetry' (1936), published in *Erläuterungen zu Hölderlins Dichtung*, 3rd edn (Frankfurt: Klostermann, 1963), pp. 31 ff.

4 Martin Heidegger, 'On the Essence of Truth' (1949), in *Basic Writings*, ed. David F. Krell (New York: Harper and Row, 1977), pp. 113–41.

5 Martin Heidegger, *Poetry, Language, Thought*, trans. Albert

Hofstadter (New York: Harper and Row, 1971; repr. 1975), pp. 15–88.

6   This is M. Dufrenne's argument in *The Phenomenology of Aesthetic Experience*, trans. Edward S. Casey et al. (Evanston: Northwestern UP, 1973).

7   This would seem to be the meaning of several of Paul Ricoeur's arguments in *The Rule of Metaphor*, trans. Robert Czerny (Toronto: Toronto UP, 1977). These kinds of ideas, though, may already be found in Dilthey's notion of poetry, for example in his *Das Wesen der Philosophie* (1907), now in *The Essence of Philosophy*, trans. Stephen A. Emery and William T. Emery (Chapel Hill: UNC Press, 1954).

8   Heidegger, 'A Dialogue on Language', in *On the Way to Language*, trans. Hertz, p. 47, discusses the connection between the respective meanings of *sagen* 'to say' and *zeigen* 'to show'.

9   Cf. 'The Nature of Language', *On the Way to Language*, trans. Hertz, p. 107.

10 On the notion of *Geviert* (the 'fourfold'), see also Heidegger's lecture on 'The Thing', in *Poetry, Language, Thought* trans. Hofstadter, pp. 163–86.

11 Cf. 'The Nature of Language', *On the Way to Language*, trans. Hertz, p. 107.

12 On this nexus between originary language and mortality, see also chapter 3 of my *Al di là del soggetto* (Milan: Feltrinelli, 1981).

13 This is what Heidegger calls the 'Geläut der Stille' ('the ringing of stillness'), in 'The Nature of Language', *On the Way to Language*, trans. Hertz, p. 108.

14 As H.-G. Gadamer points out in his *Variationen* (Tübingen: Mohr, 1977), p. 243, Husserl believes that the eidetic reduction occurs 'spontaneously' in poetry. This means that he still considers poetry as within the horizon of subject/object relations. *Variationen* constitutes the fourth volume of the *Kleine Schriften*.

15 Cf. Gadamer, *Variationen*, p. 245.

16 This may be thought of both in terms of the notion of interpretation developed by Luigi Pareyson in his *Estetica. Teoria della formatività* (2nd edn, 1954; repr. Bologna: Zanichelli, 1960), and of the concept of *Wirkungsgeschichte* ('history of effects' or 'effective history') defined by Gadamer in

Truth and Method (1960), trans. Garrett Barden and John Cummings (2nd edn, 1975; repr. New York: Crossroads, 1984) pp. 267 et passim. The historical existence of the work, though, is not to be identified so much with the kind of 'positive' efficacy that belongs to historical 'actions' in the common sense of the term as with an experience of mortality and of being used up. For this reason, Gadamer's concept of the 'history of effects' or 'effective history' ought perhaps to be replaced by another term – *trace* – which places greater emphasis on the 'residual' nature of the historical existence of the work. See also, though, chapter 7 below.

17 On the connection between illumination and darkness in the concept of *Lichtung*, see L. Amoroso, 'La *Lichtung* di Heidegger come *lucus a* (*non*) *lucendo*', in *Il pensiero debole*, ed. G. Vattimo and P. A. Rovatti (Milan: Feltrinelli, 1983), pp. 137–63.

5

Ornament/Monument

A relatively little known and minor text by Heidegger dedicated to sculpture – his lecture on 'Art and Space' (1969)[1] – ends with these words: 'it is not always necessary for the true to be embodied; it is enough if it flutters nearby as spirit and generates a sort of concord, like when the sound of bells floats as a friend in the air and as a bearer of peace.' If on the one hand this lecture seems simplistically to return to the basic concepts of 'The Origin of the Work of Art',[2] applying them this time to sculpture and the plastic arts, a careful reading reveals that this 'application' gives rise to important modifications, or rather to a new 'declension', as it were, of the definition of the work of art as a 'setting-into-work of truth'. No doubt this can be understood as a part of the general process of transformation of Heidegger's thought, and it is all the more interesting to us because it is not just a marginal aspect of the so-called *Kehre* said to separate *Sein und Zeit* from the post-1930 works. Rather, it marks a movement which takes place in the writings that are positioned after this 'turning-point' in Heidegger's work. This is not, though, the place to examine this question in such general terms.[3] In any event, it can be agreed that the 1969 lecture signals the climactic moment of a process of rediscovery of 'spatiality' by Heidegger, and thus a distancing not only from *Sein und Zeit* (in which temporality is the key dimension for the reproposition of the problem of Being), but from a number of subsequent ontological inquiries into the same problem. It is difficult to decide exactly what this rediscovery of spatiality might mean for the whole of Heidegger's thought, especially because there is a risk of seeing it as opening onto possibilities which are too clearly mystical, or so it would seem. Certainly, however, this emphasis on space in the so-called 'second period' of Heidegger's work cannot be reductively interpreted as the mere stylistic predominance of spatial metaphors, ranging from the *Lichtung* (or 'glade') to the *Geviert* (or 'four fold' of earth and sky, mortals and divinities).[4]

In specific connection to Heidegger's concept of art and the aesthetic implications of his thought, the lecture on 'Art and Space' and the new attention that it pays to spatiality appear to lead to an important clarification of the concept of the work of art as a 'setting-into-work of truth' which also bears on the Heideggerian concept of Being and the true. I propose to show that all this has significant consequences for the aesthetic analysis of ornament.

Heidegger's theory of art would seem to be opposed to a recognition of the legitimacy of ornament and decoration – at least, in its insistence on the truthfulness of the work of art, it has generally been interpreted in this way. The work as a 'setting-into-work of truth' and as an inauguration of historical worlds (as 'epochal' poetry) seems conceived above all on the model of the great classical works – at least in the ordinary sense of this term, rather than in the Hegelian one. This is the case because the 'setting-into-work of truth', as Heidegger defines it, is realized not through a harmonization and perfect matching of inside and outside, idea and appearance, but rather through the persistence of the conflict between 'world' and 'earth' within the work. In spite of this radical difference from the theory of Hegel, Heideggerian aesthetics seems to consider the work to be 'classical' inasmuch as it conceives of the work as founding history and as inaugurating and instituting models of historical/*geschicklich* existence: this constitutes precisely the work as the occurrence of truth, even if, as we shall see, it is not simply this alone.

The inaugural function of the work as a truth-event may

occur, according to Heidegger, insofar as in the work the 'exhibition of a world',[5] along with the 'production of the earth', takes place. As long as these concepts are considered in regard to poetry, they tend to give rise to a predilection for a 'strong' notion of the inaugurality of art – and it seems likely that Heidegger thinks of the relation between the interpretative tradition and the great poetic works of the past in terms of the model provided by the relation between the Christian tradition and the Holy Scriptures. What happens if the exhibition of a world and the production of the earth are instead considered in relation to an art such as sculpture? Before the lecture on 'Art and Space', certain passages of Gadamer's *Truth and Method* take a first step towards providing us with some possible answers to this question. Gadamer reconsiders Heidegger's conclusions about the work of art as the occurrence of truth in an optic that assigns to architecture a sort of 'foundational' function in regard to all other arts, at least in the sense that it makes a 'place' for them and thus also 'embraces' them.[6] The words with which Heidegger's 1969 lecture ends, over and beyond their obvious spatial implications, appear difficult to fathom in reference to his concept of poetry. Precisely the fact that Heidegger here conceives of the 'opening' function of art with reference to a *spatial* art qualifies and clarifies at last what the conflict – in a positive sense – between world and earth means, together with the very significance of the term 'earth'. 'Art and Space', therefore, by no means restricts itself to applying the ideas of Heidegger's 1936 essay to the plastic arts, but provides a decisive explanation of the meaning of that essay – which is perhaps analogous to what occurs to the notion of being-towards-death in the transition from *Sein und Zeit* to the ontological and hermeneutic works of Heidegger's final phase.[7] As is well known, in 'The Origin of the Work of Art' Heidegger theorizes a *dichterisch* essence of all the arts, both in the sense in which *dichten* means to 'create' and to 'invent', and in the more specific sense in which it indicates poetry as the art of the word. It is not entirely clear in this essay, however, how the conflict between world and earth is brought about in poetry as the art of the word; one of the clearest of the 'concrete' examples that Heidegger provides, after all, is taken from the plastic arts, namely the Greek temple (and, earlier in the essay, Van Gogh's painting). If we agree with Heidegger that earth and world are not identifiable with the matter and form of the work, then their meaning in his 1936 essay appears to be that of the 'thematized' (or 'thematizable' – that is, the world) and the 'non-thematized' (or 'non-thematizable' – that is, the earth). In the work of art the earth is still a setting forth (*hergestellt*) as such, and this alone definitively distinguishes the work of art from the thing-instrument of everyday life. The obvious temptation – to which Heidegger's followers have certainly yielded – is that of understanding this as the distinction between an explicit meaning of the work (the world that it opens up and ex-poses) and a group of meanings which are always still in reserve (the earth). This may be legitimate to the degree that the earth is still wholly conceived of in terms of the dimension of temporality: if we think in purely temporal terms, the earth's keeping itself in reserve can only appear as the possibility of future worlds and further historical/ *geschicklich* openings, that is, as an always-available reserve of further ex-positions. It should be said that Heidegger never explicitly formulates his theory along these lines, probably because of a rightful unwillingness to reduce the earth to a not-yet-present (but still capable of being present) 'world'. The decisive step, though, is taken when Heidegger turns to the plastic arts, as he does in his 1969 text. Nor is this the only place where he does so; already in *Vorträge und Aufsätze* poetic dwelling is understood as an '*Einräumen*', as a making of space in the sense that is developed by Gadamer in the passages from *Truth and Method* mentioned above. In 'Art and Space', this *Einräumen* is visible in its two fundamental dimensions: it is both an 'arranging' of localities and a positioning of these places in relation to the 'free vastness of the region [*Gegend*]'.[8] In Gadamer's text, which serves as a sort of 'commentary' to Heidegger, the essence of the decorative and secondary arts is found in the fact that they operate in a double sense: 'the nature of decoration consists in performing that two-sided mediation; namely to draw the attention of the viewer to itself, to satisfy his taste, and then to redirect it away from itself to the greater whole of the context of life which it accompanies.'[9]

May we legitimately consider this interplay between locality (*Ortschaft*) and region (*Gegend*) as a specification of the conflict between world and earth that is examined in 'The Origin of the Work of Art'? The answer is yes, if we keep in mind that Heidegger discovers this relation between *Ortschaft* and *Gegend* precisely at the point where, in 'Art and Space', he tries to explain how the 'setting-into-work of truth', which is the essence of art, could occur in sculpture. Sculpture is the 'setting-into-work of truth' insofar as it is the occurrence of authentic space (that is, in that which is proper to the latter); and this occurrence is precisely the interplay between locality and region in which the thing-work is foregrounded both as the agent of a (new) spatial ordering, and as a point of escape toward the free vastness of the region. The 'open' and the 'opening' (*das Offene*, *die Offenheit*) are the terms with which Heidegger – beginning in particular with his lecture on 'The Essence of Truth' (1930) – designates the truth in its originary meaning, that is, the one which also makes possible every occurrence of the 'true' as the conformity of the proposition to the thing. Perhaps, though, it never appears elsewhere so clearly as in this text on art and space that these terms do not only designate opening as an inaugurating and a founding, but also – and in an equally essential way – designate the act of opening as a dilation and a leaving free: it is, as it were, at once an ungrounding and a backgrounding, for what is placed in the background is also shown to possess a clearly limited and definite figure. In the play of *Ortschaft* and *Gegend* this double meaning of the opening as background is brought into focus for us. Heidegger's text on art and space thus leads us to see something that in his 1936 essay is left implicit or even not thought out: the definition of the work of art as the 'setting-into-work of truth' does not just concern the work of art, but

also and above all the notion of truth. The truth that can occur
and that can be 'set-into-work' is not simply the truth of
metaphysics (as evidence and objective stability) with the
additional characteristic of 'eventuality' rather than structure;
that truth which occurs, in an event which for Heidegger is
identified, almost without leaving any residue at all,[10] with
art, is not the evidence of the *obiectum* giving itself to
the *subiectum* but rather the play of appropriation and
expropriation which elsewhere he calls the *Ereignis*.[11] If we
look at sculpture and the other plastic arts in general, the play
of transpropriation of the *Ereignis* – which is also that of the
conflict between world and earth – arises as the interplay
between the locality and the free vastness of the region.

It is here that significant indications for thinking about the
notion of ornament may be found. In a long article on
Gombrich's *The Sense of Order*,[12] Yves Michaud observes that
Gombrich's interpretation of the urgency of the problem of
ornament in art at the turn of the century, while it supplies
crucial concepts for formulating the problem itself, does not
place in question the distinction between 'an art that attracts
attention to itself, on the one hand, and another art (that is,
decorative art), which is supposedly the object of a strictly
lateral interest, on the other'.[13] Michaud instead suggests that
we radicalize Gombrich's argument, and puts forward the
hypothesis that 'a large number of the most influential
manifestations of contemporary art may consist precisely in
the fact of shifting toward the centre and placing at the
focal point of perception that which usually remains at its
margins.'[14] This is not the place to enter into a broader and
more direct discussion of Gombrich's work, in which other
reasons for reflecting on the implications of Heidegger's
theory in regard to a 'decorative' notion of art (in music, for
instance) could easily be found; it may nonetheless be noted
that, particularly from the point of view of 'Art and Space',
the relation between centre and periphery does not have either
the meaning of founding a typology alone (the distinction
between an art that points openly and self-reflexively to itself

and one which is the object of a strictly lateral interest on the part of the spectator), nor that of supplying an interpretive key to the development of contemporary art in relation to the art of the past. For Heidegger, it would appear, it is not merely a question of defining decorative art as a specific type of art, nor of determining the particular traits of contemporary art; rather, he seeks to acknowledge the decorative nature of all art. If we keep in mind Heidegger's insistence on the verbal sense of the term *Wesen*, or 'to essentialize', then it is possible to see that this question is connected to the reversal of centre and periphery that appears to characterize contemporary art in Michaud's eyes; for we accede to the essence of art in a situation in which it arises as an *event*, with precisely those same traits defined by Michaud; and this has to do with the essence of art in general, for it is the way in which art makes itself an essence in our own epoch of Being.

The occurrence of truth in art is a problem upon which Heidegger never ceases to reflect right up to his last works. In the light of 'Art and Space', his argument in the last analysis means that: (a) the truth which may occur does not possess the nature of truth as thematic evidence, but rather that of the 'opening' of the world, which signifies at the same time a thematization and a positioning of the work on the background, or an 'ungrounding'; and (b) if truth is understood in these terms, then art, as its setting-into-work, is definable in far less grandiose or emphatic terms than those which are customarily taken to belong to Heidegger's aesthetic thought. Gadamer, who is certainly well-informed about Heidegger's work, in *Truth and Method* assigns to architecture a more or less dominant and founding position among the arts. This gesture can legitimately be taken to imply that art in general has for Heidegger, precisely inasmuch as it is the 'setting-into-work of truth', a decorative and 'marginal' essence.

The full implications of this cannot be understood unless placed within a more general interpretation of Heideggerian ontology as 'weak ontology'. The result of rethinking the meaning of Being is in fact, for Heidegger, the taking leave of metaphysical Being and its strong traits, on the basis of which the devaluation of the ornamental aspects of the work of art has always definitively been legitimated, even if through more extensive chains of mediating concepts. That which truly is (the *ontos on*) is not the centre which is opposed to the periphery, nor is it the essence which is opposed to appearance, nor is it what endures as opposed to the accidental and the mutable, nor is it the certainty of the *obiectum* given to the subject as opposed to the vagueness and imprecision of the horizon of the world. The occurrence of Being is rather, in Heideggerian weak ontology, an unnoticed and marginal background event.

If we follow the archaeological work and continual remediation that Heidegger dedicates to the poets, it is possible to see that this nevertheless does not mean that we are confronted by the inapparent nature of the peripheral occurrence of the beautiful, in a purely mystical sort of contemplation. Heideggerian aesthetics does not induce interest in the small vibrations at the edges of experience, but rather – and in spite of everything – maintains a monumental vision of the work of art. Even if the occurrence of truth in the work happens in the form of marginality and decoration, it is still true that for it 'that which remains is established by the poets'.[15] What 'remains', though, has the nature of a residue rather than an *aere perennius*. The monument is made to endure, but not as the full presence of the one whose memory it bears; this, on the contrary, remains only as a memory (and the truth of Being itself, moreover, can for Heidegger only arise in the form of a recollection). The techniques of art, for example, and perhaps above all else poetic versification, can be seen as stratagems – which themselves are, not coincidentally, minutely institutionalized and monumentalized – that transform the work of art into a residue and into a monument capable of enduring because from the outset it is produced in the form of that which is dead. It is capable of enduring not because of its force, in other words, but because of its weakness.

From a Heideggerian point of view, the work of art as the occurrence of a 'weak' truth is understandable, in so many senses, as a monument. It may even be thought of in the sense of an architectural monument that contributes to form the background of our experience, but in itself generally remains the object of a distracted perception. This is not the still grandiose metaphysical sense that can be found in Ernst Bloch's concept of ornament in *The Spirit of Utopia*;[16] for Bloch, ornament takes the form of a monument which is a revelation of our truest nature, and this monumentality is still deeply classical and Hegelian, even if Bloch tries to free it from these ties by displacing the 'perfect correspondence between inside and outside' to a future which is always yet to come. In the monument that is art as the occurrence of truth in the conflict between world and earth, there is no emergence and recognition of a deep and essential truth. In this sense as well, essence is *Wesen* in its verbal aspect; it is an occurrence in a form which neither reveals nor conceals a kernel of truth, but in superimposing itself onto other ornaments constitutes the ontological thickness of the truth-event.

We could uncover other meanings of Heideggerian weak ontology concerning an 'ornamental' and monumental notion of the work of art. In passing it could be pointed out, for instance, that Mikel Dufrenne,[17] starting from phenomenological premises, elaborates a notion of the 'poetic' which shares much of the same sense of *background* which can be found in Heidegger's work. What needs to be stressed is that ornamental art, both as a backdrop to which no attention is paid and as a surplus which has no possible legitimation in an authentic foundation (that is, in what is 'proper' to it), finds in Heideggerian ontology rather more than a marginal self-justification, for it becomes the central element of aesthetics and, in the last analysis, of ontological meditation itself – as the entire text of 'Art and Space' essentially shows. What is lost in the foundation and ungrounding which is ornament is the heuristic and critical function of the distinction between decoration as surplus and what is 'proper' to the thing and to

88 *The Truth of Art*

the work. The critical validity of this distinction today appears completely exhausted, in particular at the level of the discourse of the arts and of militant criticism. Philosophy, in returning – although not exclusively – to the results of Heideggerian hermeneutic ontology, simply acknowledges the fact of this exhaustion, and tries to radicalize it with the aim of constructing different critical models.

NOTES

1 Martin Heidegger, *Die Kunst und der Raum* (St Gallen: Erker Verlag, 1969); now in vol. XIII of the *Gesamtausgabe* (Frankfurt: Klostermann, 1983), pp. 203–10.
2 'The Origin of the Work of Art', in *Poetry, Language, Thought*, trans. Albert Hofstadter (New York: Harper and Row, 1971; repr. 1975), pp. 163–86.
3 For an extremely careful and rich analysis and discussion of this, see E. Mazzarella, *Tecnica e metafisica. Saggio su Heidegger* (Naples: Guida, 1981), part 1, chapter 3.
4 The most useful and complete of all the basic works on Heidegger's language, besides H. Feick's *Index zu Heideggers 'Sein und Zeit'*, 2nd edn (Tübingen: Niemeyer, 1968), is still E. Schöfer's *Die Sprache Heideggers* (Pfullingen: Neske, 1962).
5 Here, as well as later on, I refer to the terminology and arguments provided by Heidegger in his essay on 'The Origin of the Work of Art', though I try not to bog down my discussion with notes for each term or concept that I consider. For a more detailed analysis of this essay, see my *Essere, storia e linguaggio in Heidegger* (Turin: Ed. di 'Filosofia', 1963), chapter 3.
6 Cf. H.-G. Gadamer, *Truth and Method*, trans. Garrett Barden and John Cummings, 2nd edn (1975; repr. New York: Crossroads, 1984), p. 139.
7 Here I refer the reader to the final chapters of my *Le avventure della differenza* (Milan: Feltrinelli, 1981).
8 Martin Heidegger, *Die Kunst und der Raum*; in *Gesamtausgabe*, vol. XIII, p. 207.
9 Cf. Gadamer, *Truth and Method*, trans. Barden and Cummings, p. 140.

10 The essay on 'The Origin of the Work of Art' (in *Poetry, Language, Thought*, trans. Hofstadter), pp. 54–6, at one point discusses the different modes of occurrence of truth. None of these modes, though, not even that of philosophical thought, is taken up by Heidegger and developed in his subsequent works: the occurrence of truth remains tied to the 'setting-into-work of truth' that occurs in the work of art.

11 See especially the various texts published in *Vorträge und Aufsätze* (Pfullingen: Neske, 1954; repr. 1978).

12 E. H. Gombrich, *The Sense of Order: A Study in the Psychology of Decorative Art* (Ithaca: Cornell UP, 1979); Yves Michaud's article, 'L'Art auquel on ne fait pas attention', is found in *Critique*, 416 (Jan. 1982), pp. 22–41.

13 Michaud, *Critique*, p. 36.

14 Ibid., pp. 36–7.

15 For example, see Heidegger's lecture on 'Hölderlin and the Essence of Poetry' (1936), in *Erläuterungen zu Hölderlins Dichtung*, 3rd edn (Frankfurt: Klostermann, 1963).

16 Cf. Ernst Bloch, *Geist der Utopie* (1923), 2nd rev. edn (Frankfurt: Suhrkamp, 1977), p. 20 ff.

17 Cf. M. Dufrenne, *Le poétique* (Paris: PUF, 1963).

6

The Structure of Artistic Revolutions

I

Is it possible for us to speak of the development of the arts in the same way that Thomas Kuhn, in *The Structure of Scientific Revolutions* (1962),[1] discusses the development of science? At first glance, it would appear to be both easier and harder to speak about artistic rather than scientific revolutions. It is easier because in art the transformation of models and canons (at the level of their production and consumption) does not seem obliged to take into account the fundamental factor of truth, or even simply of validity, which for centuries has dominated scientific activity, and which today is still of some concern. In other words, there does not exist in the arts such a clear and uncontested base-value against which all changes and transformations can be measured as moments of progress or regression. This fact apparently excludes, as Croce notes, the possibility of a true history of the arts – or, better still, of art: for even the plurality of the arts and their genres is but a fact of historicity which does not reach down to the very essence of art itself. Rather, any history of the arts appears as a simple extrinsic cataloguing that also serves a functional purpose, whether it be didactic, museographic, mnemonic, or whatever. The world of art, deprived of this fundamental basis of judgement, seems to be a world in which the play of paradigms and revolutions develops freely, unfettered by the requirements of validity, truth, and verificability. Besides, this is one of the most traditional ways in which the distinction between art and science – or even between the *beaux arts* and the practical arts – is understood. This difference can be defined in terms of the difference between an area which may be thought of in terms of progress and regression (for instance, science and technology), and an area in which such terms have a rather more problematic meaning, if indeed they have any meaning at all. The problem that immediately arises, and makes the project for an aesthetic analogue to Kuhn's theory more difficult than it would at first appear to be, is that – in part thanks to Kuhn himself – the distinction between a notion of science in which progress is possible (as a cumulative process that comes ever nearer to the truth of things) and a notion of art in which this relationship with the true does not appear in such cut and dried terms, is itself already deeply in crisis. Kuhn's research, together with the debate it provokes and with the general diffusion – in various forms – of 'epistemological anarchism', seems to have done more than render impractical *this* distinction between science and technology on the one hand, and art on the other, for all these factors have combined to situate the very development of science in terms of an 'aesthetic' model. Kuhn writes that 'the choice between contrasting paradigms shows itself to be a choice between incompatible forms of social life', and 'it cannot be determined exclusively by the evaluative procedures of normal science, since these depend in part on a particular paradigm, and this paradigm is what is called into question.' If this is so, then any argument that seeks to establish through logic a choice between paradigms is necessarily circular in nature. But 'whatever its force, the status of circular argumentation is simply that of *persuasion*' (my italics). Because of this fundamental trait, which is linked more to persuasion than to demonstration, the appearance of a paradigm in the history of any given science has many – or all – of the traits of an 'artistic revolution'. Its diffusion, articulation and establishment as a canon of operative choices, evaluative criteria, and codes of 'taste' is not in fact founded on some sort of equivalence to the truth of things, but rather on its 'functionality' in regard to a form of life. This functionality is not in turn measured in terms of the criteria of 'correspondence', as if there were primary needs against which it could be measured, but rather itself becomes – in a circular fashion – an object of persuasion rather than demonstration. Even if we were to consider the appearance of new paradigms as the product of force (for instance a revolution, the seizing of power by invasion, and so on), in the end the 'aesthetic' model of historical transformation would still have to be confronted; for the emergence of a paradigm requires much more than its imposition by force from the outside. It occurs through a complex system of persuasion, active participation, interpretations and answers which are never exclusively nor principally the effects of force and violence, but involve a kind of aesthetic, hermeneutic, or rhetorical assimilation.

Kuhn's argument is employed in this chapter as representative, in very general terms, of a widespread tendency in contemporary epistemology, for in it an antithesis which is found in its clearest form in Kant's *Critique of Judgement* and *Anthropology from a Pragmatic Point of View* comes to a head and ultimately dissolves. Kant seems to envision two opposed models of historicity (I say 'seems' because he himself never actually speaks of two models of historicity), one of which could be called 'normal', if we stay with Kuhn's terminology, and the other of which could be called 'revolutionary'. Normal historicity is that which is constituted by those 'mechanical heads' – as Kant terms them – which, 'although they are not epoch-making, with their intellect that progresses every day a little further by leaning on the canes and props of experience' have perhaps made 'the greatest contribution to the growth of the sciences and [technical] arts' (*Anthropology*, para. 50).[2] For example, one 'mechanical head' of this sort – although possessed of a truly exceptional dignity and ability – would be Isaac Newton's, at least according to the description of him in paragraph 47 of the *Critique of Judgement* (although in

Anthropology from a Pragmatic Point of View Newton is considered a genius and an epoch-making mind: cf. para. 59):

thus we can readily learn all that Newton has set forth in his immortal work on the *Principles of Natural Philosophy*, however great a head was required to discover it, but we cannot learn to write spirited poetry, however express may be the precepts of the art and however excellent its models. The reason is that Newton could make all his steps, from the first elements of geometry to his own great and profound discoveries, intuitively plain and definite as regards consequence, not only to himself but to everyone else. But a Homer or a Wieland cannot show how his ideas, so rich in fancy and yet so full of thought, come together in his head, simply because he does not know and therefore cannot teach others. In science, then, the greatest discoverer only differs in degree from his laborious imitator and pupil, but he differs specifically from him who nature has gifted for beautiful art. And in this there is no depreciation of those great men to whom the human race owes so much gratitude, as compared with nature's favorites in respect of the talent for beautiful art. For . . . the former talent is directed to the ever advancing greater perfection of knowledge [*zur immer fortschreitenden grösseren Vollkommenheit der Erkenntnisse*] and every advantage depending on it . . . .[3]

The apparent non-historicity of genius stands opposed to the historicity established by mechanical 'heads', and by great scientists as well. The genius cannot teach others his ways of inventing and producing, since he himself does not know how to understand them fully. Works of genius nevertheless serve as exemplary models, and when nature gives rise to other geniuses the latter become the impulse, for any existing genius, towards new analogous works. This, perhaps more than anything else, can be called historicity: for if the kind of progress established by mechanical 'heads' appears primarily as a model of continuity and cumulation, it is still lacking in an authentically processual nature. Everything that scientists discover is presupposed as already available: in other words, scientific discoveries give articulation to already existing paradigms. In the case of the genius, as Kant also recognizes

in his *Anthropology from a Pragmatic Point of View* (para. 58),
there is instead an opening of 'new paths and new horizons'.
Yet another aspect of the genius makes him essentially
historical; that is, his 'magisterial originality' (*Anthropology*,
para. 57) and the exemplary quality of his works (without
which originality itself would appear as mere extravagance: cf.
Critique of Judgement, paras 46 and 47). Without going further
into the details of Kant's argument, it is nonetheless possible
to see in it an unresolved contradiction: only science and
technology are seen as having a history, because they alone
offer a continuous and cumulative development to which the
concept of progress is applicable; yet the genius who is 'epoch-
making', opening up new paths and new horizons, would
seem more properly to be the basis of historicity in the strong
sense of the term, namely as the new, and not merely as
continuity and development.

Contemporary epistemology's awareness of 'historicity',
which is represented but not completely embodied by Kuhn's
work, seems to take shape as a dissolution of the opposition
between a fully fledged history of science and technology and a
problematic 'history' of artistic genius. When we confront the
apparently innocent matter of transferring Kuhn's approach
from the history of science (together with the categories that he
elaborates) to artistic development, this is the problem that
faces us. This transference apparently fails because in reality
the distinction between the two fields has already dissolved.
For Kant himself, moreover, this distinction between two
kinds of historicity exists more in principle than in reality: the
genius cannot authentically exist without a sure sense of taste
and without the technical ability to produce truly exemplary
works which are epoch-making, and therefore technical rules
and procedures are for him a necessary link with the history
produced by mechanical 'heads'. Not only does this distinction
between the two kinds of historicity today seem to have
dissolved, but this very dissolution occurs through a reduction
of 'cumulative' historicity to the historicity produced by
genius. If we bear in mind that for Kant genius necessarily

implicates epoch-making and exemplary works – that is, complex mechanisms of reception and historicization – it is not difficult to see that Kuhn's scientific revolutions are largely modelled on the particular historicity (which according to Kant is not truly such) of the genius.

II

All this seems to me to signal the emergence in contemporary epistemology of an aesthetic model of historicity opposed to the notion of a process of cumulative development; furthermore, it leads also to the acknowledgement of a particular 'responsibility' for the aesthetic itself. This responsibility belongs not so much, nor only, to aesthetics as a philosophical discipline, but rather to the aesthetic as a domain of experience and as a dimension of existence that assumes exemplary value as a model for thinking about historicity in general.

The aestheticization of the history of science – if it may, with all due caution, be referred to in this way – which takes place in Kuhn's work is not a strange or exceptional event. It corresponds in fact to a much wider phenomenon, of which it is at once a symptom and a decisive instance: namely, it corresponds to what may be called the centrality of the aesthetic (aesthetic experience, art and other related phenomena) in modernity. This apparent centrality of the aesthetic could not possibly be due solely to the prejudiced point of view of philosophers and historians of art. Schelling's notion of art as the organ of philosophy, for instance, is but one of the more extreme expressions of a thematic which is found throughout modernity and which characterizes the latter. Nietzsche, in making the expression 'The Will to Power as Art' the projected title of a section of his final theoretical work (which he never finished, and which was published in fragmentary form as *Der Wille zur Macht*), summarizes in perhaps the clearest and most demythified terms this profound current of the modern spirit. Beginning with Nietzsche, it becomes possible to recognize theoretically the meaning of the centrality of aesthetics in modernity. This centrality affirms itself first of all at a practical level, in the process of the social promotion of the artist and his products starting with the Renaissance,[4] a process which gradually confers on the artist a certain dignity and superiority, along with both civil and quasi-religious functions. In a parallel fashion, this same centrality first emerges at a theoretical level in the works of Vico and the Romantics, which consider the origin of civilization and culture to be 'aesthetic'. Finally, with the advent of modern mass society, we see this same centrality in the ever greater importance which aesthetic models of behaviour (such as the various types of 'stars') and the organization of social consensus (since the strength of the mass media is above all an aesthetic and rhetorical kind of strength) continue to acquire. This process is an extremely far-ranging one; yet perhaps only in Nietzsche do we find an awareness of the authentic meaning of the function of *anticipation* that the aesthetic possesses in relation to the global development of modern civilization. In the notes at the beginning of the part of *Der Wille zur Macht* entitled 'The Will to Power as Art' (sections 794–7), which were by a stroke of good fortune placed there by the first editors of the text, Nietzsche explicitly points out the foundation of this function of anticipation and of modelling which art assumes in regard to a world which ever more openly appears as the world of the will to power. Once denied any faith in the *Grund* and in the course of events as a development toward an ultimate point, the world appears as a work of art which makes itself: '*ein sich selbst gebärendes Kunstwerk*', an expression that Nietzsche takes from F. W. Schlegel. The artist is a *Vorstufe* or a place in which the will to power can make itself known and be set in motion on a small scale (section 795); and, with the revelation of the technological organization of the world (it might be added, without betraying Nietzsche's thought), this will to power can unveil itself as the very essence of the world. The relation with technology has assumed a central importance in the arts in the twentieth century, not only in terms of the specific techniques of the different arts, which can be seen everywhere at close range, but also in terms of technology as a more general socio-historical fact involving the technological organization of production and social life (here I refer the reader to the work of Hans Sedlmayr, even if I do not agree with his own evaluation of the issue).[5] This in turn displays in a concrete manner the function – as prelude, anticipation, and model – that Nietzsche assigns to art and to artists in relation to the world as will to power. The long struggle of the aesthetics and poetics of modernity against the Aristotelian definition of art as imitation attains here its full meaning, which can only be called an ontological one ('imitation' can be understood to mean either of nature or of classical models, although the latter are still legitimated by their supposed proximity to nature and its perfect proportions). Hans Blumenberg,[6] and Edgar Zilsel before him (in his reconstruction of the origins of the notion of genius in Humanism and in the Renaissance), have shown to precisely what degree *technicity* is to be found at the basis of the concept of the artist as a creative genius. The determination of the will to power as art in Nietzsche expresses this idea and draws out all the consequences implicit in the nineteenth-century destruction of the deep roots that for Kant still link 'genius' to nature.[7] In the work of Kant, the rooting of genius in nature corresponds to the rooting of scientific knowledge in an 'objectivity' of the world of nature that impedes the identification of the scientist with the artist. From the point of view at which Nietzsche arrives, though, all these roots appear instead to be torn up: nor, for him, can a genius legitimate his own creations simply because he is inspired by nature, any more than a scientist can make progress in the knowledge of the true by discovering 'something already extant but not yet known, like America was before Columbus'.[8] In theoretical consciousness and in modern social practice, art constantly reasserts itself as a 'dense' site. This is the case both in regard to the social figure of the artist and to the special dignity (Benjamin's 'aura') assigned to artistic works from a point of view – such as Nietzsche's – which sees the notion of the will to power as the basis for a true ontology of modernity. Art thus assumes the sense of an anticipation of the essence of modernity – of its authentic nature, that is, and of the way in which its essence arises in the modern era – prior to its being completely displayed in the technological organization of today's world. The theoretical and practical centrality attributed, more or less explicitly, to art since the Renaissance reaches an extreme degree in the emergence of aesthetic models as well in the version of the history of science proposed by Kuhn. This centrality is not to be understood as a sign of a general aestheticizing tendency in the culture of the last few centuries; rather, it is an anticipation of and a prelude to the emergence of the will to power as the essence of Being in modernity. If, however, Nietzsche supplies the most radical and theoretically explicit point of view (at least in terms of the hypothesis that we are exploring here) for understanding the meaning of the centrality of art in modern consciousness, it is at the same time undeniable that he himself does not possess a perfectly clear awareness of the typically modern nature of this phenomenon. For Nietzsche, the appearance of the will to power as the essence of Being or (what amounts to the same thing) as the death of God is a historical event, and not the discovery of a 'true' metaphysical structure. It is therefore, to some extent, linked to modernity. Yet it would be difficult to argue that for Nietzsche the concept of the 'modern' is typically defined in relation to these events. It is more likely that he offers an extreme example of the consciousness of modernity in the subjective meaning of the genitive, not in the objective one: the numerous texts in which Nietzsche discusses modernity as a phenomenon of decadence cannot be easily reconciled to those in which he instead speaks of the necessity of fulfilling nihilism (and therefore decadence) through a passage from the reactive stage of nihilism to the active and affirmative stage. Even the central function of art, as the principle of a

Gegenbewegung against the various forms of reactive nihilism (religion, morality, and philosophy: cf. section 794 of *Der Wille zur Macht*), is not thought of by Nietzsche in terms of a specific relation to modernity, but rather in far more general terms. This difference between our point of view today, which is nonetheless linked to Nietzsche's, and Nietzsche's own is far more theoretically charged than it would appear to be at first glance. If this difference means that in Nietzsche's work we find the culmination of the consciousness of modernity only in the subjective meaning of the genitive, then this also means that we can never simply re-use his arguments, but must instead situate ourselves – or recognize that we find ourselves – in terms of a different displacement. This 'displacement' not only distances us from Nietzsche, but also places us in a position distinct from his as regards the significance of the centrality of art in modernity.

Passing over a few passages and a more detailed analysis of the difference between the subjective and objective meanings of the genitive in the phrase 'Nietzsche, philosopher of modernity', while at the same time keeping this difference firmly in mind, it is necessary to recognize that the particular connection between the centrality of art and modernity may appear more clearly to us than it does to Nietzsche, thanks to the light cast on it by a concept that Nietzsche never thematizes (perhaps because it is still too close to him). This concept is the value of the new, or the new as value. Here we need to introduce explicitly a definition of modernity which, even if not formulated in exactly the terms that we aim to use in the present work, can still be considered widely present in the work of many theoreticians of the modern, from Weber to Gehlen, Blumenberg, and Koselleck.[9] This definition, which certainly reflects a Nietzschean thematics as well, goes as follows: modernity is that era in which being modern becomes a value, or rather, it becomes *the* fundamental value to which all other values refer. This formula may be corroborated if we see that it coincides with the other, and more widely disseminated, definition of the modern in terms of secularization. Secularization, as the modern, is a term that describes not only what happens in a certain era and what nature it assumes, but also the 'value' that dominates and guides consciousness in the era in question, primarily as faith in progress – which is both a secularized faith and a faith in secularization.[10] But faith in progress, understood as a kind of faith in the historical process that is ever more devoid of providential and meta-historical elements, is purely and simply identified with faith in the value of the new. Against this background we must see, first of all, the grandiosity invested in the concept of genius, and, secondarily, the centrality that art and artists acquire in modern culture. Modernity is primarily the era in which the increased circulation of goods (Simmel[11]) and ideas, and increased social mobility (Gehlen[12]), bring into focus the value of the new and predispose the conditions for the identification of value (the value of Being itself) with the new. A good deal of twentieth-century philosophy describes the future in a way deeply tinged with the grandiose. Such descriptions range from the early Heidegger's definition of existence as project and transcendence to Sartre's notion of transcendence, to Ernst Bloch's utopianism (which is emblematic of all Hegelian/ Marxist philosophy), and to the various ethics which seem ever more insistently to locate the value of an action in the fact of its making possible other choices and other actions, thus opening up a future. This same grandiose vision is the faithful mirror of an era that in general may legitimately be called 'futuristic', to borrow an expression from an essay by Kryzstof Pomian to which I will refer again later.[13] The same may naturally be said of the twentieth-century artistic avant-garde movements, whose radically anti-historicist inspiration is most authentically expressed by Futurism and Dadaism. Both in philosophy and in avant-garde poetics, the pathos of the future is still accompanied by an appeal to the authentic, according to a model of thought characteristic of all *modern* 'futurism': the tension towards the future is seen as a tension aimed towards a renewal and return to a condition of originary authenticity.

A visible first link between modernity, secularization and the value of the new can therefore be discovered when the following points are brought into focus. (a) Modernity is characterized as the era of *Diesseitigkeit*, namely the abandonment of the sacred vision of existence and the affirmation of the realm of profane value instead, that is, of secularization. (b) The key point of secularization, at the conceptual level, is faith in progress (or the ideology of progress), which takes shape through a resumption of the Judeo-Christian vision of history, from which all references to transcendence are 'progressively' eliminated.[14] This occurs because progress depicts itself ever more insistently as a value in and of itself, in order to escape from the risk of theorizing the end of history (which is a risk when there is no longer a belief in the afterlife as defined by Christianity). Progress is just that process which leads toward a state of things in which further progress is possible, and nothing else. (c) This extreme secularization of the providential vision of history is simply the equivalent of affirming the new as the fundamental value.

In this process of secularization and the affirmation of the value of the new – a process which, historically speaking, is not at all as linear as it appears when its theoretically essential traits are retrospectively reassembled – art functions as an anticipation or emblem. This is the same as saying that, while for much of the modern age the discoveries made by 'mechanical heads' have still been limited and directed – at the level of science and technology – by the value of 'truth' or by the value of 'usefulness for life', for art these limitations and forms of metaphysical founding have long since been abandoned. Thus from the beginning of the modern era or thereabouts, art (although there are of course differences in the development of the individual arts) has found itself in the same ungrounded condition that science and technology only today explicitly recognize themselves to be in.

In his 1967 essay on 'Die Säkularisierung des Fortschritts', Arnold Gehlen describes this process in rather different terms, which by and large, however, fit in with the argument that we

have put forward here. He sees the secularization of progress
to be articulated in different ways, depending upon whether it
occurs in the field of science and technology (more precisely,
what he calls the operative connection – *Zusammenarbeit* – of
'exact sciences, technological development and industrial
application'[15]), or in the field of culture as constituted by the
arts, literature, and the *schöne Wissenschaften* in general. In the
former, progress represents a kind of fatalism, for it becomes
'routine': in science, technology and industry what is new
simply signifies survival of these domains of activity (as
economics reasons solely in terms of the rate of development,
not in terms of the satisfaction of vital basic needs). The
transformation of progress into a routine in these fields,
Gehlen argues, discharges all the pathos of the new onto the
other field, that is, that of the arts and literature. Here,
though, in a way and for reasons that Gehlen's text does not
seem to explain clearly, the value of the new and the pathos of
development undergo a still more radical secularization than
that which occurs in the passage from faith in the history
of redemption to the profane ideology of progress. For
different reasons, both in the becoming 'routine' of scientific/
technological/industrial progress and in the displacement of
the pathos of the new towards the territory of art, there occurs
a true dissolution of progress itself. This dissolution is linked
on the one hand to the very process of secularization itself.
Gehlen writes that secularization:

consists in general in this – that the specific laws of the new world
suffocate faith, or rather, not faith as much as its triumphalistic
certitude (*die siegesbeglückte Gewissheit*). At the same time, the
overall project – following an objective impulse of things – fans out
(*fächert auf*) in divergent processes that develop their own internal
legality ever further, and slowly progress (since in the meantime we
want to keep on believing in it) is displaced towards the periphery of
facts and consciousness, and there is totally emptied out.[16]

Secularization itself, in short, contains a tendency toward
dissolution which is accentuated with the passage of the pathos

of the new toward the field of art. This is in itself a peripheral field, according to Gehlen, in which the need for the new – and its progressively becoming inessential – is intensified.[17] Secularization, as the establishment of laws proper to each of many different fields and domains of experience, thus appears as a menace to the notion of progress inasmuch as it can eventually thwart that very notion. This can be seen in the work of Bloch, for instance, who wants to remain faithful to a vision of the progressive and emancipatory movement of history, but who examines with concern the 'differentiations in the concept of progress'[18] and seeks to find in them a unitary design, in spite of the multiplicity of historical time (which is linked to the nature of class conflict). The discovery of this same design is also the objective of Benjamin's critique in his 'Theses on the Philosophy of History'.

III

Gehlen is the first to use the term *post-histoire* in regard to late modernity. He claims to take this from the mathematician Antoine Augustin Cournot, who, however, never seems to have employed exactly this term; Gehlen probably borrows it from Hendrik de Man instead.[19] The *extreme secularization* which Gehlen describes offers us the opportunity to go one step further and to try to answer the question (already apparent in my earlier allusion to Nietzsche) that asks for the difference between a consciousness of modernity in the subjective meaning of the genitive, on the one hand, and in the objective meaning of the genitive, on the other. The definition of modernity as the era in which being modern is the base-value is not a definition which modernity could give of itself. The essence of the modern becomes truly visible only from the moment in which – in a way that needs to be examined more carefully – the mechanism of modernity distances itself from us. Gehlen, in speaking of the dissolution and emptying-out of the notion of progress both in the domain of science/

technology/industry and of the arts, supplies a clue to understanding this distancing of modernity. The fact (noted by Gehlen) that the final condition sought by the radically 'future-oriented' utopias, like the great revolutionary ideologies themselves, reveals noticeable traits of ahistoricity, can perhaps be placed together with this same tendency to dissolution. 'Where we effectively try to make the new man, our relationship with history also changes . . . The French revolutionaries called 1793 the year One of a new era.'[20] Gehlen detects this trait of ahistoricity in a typical eighteenth-century utopia, Sebastien Mercier's *L'an 2240* (published in 1770). In the future world described by Mercier, which is governed by Rousseauian sobriety and virtue, all forms of credit have been abolished, everyone pays for everything in cash, and classical languages are no longer studied, since they are not needed in order for men to be virtuous.[21] The suppression of all credit and classical languages emblematically embodies a reduction of existence to the naked present, that is, the elimination of any historical dimension.

Progress seems to show a tendency to dissolve itself, and with it the value of the new as well, not only in the effective process of secularization, but even in the most extremely futuristic utopias. This dissolution is the event that enables us to distance ourselves from the mechanism of modernity, much more than Gehlen ever acknowledges. Krzysztof Pomian's essay on 'The Crisis of the Future', although it does not refer directly to Gehlen's work, takes up the line of reflection developed by the latter. Pomian adds some useful ideas for the present discourse, for he thematizes more openly the crisis of the value of the new which seems to characterize the present-day situation (it might be added that it is on this basis that it is defined as *post-histoire*, in a more precise sense of the term than Gehlen's). In his discussion of the characterization of modernity as a 'futuristic' era, Pomian makes explicit the nexus between the emergence of the value of the new and the constitution of the modern state. We have already seen that Mercier's utopia calls for the end of all credit arrangements;

Pomian writes that 'the future is, literally, injected into the very texture of the present in the form of paper money . . . The history of more than two thousand years of monetarization of the economy is also the history of a growing dependence of the present on the future' (102). Even if this dependence already exists in principle in every agricultural society in which there is an interval between planting and harvest-time, it becomes a decisive dimension only in modern society. 'Only large-scale commerce, in the form that first appears in the twelfth century in Italian, Flemish and Hanseatic cities, together with the concomitant development of credit and maritime insurance, granted the future the role of a constitutive dimension' (103). The value assigned to the reproductive role of the family as a secularized form of eternity, and the consequent recognition of childhood and youth as conditions possessed of specific values which are entirely future-related, are connected to this basic mechanism of the modern form of society. More clearly than Gehlen, Pomian recognizes the crisis of the value of the future in contemporary culture that runs parallel to the crisis – with its tendencies to dissolution – that plagues the very institutions that conditioned the emergence of that value, in particular the modern state. The institutions which embody the futuristic orientation of the modern world 'appear to be plagued by serious malfunctions' (112), ranging from inflation (which destabilizes the purchasing power of money) to the complexity and uncontrolled growth of the state apparatus, etc. If we leave aside Pomian and matters of macrosociology, and turn instead to the field of the arts, here too we are struck by the dissolution of the value of the new. This is the meaning of the post-modern, to the degree in which it cannot be reduced to a mere fact of cultural fashion. From architecture to the novel to poetry to the figurative arts, the post-modern displays, as its most common and most imposing trait, an effort to free itself from the logic of over-coming, development, and innovation. From this point of view, the post-modern corresponds to Heidegger's attempt to prepare a post-metaphysical kind of thought which would not be an *Überwindung* but rather a *Verwindung* of metaphysics (see chapter 10 of the present study). This latter term, despite all its ambiguities, deserves to be placed alongside those of 'secularization' and (Nietzschean) 'nihilism' in any consideration of modernity that is philosophical and not merely *historisch*. Seen in the light not only of Nietzsche's 'Wille zur Macht als Kunst', but also especially of Heidegger's post-metaphysical ontology, the post-modern experience of art appears as the way in which art occurs in the era of the end of metaphysics. This holds good not only for what we today call 'post-modern' figurative art, literature, and architecture, but also for the dissolutive tendencies already apparent in the great early twentieth-century avant-garde movements, such as, for instance, Joyce's transition from *Ulysses* to *Finnegan's Wake*, which Ihab Hassan correctly sees as a key event for the definition of the post-modern.[22]

IV

Post-modern art appears as the most advanced point at which the process of secularization described by Gehlen has arrived. It is also a preparatory phase for the conditions in which the consciousness of modernity may become such, even in the objective meaning of the genitive. In the phantasmagoric (as Adorno calls it) play of a society built around the marketplace and technological mass media, the arts have experienced without any further metaphysical mask (such as the search for a supposedly authentic foundation of existence) the experience of the value of the new as such. This experience occurs in a purer and more visible way than it does for science and technology, which are still to a degree tied to truth-value or use-value. For the arts, the value of the new, once it has been radically unveiled, loses all possibility of foundation or value. The crisis of the future which permeates all late-modern culture and social life finds in the experience of art a privileged locus of expression. Such a crisis, obviously, implies a radical change in our way of experiencing history and time, as is somewhat obscurely anticipated by Nietzsche in his 'doctrine' of the eternal return of the Same. It is not perhaps an insignificant coincidence that certain 'epoch-making' works of the twentieth century – from Proust's *Remembrance of Things Past* to Musil's *The Man Without Qualities* to Joyce's *Ulysses* and *Finnegan's Wake* – concentrate, even at the level of content itself, on the problem of time and on ways of experiencing temporality outside its supposedly natural linearity.[23] This suggests a positive direction for Gehlen's *post-histoire*, not just a purely dissolutive one, while at the same time avoiding all Spenglerian nostalgia for 'decline'. If in this way the very notion of artistic revolution, caught up in this game of ungrounding, loses some of its meaning, at the same time it perhaps supplies a means of establishing a dialogue between philosophical thought and poetry, in view of that which in contemporary philosophy continually reasserts itself as the possible – though problematical – overcoming of metaphysics.

NOTES

1 Thomas S. Kuhn, *The Structure of Scientific Revolutions*, 2nd edn (Chicago: Chicago UP, 1970).

2 This and the following quotations are taken from Kant's *Anthropology from a Pragmatic Point of View*, trans. Mary J. Gregor (The Hague: Nijhoff, 1974) paras 46–59.

3 Kant, *Critique of Judgement*, trans. J. H. Bernard (New York/ London: Hafner Press and Collier-Macmillan, 1951), para. 47.

4 On this point, cf. Mario Perniola, *L'alienazione artistica* (Milan: Mursia, 1971).

5 See especially Sedlmayr's *Art in Crisis, the Lost Center* (1948), trans. Brian Battershaw (Chicago: H. Regnery Co., 1958), and *The Revolution of Modern Art* (1955).

6 Cf. Hans Blumenberg, *Wirklichkeiten in denen wir leben* (Stuttgart: Reclam, 1981), especially the essay 'Nachahmung der Natur'; and, more generally, *Die Legitimät der Neuzeit* (Frankfurt: Suhrkamp, 1966).

7   On this point, see the first part of H.-G. Gadamer, *Truth and Method*, trans. Garrett Barden and John Cummings 2nd edn, 1975; repr. New York: Crossroads, 1984).

8   Kant, *Anthropology from a Pragmatic Point of View*, trans. Gregor, para. 57.

9   See Max Weber, *The Sociology of Religion*, trans. Ephraim Fischoff (Boston: Beacon, 1964). For Arnold Gehlen, see his *Man in the Age of Technology* (1957), trans. Patricia Lipscomb (New York: Columbia UP, 1980), and his 1967 essay on 'Die Säkularisierung des Fortschritts', in vol. VII of his collected works, entitled *Einblicke*, ed. K. S. Rehberg (Frankfurt; Klostermann, 1978). For K. Koselleck, see esp. *Vergangene Zukunft. Zur Semantik geschichtlicher Zeiten* (Frankfurt: Suhrkamp, 1979).

10 The best overall history of the concept of secularization is H. Lübbe's *Säkularisierung. Geschichte einen ideenpolitischen Begriffs* (Freiburg: Alber, 1965).

11 Cf. Georg Simmel's essay on 'Fashion' (1895), in *On Individuality and Social Forms*, ed. Donald N. Levine (Chicago: Chicago UP, 1971), pp. 294–323.

12 Cf. above all Gehlen's essay on 'Die Säkularisierung des Fortschritts'.

13 K. Pomian, 'The Crisis of the Future', published in Italian ('La crisi dell'avvenire') in *Le frontiere del tempo*, ed. R. Romano (Milan: Il Saggiatore, 1981).

14 The classic argument concerning modern historicism as the secularization of the theology of Judeo-Christian history is found in Löwith's *Meaning in History* (1949; repr. Chicago: Chicago UP, 1957).

15 Gehlen, 'Die Säkularisierung des Fortschritts', p. 410.

16 Ibid., p. 409.

17 Ibid., p. 411.

18 Ernst Bloch, 'Differenzierungen im Begriff Fortschritt', in *Tübinger Einleitung in der Philosophie* (Frankfurt: Suhrkamp, 1964), vol. I, pp. 160–202. On Bloch's notion of history, specifically in regard to a 'plurality' of historical times, cf. R. Bodel, *Multiversum. Tempo e storia in Ernst Bloch* (Naples: Bibliopolis, 1979).

19 Gehlen, 'Die Säkularisierung des Fortschritts', note for pp. 468–70.

20 Ibid., p. 408.
21 Ibid., p. 409.
22 Cf. Ihab Hassan, *Paracriticism* (Urbana: Illinois UP, 1975).
23 See Alberto Asor Rosa's essay, 'Tempo e nuovo nell'avanguardia ovvero: l'infinita manipolazione del tempo', in *Le frontiere del tempo*, ed. Romano.

PART III

The End of Modernity

PART III

7

Hermeneutics and Nihilism

The work that ushers into contemporary philosophical thought what has become known as hermeneutic ontology is H.-G. Gadamer's *Truth and Method* (first published in 1960).[1] It begins with a long first section dedicated to bringing the question of truth into focus 'as it emerges in the experience of art'. This first section takes its theoretical impetus from a later chapter devoted to the 'retrieval of the question of artistic truth' and to a critique of the abstract nature of aesthetic consciousness. With this critique of aesthetic consciousness, Gadamer develops in an original manner the conclusions reached by Heidegger in his meditation on art, which sees the work of art as 'the truth of Being setting itself to work'.[2] Gadamer's critique of aesthetic consciousness aims to show the historical character of aesthetic experience, but it seems in the last analysis to reduce aesthetic experience to historical experience. Hermeneutic ontology has, however, seen a number of other important developments since the publication of *Truth and Method*.[3] Many of these have – especially in contemporary German thought (and here I am thinking of the work of K. O. Apel in particular[4]) – emphasized the nature of hermeneutics as a sort of 'philosophy of social communication'. Apel has attempted to bring about a synthesis of the analytic philosophy of language (with its origins in pragmatics and empiricism) and Heideggerian existential philosophy precisely by insisting on what he calls the 'a priori' of an unlimited community of communication.[5]

Other recent work in hermeneutics, such as H. R. Jauss's literary hermeneutics,[6] also seems to be oriented toward the historically 'constructive' character of the philosophy of interpretation. For Apel, the ideal of *Verstehen* that guides hermeneutics is the model which a society freed from the darkness of neurosis, inequality, and want should seek to realize. Jauss argues that a more acute hermeneutic awareness alone would allow a more comprehensive literary and artistic criticism to be established. He shows how this may be accomplished by giving greater consideration to the historical context in which a work has arisen and to that in which it lives on and continues to act. Apel and Jauss seem to be noteworthy examples of a 'constructive interpretation' of hermeneutics, which develops – on the whole, quite coherently – premises already present in Gadamer's work. In these constructive interpretations, however, hermeneutics seems to move ever further from its Heideggerian origins. This process reaches an extreme point in Apel's work, where the hermeneutic problem is rethought by using neo-Kantian terminology within a neo-Kantian horizon,[7] despite the fact that neo-Kantianism serves as a constant polemical target for Heidegger. Although Gadamer does not share this neo-Kantian perspective, some of its premises seem to be already present in *Truth and Method*. The book opens with a 'critique of aesthetic consciousness' which displaces all the 'nihilistic' implications of Heidegger's ontology, and thus exposes hermeneutics to the possible risk of becoming a philosophy of history of a basically 'humanistic' – and, ultimately, neo-Kantian – kind.

Let us leave aside for now these broad questions which would require a critical reconstruction of the meaning of the whole of modern hermeneutics. I will limit myself here to examining what seem to be the 'nihilistic' aspects of Heidegger's hermeneutics, and to showing how 'aesthetic consciousness' may be defended against Gadamer, who so severely criticizes its links to nineteenth- and twentieth-century subjectivist philosophy, on the basis of these very same 'nihilistic' aspects. Indeed, 'aesthetic consciousness' may be recuperated as an experience of truth precisely insofar as this experience is substantially nihilistic.

Heidegger is generally considered to provide the basis of hermeneutic ontology insofar as he asserts a connection – almost, one might say, an identification – between Being and language. Yet while this thesis is itself rather problematical, there exist other aspects of Heideggerian philosophy that are of fundamental importance for hermeneutics. These can be summarized as (a) the analysis of Dasein (that is, human existence) as a 'hermeneutic totality', and (b) in the late works, the effort to define a kind of thought beyond the limits of metaphysics in terms of *An-denken*, or 're-collection' ('keeping in mind'), and, more specifically, in terms of the relationship to tradition. Precisely these two elements impart content to the general notion of a link between Being (*Sein*) and language (*Sprache*), and define that link in a nihilistic sense.

The first nihilistic element in Heidegger's hermeneutic theory may be found in his analysis of Dasein as a hermeneutic totality. Dasein, we know, means essentially being-in-the-world; but this, in turn, can be understood only as the threefold existential structure of State of Mind (*Befindlichkeit*), Understanding-Interpreting (*Verstehen-Auslegung*), and Discourse (*Rede*).[8] The circle of understanding and interpretation is the constitutive central structure of Dasein's own being-in-the-world. Being-in-the-world does not mean being effectively in contact with all the different things that constitute the world, but rather being always already familiar with a totality of meanings, that is, with a context of references. In Heidegger's analysis of the world-character of the world, things give themselves to Dasein only within a project, or, as Heidegger says, as tools. Dasein exists in the form of a project in which things *are* only insofar as they belong to this project, or, in other words, only insofar as they have a specific meaning in this context. This preliminary familiarity with the world, which is identified with the very existence of Dasein, is what Heidegger calls 'understanding' or 'pre-understanding'. Every act of knowledge is nothing other than an articulation or an interpretation of this preliminary familiarity with the world.

This definition of the hermeneutic structure of existence, though, is by no means a complete one. The second section of the first part of *Sein und Zeit*, in fact, takes up this problem once again and subsequently develops it in a way that eliminates any misunderstanding about a possible form of neo-Kantian 'transcendentalism' in Heidegger's thought in *Sein und Zeit*. The hermeneutic totality that is Dasein may not be in fact identified with some Kantian *a priori* structure. The world with which Dasein is always already familiar is neither a transcendental screen nor a categorial schema, for the world is always already given to Dasein in an historical and cultural *Geworfenheit*, or 'thrown-ness', which is profoundly linked to its mortality. At the beginning of the second section of *Sein und Zeit*, Heidegger demonstrates the connection between the project of Dasein and being-toward-death by posing the problem of the totality of the structures of Dasein. Dasein may be a totality only by anticipating, and resolving upon, its own death. Among all the possibilities that constitute Dasein's project, that is, its being-in-the-world, dying is the only possibility that Dasein cannot avoid. Moreover, as long as Dasein exists, death is also that possibility which must remain pure possibility. Death – if realized – would render impossible all other possibilities beyond itself (namely the concrete possibilities by which humanity in fact lives). Precisely through its remaining a permanent possibility, though, death also acts as the factor which allows all other possibilities to manifest themselves *as* possibilities. It therefore confers upon existence the mobile rhythm of a kind of *dis-cursus*, of a context whose sense is constituted as a sort of ever-moving musical composition that never comes to rest on a single note.

Dasein establishes itself as a hermeneutic totality only insofar as it continually lives the possibility of no-longer-being-there. This condition may be described by saying that the foundation of Dasein coincides with its groundlessness: the hermeneutic totality of Dasein exists only in relation to the constitutive possibility of no longer being (there).

This relation between founding and ungrounding, introduced in *Sein und Zeit* in the analysis of being-toward-death, is a constant in all the successive phases of development of Heidegger's thought, even though the problematic of death seems to disappear (or nearly so) in his final works. Founding and ungrounding are also the basis for the notion of the *Ereignis* or the event of Being. In the late works of Heidegger, the set of problems that are linked in *Sein und Zeit* to the concept of authenticity (*Eigentlichkeit*) are instead transferred to this term. In *Vorträge und Aufsätze* (1954), for instance, the *Ereignis* is the event in which the thing is given *als etwas*, that is, as something. A thing can be given 'as something' – or, in other words, appropriate itself (*eignen*) – only insofar as it is taken up in 'the mirror-play of the world' or in the 'round dance' (*Ring*). While appropriating itself in this fashion, however, it is also expropriated (*Ent-eignet*), since in the last analysis appropriation is always an *Über-eignen* or transpropriation.[9] This conception of the event as *ereignen*, which is ultimately also *über-eignen*, corresponds in Heidegger's late works to the link between founding and ungrounding in *Sein und Zeit*. And this should hardly be surprising, for such a conception of the event is developed by Heidegger out of the same line of thought already present in *Sein und Zeit*: the thing comes to Being only as an aspect of a total project that, while it allows the thing to appear, also consumes it in a network of references. In *Sein und Zeit*, hermeneutic totality is established only in relation to the possibility of its not being there anymore. Each thing appears as itself (as what it is) only insofar as it dissolves into a circular reference to all other things. This does not possess the nature of a dialectical insertion in a foundational totality, but rather has the character of a 'round dance', as Heidegger explicitly states in his lecture on 'The Thing'.

In what sense can this vision of the hermeneutic constitution of Dasein be called 'nihilistic'? First of all, we need to look at it in one of the senses that Nietzsche attributes to the term 'nihilism', in a note placed by the editors at the beginning of the 1906 edition of *The Will to Power*. Nihilism is described by Nietzsche as that situation in which 'man rolls from the centre towards X', as in the Copernican revolution. For Nietzsche, this means that nihilism is the situation in which the human subject explicitly recognizes that the lack of foundation is a constitutive part of its condition (what Nietzsche calls elsewhere 'the death of God'). Now, the non-identification of Being and foundation is one of the most evident points of Heidegger's ontology: Being is not foundation, and every foundational relation is always already given within a specific epoch of Being. These epochs, however, are in themselves *opened up* – rather than founded – by Being. In a passage in *Sein und Zeit*, indeed, Heidegger explicitly discusses the need to 'forget about Being as foundation'[10] if we are to draw any closer to a kind of thought which is no longer metaphysically oriented towards object-ness alone.

Nevertheless, it would appear that Heidegger's mode of thought is the opposite of nihilism, at least in the sense in which nihilism signifies that process which not only eliminates Being as foundation but forgets about Being altogether. Nihilism, according to a passage from Heidegger's *Nietzsche*, is that process in which in the end 'there is nothing left of Being' as such.[11] Is it legitimate to call Heideggerian hermeneutics 'nihilistic' in this latter sense, since it means going against the letter of Heidegger's own text?

In order to see how this second meaning of nihilism can also be applied to Heidegger's philosophy, let us look at the second of the two 'nihilistic traits' which – at least according to my interpretation – are fundamental for Heidegger and for his hermeneutics, that is, his conception of thinking as *An-denken*. *An-denken*, as noted above, is the form of thought that Heidegger opposes to metaphysical thought (which is dominated by the forgetting of Being). *An-denken* is also what he himself attempts to do in the works that follow *Sein und Zeit*, in which Heidegger no longer develops a systematic discourse, but instead limits himself to retracing the great moments of the history of metaphysics which are expressed in the great works of poets and thinkers. It would be an error to consider this work of retracing the history of metaphysics as simply a preparatory stage which would then serve in the subsequent construction of a positive ontology. Recollection as a retracing of the decisive moments of the history of metaphysics is instead the *definitive* form of the thought of Being that we are to carry out. *An-denken* corresponds to what Heidegger describes in *Sein und Zeit* as an anticipatory decision regarding death that is supposed to be found at the basis of authentic existence. In *Sein und Zeit* this decision is discussed as a possibility but is defined only in rather vague terms. The fact of mortality, which founds the hermeneutic totality of existence, appears more clearly in Heidegger's late works as *An-denken* or recollective thought. It is by retracing the history of metaphysics as the forgetting of Being that Dasein decides for its own death and in this way founds itself as a hermeneutic totality whose foundation consists of a lack of foundation. A passage from *Der Satz vom Grund*[12] provides one of the relatively few instances where in his late works Heidegger discusses death and mortality. In it the appeal to a principle of sufficient reason (*Grund*) to indicate the cause of any and every phenomenon, and thus give a rational ordering to the world, is turned upside down by Heidegger's reading. He calls instead for a leap into the *Abgrund*, or, in other words, into the abyss in which we, as mortals, always already find ourselves. This leap is nothing other than *An-denken*: for the latter means 'thinking from the point of view of the *Geschick* [the mission-destiny-gift of Being], and that is an entrusting of oneself – through recollection – to the liberating bond that positions us within the tradition of thought'. Even if Heidegger does not explicitly make this same connection in *Sein und Zeit*, it is fair to assume that what he defines there as an anticipatory decision towards death becomes, in the late works, thought as recollection. This kind of thought is carried out insofar as Dasein entrusts itself to the liberating bond that positions it in the *Über-lieferung* ('tradition'). *An-denken* is that recollection which is counterpoised to the forgetting of

Being that characterizes metaphysics itself, and is thus defined as a leap into the abyss of mortality or, in what amounts to the same thing, an entrusting of oneself to the liberating bond of tradition. Thought that frees itself from metaphysical forgetting does not, therefore, directly accede to Being by re-presenting it, namely by making it present or by recuperating its presence. On the contrary, this is precisely what constitutes the metaphysical thought of objectivity. Being can never really be thought of as a presence, and the thought that does not forget it is only that which remembers it or, in other words, already thinks of Being as absent, vanished, or gone away. In a certain sense, what Heidegger says about nihilism is therefore also true of recollective thought, for in the latter too 'there is nothing left' of Being as such. Tradition is the transmitting of linguistic messages that constitute the horizon within which Dasein is thrown as an historically determined project: and tradition derives its importance from the fact that Being, as a horizon of disclosure in which things appear, can arise only as a trace of past words or as an announcement that has been handed down to us. This transmitting or handing down is closely connected to Dasein's mortality, for Being is an announcement that is handed down only because the generations of mankind follow one another in the natural rhythm of birth and death.

The task of hermeneutics in regard to tradition is never a making-present in any sense of the term. Above all, it cannot be understood in the historicist sense of reconstructing the origins of a certain state of affairs or things in order better to appropriate them, according to the traditional notion of knowledge as knowledge of causes and principles. In entrusting oneself to tradition, what proves liberating is not cogent evidence of principles or *Gründe* which, when we arrive at them, would finally allow us to explain clearly what happens to us; instead what is liberating is the leap into the abyss of mortality. As happens also in Heidegger's etymological reconstructions of the great words of the past, the relationship with tradition does not supply us with a fixed point of support, but rather pushes us on in a sort of return *in infinitum* to the past, a return through which the historical horizons that we inhabit become more fluid. The present order of entities – which in the objectifying thought of metaphysics claims to be identified with Being itself – is instead unveiled as a particular historical horizon. This is not, however, to be understood in a purely relativistic sense. What Heidegger is seeking is still the meaning of Being, and not the irreducible relativity of the different epochs. The meaning of Being is precisely what is recalled through this re-ascent *in infinitum* through the past and the fluidification of historical horizons. This meaning of Being, which is given to us only through its link to mortality and to the handing down of linguistic messages from one generation to another, is the opposite of the metaphysical conception of Being as stability, force, *energheia*. It is instead a *weak* Being, in decline, which discloses itself through a weakening and fading: it is that *Gering*, so unapparent and irrelevant, which Heidegger discusses in his lecture 'The Thing'.

If this is so, then the hermeneutic constitution of Dasein does not only have a nihilistic character because man is founded by rolling 'from the centre toward X', but because Being, whose meaning we seek to recuperate, tends to identify itself with nothingness, with the fleeting traits of an existence enclosed between the boundaries of birth and death.

In contrast, hermeneutic experience as defined in Gadamer's work can hardly be considered as a leap into the *Ab-grund* of mortality, at least not in the sense in which Heidegger discusses it in *Der Satz vom Grund*. This ought to be obvious if we recall Gadamer's critique of aesthetic consciousness in the first section of *Wahrheit und Methode*. Aesthetic consciousness (*aesthetische Bewusstsein*) is the term that sums up the notion of aesthetic experience developed by the various neo-Kantian philosophies of the early part of the twentieth century. The aesthetic quality of a natural object or of a human artifact is the correlate of a purely contemplative stance, deliberately chosen by consciousness, which does not assume a theoretical or practical position with respect to the object. This notion originates in Kant, where disinterested contemplation is focused on the object considered as a work of genius, that is, as a display of a creative force embedded in nature itself. Aesthetic quality is no longer ontologically rooted, and remains defined negatively as lacking any practical or cognitive points of reference, for it is intrinsically tied to a specific stance assumed by the observer. Gadamer recalls in this context Valéry's 'hermeneutic nihilism': 'mes vers ont le sens qu'on leur prête.' We might also mention here certain aspects of Croce's aesthetics, which distinguishes the beautiful from any other type of cognitive, ethical, or political value. The dominion of art is thus constituted as a dimension of an abstractly considered 'aesthetic quality', whose meaning is nothing other than the crystallization of a particular social taste which, moreover, appreciates the beautiful only as a sort of fetish cut off from any effective historical and existential reference. The museum as a public institution corresponds to this notion of aesthetic consciousness, and it is no mere coincidence that this phenomenon develops over the course of the last few centuries in parallel to the theoretical genesis of aesthetic subjectivism. The museum, where works of art of the most diverse styles and schools are gathered together, is the place where this abstract and historically uprooted sort of aesthetic quality is most evident. Whereas the personal and private collections of princes or aristocrats represent a certain taste and particular individual preferences, the museum accumulates everything that is 'aesthetically valid', but only inasmuch as the objects are endowed with a 'contemplativity' totally cut off from historical experience.

Thus abstractly defined, aesthetic quality is given to the individual in an experience that has the nature of the *Erlebnis*, namely as a lived, momentary, and ultimately epiphanic experience. Gadamer quotes in this context a relevant passage from Dilthey's *Leben Schleiermachers*: 'each one of the *Erlebnisse* is complete in itself, it is a particular image of the universe which eludes any explicative connection.'[13] But this meaning of the romantic *Erlebnis* is still linked to a pantheistic vision of the universe. The *Erlebnis* of twentieth-century culture, and of Dilthey himself, is instead an experience whose meaning is totally subjective and devoid of any ontological legitimation: whether in a poem, in a landscape, or in a musical score, the sovereign subject distils the totality of meaning in an entirely arbitrary way, depriving it of any organic connection with its existential and historical situation or with the 'reality' within which it lives. Founding aesthetics on the concept of *Erlebnis* leads to a dissolution into an 'absolute series' of discrete temporal points, or discontinuous 'punctuality', that 'annihilates both the unity of the work and the identity of the artist with himself, and the identity of the person understanding or enjoying the work of art'.[14] When understood in this way, aesthetic consciousness subsumes those negative traits signalled by Plato in his distrust of tragic actors who can feign any kind of feeling, and thus somehow lose their own identity; and it also comprises the nihilstic and self-destructive traits that for Kierkegaard belong to the aesthetic phase of existence. Gadamer substitutes an experience of art characterized by the historical continuity and constructivity that Kierkegaard locates in the ethical choice of marriage in place of an aesthetic consciousness defined (as in Kierkegaard's *Don Juan*) in terms of its transitory and ephemeral nature. Gadamer's aim is to recuperate art as an experience of truth. In this, he goes against the contemporary scientistic way of thinking that has limited truth to the field of the mathematical sciences of nature, relegating all other experiences more or less explicitly to the domains of poetry, aesthetic 'punctuality', and the *Erlebnis*. In order to recuperate art as an experience of truth, the notion of truth as the conformity of the proposition to the thing must be replaced with a more comprehensive notion founded on the concept of *Erfahrung*, that is, on experience as a modification that the subject undergoes when it encounters something that truly has relevance for it. It may then be said that art is an experience of truth if it is an authentic experience or, in other words, if the encounter with the work actually modifies the observer. This notion of experience is quite obviously of Hegelian origin, for its model is the itinerary described in the *Phenomenology of the Spirit*. Hegel profoundly influences Gadamer here insofar as, in order to be lived as an experience of truth, the encounter with the work of art must be set in the dialectical continuity of the subject with itself and with its own history. The work does not speak to us in the abstract succession of discrete instants of the *Erlebnis*: the work is an historical event, and our encounter with it is also an historical event in that in it we are changed, just as the new interpretation of the work also has a bearing upon its being by extending it in the act of interpretation. In fact, all this defines aesthetic experience as an authentic historical experience. Furthermore, it ultimately identifies the experience of art with historical experience *tout court*, in such a way that the specificity of the work can no longer be perceived. There is, after all, a good reason why one of the central concepts of Gadamer's hermeneutics is that of the 'classic', for the aesthetic quality of the classic work of art is recognized as an historically founding one, and is therefore the exact opposite of any abstract *Erlebnis*. Aesthetic quality is the force of historical foundation, the capacity to exert a *Wirkung* or effect that shapes not only taste but also language, and therefore the realms of existence of future generations.

Heidegger always keeps in mind Hölderlin's lines: 'Voll Verdienst, doch dichterisch/wohnet der Mensch auf dieser Erde' ('Full of merit, yet poetically/does Man dwell upon this earth'). But why should the poet say 'doch' ('yet')? From Gadamer's standpoint, in which the work of art and the encounter with it are historical events fully couched in the continuity of effects, namely of the *Wirkungen* that constitute the texture of history, it is not clear why there should be an opposition between the 'merit' – that is to say, human labour and the production of historical effects – and the poetic quality of man's dwelling upon the earth. Yet Heidegger continually insists on this opposition. In fact, in his hermeneutics and in the aesthetics that derive from it, the concept of the experience of the truth of art does not allow itself to be reduced to the historical and constructive terms defined by Gadamer. As a result of this, it also calls for a revision of the critique of aesthetic consciousness. It could be said that the discontinuous and ephemeral quality of aesthetic consciousness that Gadamer criticizes expresses precisely the meaning of Hölderlin's 'doch': what takes place in the work of art is a particular instance of the ungrounding of historicity, which is announced as a suspension of the hermeneutic continuity of the subject with itself and with history. Aesthetic consciousness, as an abstract series of discrete instants in time, is the mode by which the subject lives the leap into the *Ab-grund* of its own mortality.

When Heidegger speaks of the work of art as 'the setting-into-work of truth', he explains that it is such insofar 'as it sets up [*stellt auf*] a world' and 'it sets forth [*her-stellt*] the earth.' The setting up of a world is the meaning of the work's historical opening. This opening function of the work can be read both in a utopian sense that would bring this aspect of Heidegger's aesthetics close to the aesthetics of Bloch and Adorno, and in a transcendental sense, as the capacity of the work to project alternative possibilities of existence as pure possibility, as argued for instance by Ricoeur.[15] The setting up of a world is also the truth of art as Gadamer sees it in *Truth and Method*. But what is the setting forth of the earth? In Heidegger's terms, it is the fact of bringing into the open the earth as the obscure element upon which every world takes root and from which every world draws its vitality, but without ever managing to bring it completely out of obscurity. If we look elsewhere in Heidegger's work for suggestions on how better to understand what meaning to attribute to the terrestrial nature of the work of art, we find that the term *Erde* figures in the doctrine of the *Geviert* as one of the 'fourfold' of the world which is unfolded in earth and sky, mortals and divinities.[16] Although the *Geviert* presents some of the greatest difficulties in all of Heidegger's conceptual terminology, his works are clear at least on the following: the earth is *inhabited* by human beings insofar as they are mortals. From the earth we are therefore sent back to mortality, which as we have seen constitutes the basic nihilistic trait of Dasein as a hermeneutic totality. We may then say that the work of art is a 'setting-into-work of truth' because it sets up historical worlds; it inaugurates and anticipates, as an original linguistic event, the possibility of historical existence – but always shows this only in reference to mortality. The union of founding and ungrounding that runs through all of Heidegger's ontology is realized in the work of art and in the nexus that it constitutes between world and earth. The Greek temple which Heidegger discusses in his essay on 'The Origin of the Work of Art' exhibits all its own historical meanings solely on the basis of its physically staying within nature, registering on its own stony body the passing of the seasons, and with it the passing of historical time. So it is, in the same essay, that in his discussion of the concept of the thing Heidegger takes as an example the peasant's shoes in Van Gogh's painting – for they show cracks that are not to be seen, according to Heidegger, as a realistic representation of life in the fields, but rather as the presence of earthliness as lived temporality in the form of birth, ageing, and death. Already in this essay, then, the earthly element shows itself to be the aspect of the work of art which is rooted in the natural. This has to do with its being a kind of matter in which lives the *physis*, which is always to be understood as a ripening (*Zeitigung*) or growth of an organism that is born and is destined to die. Unlike practical products, the work of art displays its earthliness, its mortality, and its being subject to the action of time – like, for instance, the patina on a painting, or the growing corpus of interpretations, or the disappearance and rediscovery of certain works of art according to the vicissitudes of taste – not as a limit, but as a positively constitutive aspect of its meaning.

This presence of mortality, and of nature as the place of birth and death, cannot at any rate be articulated in the interpretations of the work of art except as a limiting idea. Adorno's use (in his *Aesthetic Theory*) of the term 'expression' may be of help to us here.[17] For Adorno, this term serves to indicate the fact that in every work there exists – beyond its structure, techniques, and even dissonances – 'something more' in its meaning that is akin to its expressivity. Insofar as this 'something more' does not become discourse – that is, it cannot be defined in terms of a conceptual mediation – it may be the precise correlative of the aesthetic *Erlebnis*. That sense in which the work of art is always also a 'symbol' of the experience of birth and death is something that interpretation and critical discourse cannot articulate except at the cost of lapsing into tautology. And yet our aesthetic experience bears witness to the fact that all the discursive work of interpretation and criticism would be in vain if it did not lead to that 'final' moment which is perhaps what Aristotle's *Poetics* means by the notion of *katharsis*. In each work of art there is an earthly element that does not become a part of the world, and that does not turn into discourse or a fully displayed meaning: this element alludes to mortality, often at the level of the contents of the work (for instance, in the archetypes that may be discovered in it), or sometimes at the level of its material nature (the patina of time, the vicissitudes a work undergoes in the course of history, or even its physical decay). This terrestrial element, insofar as it cannot be the object of any possible '*dis-cursus*', is given to a kind of experience that can be described only as *Erlebnis*. It is not true, however, that once the *Erlebnis* is freed from the romantic metaphysics of genius and its ontological foundation in nature, it must necessarily fall back into the horizon of subjectivism. It is precisely the analysis of Dasein performed by Heidegger in *Sein und Zeit* which allows us to see the constitutive structure of existence outside the subjectivity/objectivity opposition. In the experience of the constitution of Dasein as a hermeneutic totality, in the experience of recollective thought, and in the encounter with the work of art as the 'setting-into-work of truth', there is an element of ungrounding which is inseparable from founding itself. Art is in fact defined as a 'setting-into-work of truth' precisely because it keeps the conflict between earth and world alive – that is to say, because it founds the world while showing at the same time its lack of foundation. In order to describe, on a subjective level, this experience of ungrounding, or the leap into the *Ab-grund* of mortality in which we already and always are, the only model we have at our disposal is precisely that of the *Erlebnis*, of aesthetic consciousness in its abstract ahistoricity and discontinuity – in other words, in the traits through which it appears as an experience of mortality. Even if in this momentary experience Dasein does not encounter the ontological transcendence of nature that is supposedly present in the work of genius, as the Romantics believe, this in turn does not mean that Dasein encounters only itself as subject: it encounters itself instead as existing, as mortal, as something that – in its capacity for death – experiences Being in a radically different manner from that which is familiar to the metaphysical tradition.

NOTES

1   H.-G. Gadamer, *Truth and Method*, trans. Garrett Bardon and John Cummings, 2nd edn (1975; repr. New York: Crossroads, 1984). 'Hermeneutic ontology' begins with this seminal work of Gadamer's, although its basis is already clearly present in Heidegger's work. Other thinkers, moreover, follow Heidegger's lead in directions that radically differ from the one that Gadamer takes in *Truth and Method*. For instance, in Italy Luigi Pareyson develops an original philosophy of interpretation; his intellectual itinerary starts with *La filosofia dell'esistenza e Carlo Jaspers* (1940), 2nd edn (Casale Monferrato: Marietti, 1983), and continues with *Esistenza e persona* (Turin: Taylor, 1950) (which he has revised and republished a number of times), *Estetica. Teoria della formatività*, and *Verità e interpretazione* (Milan: Mursia, 1971).

2   Cf. Heidegger's essay on 'The Origin of the Work of Art', *Poetry, Language, Thought*, trans. Albert Hofstadter (New York: Harper and Row, 1971; repr. 1975), pp. 163–86.

3   See my introduction to the second edition of the Italian translation of *Truth and Method* – *Verità e metodo*, trans.

G. Vattimo (Milan: Bompiani, 1983) – for a brief overview of the leading interpretations of Gadamer's work over the past twenty years or so.

4 See especially K. O. Apel, *Transformation der Philosophie* (Frankfurt: Suhrkamp, 1973).

5 See my introduction to the Italian translation of a set of selected essays from Apel's *Transformation der Philosophie*, entitled *Comunità e comunicazione*, trans. G. Carchia (Turin: Rosenberg e Sellier, 1977).

6 Cf. Hans Robert Jauss, *Toward an Aesthetic of Reception*, trans. Timothy Bahti (Minneapolis: Minnesota UP, 1982).

7 On this point see my *Al di là del soggetto* (Milan: Feltrinelli, 1981), chapter 4.

8 These themes are discussed in the first section of *Sein und Zeit*. Regarding the theory of interpretation that is found in *Sein und Zeit*, see M. Bonola's recent and penetrating study, *Verità e interpretazione nello Heidegger di 'Essere e Tempo'* (Turin: Ed. di 'Filosofia', 1983).

9 Cf. Heidegger's lecture on 'The Thing', in *Poetry, Language, Thought*.

10 Cf. Heidegger, 'Time and Being', in *On Time and Being* (1962), p. 6. See the final note of chapter 1 for the full English translation.

11 Cf. Heidegger, *Nietzsche*, vol. II: *The Eternal Recurrence of the Same* (1961), trans. David F. Krell (New York: Harper and Row, 1984).

12 Cf. Heidegger, *Der Satz vom Grund* (Pfullingen: Neske, 1957), p. 186.

13 Wilhelm Dilthey, *Leben Schleiermachers*, ed. Mulert, 2nd edn (Berlin, 1922), vol. I, p. 341.

14 Gadamer, *Truth and Method*, trans. Burden and Cummings, p. 85.

15 See, for instance, P. Ricoeur, *The Rule of Metaphor*, trans. Robert Czerny (Toronto: Toronto UP, 1977).

16 Heidegger discusses the notion of *Geviert*, for instance, in his lecture on 'The Thing' (in *Poetry, Language, Thought*), and in a number of different places in *On the Way to Language*, trans. Peter D. Hertz (New York: Harper and Row, 1971).

17 Cf. Theodor Adorno, *Aesthetic Theory*, trans. C. Lenhardt, ed. Gretel Adorno and Rolf Tiedemann (London: Routledge and Kegan Paul, 1984), p. 148 ff.

8

Truth and Rhetoric in
Hermeneutic Ontology

I

What we call 'hermeneutic ontology' is, in contemporary
thought, a very distinct and well-developed philosophical
position. Besides Gadamer, one need only think of the original
and highly articulate theories put forward by philosophers
such as Luigi Pareyson, Paul Ricoeur, or (more recently)
Richard Rorty. These thinkers have contributed decisively,
though often in divergent directions, to the philosophy of
interpretation. My consideration of the problem here cannot
therefore be an exhaustive one; I shall seek to examine the
relationship between truth and rhetoric solely from the
specific hermeneutic perspective of Gadamer. For among the
authors mentioned above, Gadamer more than any other has –
and in the most influential fashion – thematized such a
relationship in his work.

Gadamer's interest in rhetoric is amply documented in his
great work, *Truth and Method* (1960),[1] and is given even
greater emphasis and consideration in the essays produced in
the following years, now collected in his *Kleine Schriften* and
Die Vernunft im Zeitalter der Wissenschaft (*Reason in the Age of
Science*).[2] Gadamer returns to, and elaborates, Heidegger's
'connection' or 'identification' between Being and language in
a direction that stresses ever more emphatically the pole of
language rather than of Being. This is in essence the meaning
of the 'urbanization' – to borrow Jürgen Habermas's term for
it – performed by Gadamer on Heidegger's philosophy.[3]
Probably only thanks to this urbanization is it today possible,

for example, to set Heidegger and Wittgenstein in proximity to each other in an increasingly convincing manner, one that has ever more distinct consequences for philosophy. This proximity was suggested many years ago by such writers as Pietro Chiodi[4] and, at the beginning of the 1960s, K. O. Apel.[5] However, particularly in Chiodi's work, emphasis is always placed on the 'irrationalistic' and mystical elements that are supposedly to be found in Wittgenstein's work as well as Heidegger's, and no serious attempt is made instead to read Heidegger in light of the analytical philosophy of language. Only after Gadamer's 'urbanization', in short, does it become possible to make the kind of comparison upon which, for example, Rorty's *Philosophy and the Mirror of Nature* depends.[6] Indeed, the latter sees in twentieth-century philosophy a line of descent that is to be defined in terms of just three names: Dewey, Wittgenstein, and Heidegger.

The very possibility of seeing a resemblance between Wittgenstein and Heidegger is based upon a reading of the latter which 'urbanizes' his notion of language as the house of Being by emphasizing the pole of language itself, or even dissolving altogether – at least implicitly – the pole of Being. This dissolution is to a degree undertaken by Heidegger himself, so much so that we may speak legitimately of the nihilistic vocation of his philosophical thought.[7] Gadamer's fundamental argument is that 'the Being that can be understood is language', and this announces a development of Heideggerian thought in the direction of a dissolution of Being into language – or, at the very least, its resolution into language. As proof of this, it may be recalled that such central notions for Heidegger as metaphysics and the forgetting of Being find no systematic collocation in Gadamer's work.

Nevertheless, it would be an error to think that Gadamer's 'urbanization' of Heideggerian philosophy could be entirely explained in terms of this emphasis on the pole of language, perhaps in connection with the leading role widely assigned to linguistics (precisely in the period in which Gadamer published *Truth and Method*) as a model for those human

sciences inclined toward structuralism. Nor could it be
explained entirely in relation to the fact that interpretation and
hermeneutic tradition, which lie at the centre of Gadamer's
concerns, determine from the first his reflections on language.
What is already clear in *Truth and Method*, and what becomes
even clearer later on, is that the expanded role assigned to
language is accompanied by – or rather, has its true origin in –
the ethical concerns that govern Gadamer's hermeneutics.
Already in *Truth and Method* such key notions as the
fusion of horizons or the *wirkungsgeschichtliches Bewusstsein* are
generally constructed with reference to Aristotelian ethics and
the concept of 'application'. In subsequent essays it becomes
clearer that language, as a locus of total mediation of every
experience of the world and every occurrence of Being ('the
Being that can be understood is language'), is characterized
even more fundamentally – or in an equally originary way – in
ethical rather than purely linguistic terms. For Gadamer it is
not so much, or not principally, a matter of showing that every
experience of the world is made possible for the individual by
the possession of language; language is not primarily that
which the individual speaks, but rather that which speaks the
individual.[8] Above all, language is for Gadamer a locus, or a
place of concrete realization of the collective *ethos* of a
historically determined society, and thus it functions as a total
mediation of the experience of the world. In this sense, he
understands it to signify an historically determined language,
not the general human faculty of speaking. In it we experience
that world 'that we possess and share, which embraces past
history and the present, and which receives its linguistic
articulation in the discourse that men reciprocally address to
each other'.[9] This shared world that is articulated in language
possesses the traits of rationality; the *logos*, understood as at
once the language and the rationality of the real, is identified
with it. According to Gadamer, the Greek concept of the
rationality of nature and the Hegelian concept of the presence
of reason in history intersect in this concept of language as the
living *logos*.[10] It might be added that the vision of natural

language found in post-Wittgensteinian analytical philosophy
also intersects with this same concept. Gadamer describes the
linguistic and ethical dimension which governs experience by
referring back to the Greek notion of *kalon* in connection with
that of *theoria*. In the earliest linguistic usage of the term by
the Greeks, *theoria* is not primarily a formalized conceptual
construct that entails an 'objectifying' split between subject
and object. It is, rather, related to the participation in the
gods' procession, a participation in which the *theoroi* function,
moreover, as the delegates of their *polis*. It is thus a 'looking at'
which is also a 'participating in' and, in a certain way, a
'belonging to', rather than a possessing of the object. *Kalon*,
Gadamer notes in one of his essays in *Die Vernunft im Zeitalter
der Wissenschaft*, did not designate only artistic and religious
creations, but also included that which was without a shadow
of a doubt desirable and which did not require justification
through a demonstration of its utility: 'this is what the Greeks
called *theoria*: to have been given away to something that in
virtue of its overwhelming presence is accessible to all in
common. . . .'[11]

As the place of total mediation, language is precisely this
kind of reason and this *logos* that lives in the collective
belonging to a web of living tradition or an *ethos*. When
understood in this way, language/*logos*/*kalon* has a constitutive
nexus with the good: both serve as ends in themselves, or as
highest values which are not sought after for some other end,
and beauty is the perceptibility, or shining forth, of the idea of
the good – as Gadamer observes in the final paragraph of *Truth
and Method*.[12] Rationality in the historical experience of
individuals and groups may be defined only in reference to this
logos which is at once world and language. The *logos* does not
possess the infinite quality of self-transparence of the Hegelian
absolute spirit; it is dialectical only insofar as it lives in the
always finite and qualified dialogue of historical human
beings. Gadamer also calls it 'social understanding' (*sozialer
Einverständnis*) and social consciousness.[13]

II

Unquestionably this emphasis on the nexus between language and the *ethos* of a given linguistic community confers a particular meaning to Heideggerian thought (to which Gadamer makes explicit reference), one which is perhaps new even in respect to Heidegger himself. It is here that we may see a specific connection between truth and rhetoric. As is well known, *Truth and Method* opposes an idea of truth which takes the experience of art as its own model to the scientific notion of the true as a methodical verifiability in accordance with public and controllable criteria. The relationship between the initial reference to the experience of art and the final identification of the *logos*/world with the *kalon* is not, however, a vicious circle in the logical sense of the term. On the contrary, the final concept of the *kalon* explains, and grants content to, the modelling function originally assigned to art. In other words, art is also an experience of truth only because the experience of the true is the experience of belonging to language as the place of a total mediation of existence in the living collective consciousness. An entire branch of the tradition of aesthetic philosophy is implicated in this idea, that branch which – ranging from the special 'subjective' universality of the beautiful for Kant to Hegel's connection between art and the self-awareness of a people – has brought into focus the connection between the work of art and collective consciousness. Our encounter with the work of art is not an encounter with a determinate truth (which explains the evident clumsiness of all attempts to explain the 'truth-content' of a given work); it is rather, in the last analysis, an experience of our belonging, and of the work's belonging, to that horizon of collective consciousness represented by language itself and the tradition that it continues.

What does any of this have to do with the relationship between truth and rhetoric? 'Rhetoric' is taken here, as Gadamer takes it, in the most general and generic sense of an art of persuasion through discourse. The insistence and force of conviction with which the inheritance of collective consciousness (that is, the *kalon*) impresses itself upon us are of a rhetorical kind: Gadamer notes that 'the *eikos*, the verisimilar and the evident (*das Einleuchtende*) belong to a series of concepts that claim legitimacy for themselves over and against the truth and the certainty of that which is demonstrated and known.'[14] Hermeneutic truth, which is the experience of truth to which hermeneutics refers and which it understands to be exemplified by the experience of art, is essentially rhetorical:

To what should theoretical reflection on understanding refer if not to rhetoric, which from ancient times has always been presented as the sole advocate of a claim for truth which would defend the verisimilar, the *eikos*, and the evidence of common sense against the pretensions of science to certainty and demonstrativity? To convince and to explain without being able to adduce proofs are clearly the scope and the aim of not only understanding and interpretation, but of the art of discourse and rhetorical persuasion.[15]

This is not, however, a matter of a kind of truth that could be considered, in some sort of ideal classification, as different and distinct from the methodical kind of truth proper to science. Gadamer adds that the dominion of rhetorical persuasion, whose content is made up of collective consciousness and tradition, not only does not yield ground in the face of scientific progress, but rather 'extends itself with every new scientific discovery, in order to reassert its rights over science and to adapt it to itself'. Only rhetoric and hermeneutics, when understood in this way, make 'science a social factor of life'.[16] The *logos*/common language reaffirms its own rights over science and its discoveries, but not simply by transferring scientific ideas and terminology into everyday language and collective consciousness: such a transference occurs through popularization, obviously enough, and therefore through both a certain impoverishment of the meaning of scientific utterances and an emphasis on the rhetorical aspects that all scientific theories possess.[17] There is more to the problem than just this, however, as can be seen in Gadamer's essays in *Die Vernunft im Zeitalter der Wissenschaft*. The *logos*/collective consciousness exercises its rights as an ethical stance toward the use and development of the results of scientific research. The practicability that science and technology offer is never enough on its own to bring about a certain social use of science; an ethical kind of decision (even if only an implicit one) is always required, which sometimes even leads us to choose not to pursue a certain course of technological development. According to Gadamer, this is what is happening today to genetic engineering, which because of certain moral decisions is not being developed in certain directions.

This 'reconnection', so to speak, of the results of scientific research to collective consciousness is not merely an aspect of the becoming of language, but is primarily an ethical fact; and these two phenomena are, moreover, inseparable from each other. If we take seriously Gadamer's discourse concerning the *theoria* and the *kalon* as sites of truth, then we must say that the moment of truth for science is not primarily that of the verification of its propositions or the laws that it discovers; rather, it consists in a 'reconnection' to collective consciousness, and it too is therefore to be characterized in essentially rhetorical terms, though necessarily deeply coloured with pragmatic concerns. Heidegger's argument that science does not think may also be understood in this light: for the moment of truth for science is not the one that science believes it to be, that is, verification and demonstration. From this point of view, though, what happens to the notion of the truth as being publicly controllable in terms of agreed criteria that may be employed (at least in principle) by all? On the basis of the premises that have been examined here thus far, this cannot be understood either as a pacific distinction between *Natur-* and *Geisteswissenschaften* or as a simple reduction of science to 'economic' activity *à la* Croce.

On the contrary, rhetoric and hermeneutics – that is, the *logos*/collective consciousness – reaffirm their rights over the demonstrative discourse of science as a *radicalization* of the essentially rhetorical nature of science itself. This takes a direction, one might say, that proceeds from form to content. The rhetorical nature of science, in a purely formal sense, can be seen in its effective dependence upon paradigms that are always historical and mutable. Thomas Kuhn's hypotheses, at least in general, are no longer particularly shocking ones; or at least a hermeneutic notion of science can more willingly refer back to them.[18] Scientific theories are proven on the basis of observations that are possible, and that have a meaning, only within the confines of those same theories and their paradigms. For this reason, the emergence of a paradigm is not in turn a fact that can be described in terms of a scientific demonstration. Kuhn, as is well known, effectively leaves open the question of how we are to conceive of the historical event of a shift in paradigms. Hermeneutics may significantly contribute to thinking through this problem from beyond the limits of a notion of history as a pure play of forces or, on the contrary, as progress towards the objective knowledge of a stable reality.[19] Whatever difficulties there are in the framework of Kuhn's theory, the general meaning (perhaps a more generally acceptable one) of his theory of scientific revolutions may be formulated in terms of a reduction of scientific logic to rhetoric, in the restricted sense in which this means that scientific theories are demonstrable only from within paradigms which in turn are not 'logically' verifiable, but are accepted on the basis of a rhetorical kind of persuasiveness, no matter how this in fact occurs.

This recognition of the rhetorical essence, in this sense, of scientific logic itself is for the most part limited, however, to a generic acceptance of the conventionality of scientific paradigms. Kuhn's chief merit probably consists in having reconnected this general and generic conventionalism to an historical perspective. It might be said that conventions upon which the demonstrative methods of science rest are not assumed 'arbitrarily' or on the basis of abstract criteria of economy or practical utility, but rather on the basis of their 'conformity' to 'forms of life', and thus also to historically defined traditions and cultures. Hermeneutics effects a radicalization in respect to this general and generic acceptance of the rhetorical nature of science, which consists precisely in pursuing this path of historicization. It thus makes clear that the *public* nature of the rules of verification for scientific propositions is not only a formal universality (which at most would refer to the research community, already itself conceived on the model of the 'pure' scientific subject): the public nature of these rules is their effective grounding in an historically and culturally determinate public domain. The truth of a scientific proposition is not its verificability, which is controllable in terms of publicly stipulated rules which may ideally be employed by all; this would be a way of reducing the link between logic and rhetoric to a purely formal meaning. It is rather the reconnection of the governing rules of verification in the different scientific disciplines to a public domain that is the *logos*/common language, continually woven and rewoven in rhetorical and hermeneutical terms because its substance is the continuity of a tradition that is sustained and renewed through a process of reappropriation (of the object-tradition on the part of the subject, and vice-versa)[20] which occurs on the basis of 'evidence' of a rhetorical kind.

III

All this would seem to suggest a further and more essential link between truth and rhetoric, one in which hermeneutics draws closer to the kind of philosophy whose origins are found in empiricism and positivism. Gadamer describes the persuasive evidence provided by the content of the *logos*/collective consciousness in terms of a shining forth of the beautiful, the true, and the good, an experience which is, in the last analysis, an intuitive one that occurs in the consciousness of each individual. Yet his insistence on language as the locus of this experience entails – although this is only implicit in Gadamer's work, and perhaps making it explicit here opens up a new set of problems – an accentuation of the prevalently *public* nature of the true, which probably limits any reference to the intimate evidence of consciousness. To arrive at the truth does not so much mean to attain that state of luminous interiority which traditionally is considered 'evidence', as rather to pass to the level of those shared and commonly elaborated assumptions that appear obvious (rather than evident) and not in need of interrogation. The latter, perhaps, do not even therefore appear to be understandable as authentic evidence in the strong sense of the term. In this context we might think of Lacan's interpretation of the Freudian motto '*Wo Es war soll Ich werden.*'[21] Collective consciousness serves as the basis of our judgements, although this is not always apparent to us, and may even remain at an 'unconscious' level. As a 'background' it has, therefore, in this sense a weak nature which cannot truly be theorized in terms of the splendour and luminosity that Gadamer sees in the notions of *kalon* and *theoria*. The nature of collective consciousness as a background must be emphasized and taken as the central theme for any further reflection on the meaning of hermeneutics. Besides, to conceive of the *logos*/collective consciousness as language undoubtedly requires an accentuation of the experience of truth as a setting-into-work of explicitly thematized linguistic procedures – this latter understood not so much in the sense of public controllability of scientific utterances, but rather as an analysis of different languages in terms of their use. Even in this less formalized sense, the experience of truth is reconnected to the practice of analytical and control procedures which are essentially public in nature. From the point of view of the philosophical tradition from which hermeneutics derives, this would in any event appear to be an important acquisition. The 'urbanization' of Heidegger's thought here appears in a very literal sense, namely as an acceptance of the more 'external' rather than the intimate nature of truth on the part of a philosophy whose approach is originally an existentialist one. It is an acceptance as well of the predominance of the procedural moment over the intuitive moment, and of the moment of 'civil' communication – organized according to rules – over the moment of the interior vision of truth. In this way Heidegger's anti-humanism becomes easier to see; it appears above all else to be opposed to any special emphasis on consciousness, and thus distrustful of the subject of modern metaphysics – a distrust which has a precedent in Nietzsche and his rejection of the ultimate nature of the evidence of consciousness.

If, however, we are willing to allow that this separation of the true from the dominion of intuition and interior evidence represents an important acquisition for philosophy in numerous ways which remain to be fully explored, nevertheless it also involves more than a few problems which hermeneutics shares with certain strands of analytical philosophy deriving from the so-called 'second period' of Wittgenstein's work. For Wittgenstein poses in a particularly acute way the question of whether or not the majority of speakers of a given language could possibly be in error.[22]

In Gadamer's hermeneutics, this problem is posed in essentially analogous terms: to arrive at the truth fundamentally means to refer back to the *logos*/collective consciousness, and also to reconnect to it the discourses – no matter how partial – of science, technology, and perhaps even of particular groups in a society. But the *logos*/collective consciousness, together with its content, can itself never be placed in doubt – except, perhaps, with reference to effective historical mutations of the community and to extensions of the latter, though here too this appears quite problematical, unless we want to revert to an image of history as a pure play of forces of which the 'truth' is but a reflection and a consequence. From the specific point of view of the critical nature that philosophy has always claimed for itself and for thought in general in the Western tradition, is it sufficient simply to maintain that the road towards the truth is the same one that leads 'particular' discourses back, in cognitive and ethical terms, to the consciousness of the *sensus communis*? Is the 'leap into the *logoi*' of Plato's Socrates, which Gadamer considers constitutive of philosophy and reason in its hermeneutic meaning, truly a leap if it consists principally in reasserting the rights of collective consciousness over the often dogmatic claims of the discourses of the different sciences? Does not this leap, in such a way, become an 'apology of what already exists'? In the name of what can a critique of the majority opinion by prophets, revolutionaries, or even ground-breaking scientists, be made legitimate?

Gadamer sees the problematic nature of his notion of the *logos*/collective consciousness only in the form of the effective occurrence of such a consciousness. He maintains that, despite all appearances to the contrary, a collective consciousness – that is, a continuity of the ethical tradition – may still occur in our scientific and technological society.[23] He does not consider the question of rights themselves; in other words, he does not consider in the name of what particular right the collective consciousness should predominate and prevail over individuals.

This is, probably, another aspect of Gadamer's 'urbanization' of Heidegger's work, which could be termed in this instance an excess of 'urbanity'. At the beginning of this chapter I noted that in Gadamer's own work some of Heidegger's essential themes, such as the notion of metaphysics or of ontological difference, seem to disappear altogether. This point comes to mind again when the problem is posed of the critical nature of thought in the hermeneutic and rhetorical perspective that Gadamer outlines with his notions of *kalon* and *theoria*. Whatever the reason, it is certain that a great deal of Heidegger's critical pathos in regard to the world of the forgetting of Being, and of a metaphysics that has been accomplished in the global dominion of technology, is greatly attenuated, or completely absent, in Gadamer's work. For the latter, what counts is the ability to limit the dogmatic claims of science and technology in favour of a social rationality which sees no need to take too great a distance from Western metaphysics, but rather positions itself in a relation of fundamental continuity with it. This is the reason – above and

beyond the greater importance that his philological training
has for him – for the way in which Gadamer distances himself
from Heidegger's interpretations of the philosophers and
poets of the past.[24] For these are the texts in which Heidegger
appears at his most oracular and least 'urbane', and those
which appeal least to a reader such as Habermas. Yet,
paradoxically, these are the very same texts in which
Heidegger remains most faithful to a critical stance regarding
what already exists that in Gadamer's work is minimized to
the point of vanishing altogether.

The fact is that, in his archaeological enterprise of rereading the poets and philosophers of the past, Heidegger goes
in search of 'dense' zones of language in which the event of
Being resounds in a more intense and more recognizable
manner. These zones thus also become the points of greatest
strength for a critique of the subjection of common language
to metaphysics and technology. Gadamer claims instead to be
able to criticize technicity and scientificity from the point of
view of a language/collective consciousness which seems to
him to be fundamentally in order, and in regard to which
hermeneutics does not have a true critical function, but only a
reconstructive and reconstitutive one.

How could the originary critical force of Heidegger's
thought be recuperated today as a possible alternative to
Gadamer's? This might quite probably be achieved by
returning to Heidegger's reflections on art and poetry, or in
general on the 'dense zones' of language. It would probably
then emerge that, at the source of the divergence between
Heidegger and Gadamer, there is a bracketing of the more
'existential' elements of Heideggerian philosophy (authenticity,
the anticipatory decision for death, and so on), and even a
different conception of the experience of art, although the
latter functions for both thinkers as an emblematic locus of the
occurrence of truth. The final pages of *Truth and Method*,
where Gadamer describes the *kalon*, are entirely dominated by
a reversion to a metaphysics of light and, more generally, of
the splendour of form. Gadamer's words seem to take us far

from the idea of the work of art as an ever-open conflict between world and earth which Heidegger proposes in his essay on 'The Origin of the Work of Art'.[25] It is precisely by taking up and reflecting on these 'repressed' elements of Heidegger's philosophy, which are also the most frankly existential elements of his work, that it may be possible to lead hermeneutics beyond a simple acceptance of collective consciousness and beyond the risk of being reduced to an apology for what already exists.

NOTES

1 H.-G. Gadamer, *Truth and Method*, trans. Garrett Barden and John Cummings, 2nd edn (1975; repr. New York: Crossroads, 1984).

2 H.-G. Gadamer, *Kleine Schriften*, 4 vols. *op. cit. Die Vernunft im Zeitalter der Wissenschaft* was published by Suhrkamp (Frankfurt, 1976) and appeared in English as *Reason in the Age of Science*, trans F. G. Lawrence (Cambridge: MIT Press, 1981).

3 Cf. Jürgen Habermas, 'Urbanisierung der Heideggerschen Provinz', now in H.-G. Gadamer and J. Habermas, *Das Erbe Hegels* (Frankfurt: Suhrkamp, 1979), pp. 9–51.

4 P. Chiodi, 'Essere e linguaggio in Heidegger e nel *Tractatus* di Wittgenstein', *Rivista di filosofia* (1955), pp. 179–91.

5 K. O. Apel, *Transformation der Philosophie* (Frankfurt: Suhrkamp, 1973), vol. I, p. 225 ff.

6 Richard Rorty, *Philosophy and the Mirror of Nature* (Princeton: Princeton UP, 1979).

7 Here I refer the reader to my *Le avventure della differenza* (Milan: Garzanti, 1979) (esp. section 3), and *Al di là del soggetto* (Milan: Feltrinelli, 1981).

8 Gadamer pays explicit homage to Jacques Lacan in one of his post-*Truth and Method* essays; cf. *Kleine Schriften*, vol. I, p. 129.

9 Ibid., vol. I, p. 118.

10 Gadamer, *Reason in the Age of Science*, pp. 59–60.

11 Ibid., p. 77.

12 Cf. Gadamer, *Truth and Method*, pp. 497–8.

13 Gadamer, *Kleine Schriften*, vol. I, pp. 129–30.

14   Gadamer, *Truth and Method*.

15   Gadamer, *Kleine Schriften*, vol. I, p. 117.

16   Ibid.

17   Cf., for instance, Gadamer, *Kleine Schriften*, vol. I, pp. 117–18.

18   Cf. Gadamer, *Reason in the Age of Science*, p. 164. Gadamer refers here to Thomas S. Kuhn's *The Structure of Scientific Revolutions*, 2nd edn (Chicago: Chicago UP, 1970).

19   One could, in order to develop this hypothesis further, take as a point of departure either the parallel established by Rorty in *Philosophy and the Mirror of Nature* between the terms normal science and revolutionary science (Kuhn) or epistemology and hermeneutics, or Gadamer's remarks concerning Habermas's ideas on tradition and power (*Kleine Schriften*, vol. I, p. 125).

20   This reciprocal reappropriation between 'subject' and 'object' in the hermeneutic act is related to the transpropriation that occurs in the *Ereignis* of Being as it is described by Heidegger. Cf., for instance, *Vorträge und Aufsätze* (Pfullingen: Neske, 1954; repr. 1978), especially the essay on 'The Thing'.

21   Cf. Jacques Lacan, *Écrits: A Selection*, trans. Alan Sheridan (New York: Norton, 1979).

22   Concerning this problem, see the essay by C. M. Leitch and S. H. Holtzman, 'Communal Agreement and Objectivity', which serves as an introduction to the volume *Wittgenstein. To Follow a Rule*, ed. C. M. Leitch and S. H. Holtzman (London: Routledge, 1981).

23   Cf. Gadamer, *Reason in the Age of Science*, pp. 82–3, 86–7.

24   On this matter, see A. Fabris's interview with Gadamer, entitled 'Interpretation and Truth', *Teoria*, 2 (1982), pp. 157–75.

25   Contained in *Poetry, Language, Thought*, trans. Albert Hofstadter (New York: Harper and Row, 1971; repr. 1975), pp. 163–86.

9

Hermeneutics and Anthropology

In the final chapter of his *Philosophy and the Mirror of Nature*,[1] Richard Rorty offers a rigorous critique of the mixture of the respective points of view of anthropology and transcendental philosophy which (according to him) occurs in Habermas's work. Rorty specifically refers to the following passage in Habermas's 'Nachwort' to the second edition of *Erkenntnis und Interesse* (1973):[2]

the functions knowledge has in universal contexts of practical life can only be successfully analysed in the framework of a reformulated transcendental philosophy. This, incidentally, does not entail an empiricist critique of the claim to absolute truth. As long as cognitive interests can be identified and analysed through reflection upon the logic of inquiry in natural and cultural sciences, they can legitimately claim a 'transcendental' status. They assume an 'empirical' status as soon as they are analysed as the result of natural history – analysed, as it were, in terms of cultural anthropology.

Rorty comments that, contrary to what Habermas believes, 'there is no point in trying to find a general synoptic way of "analysing" the "functions knowledge has in universal contexts of practical life"', and that 'cultural anthropology (in a large sense which includes intellectual history) is all we need.'[3]

This critique of the 'transcendentalization', so to speak, of anthropology, which seems to be at the basis of Habermas's (and Apel's) recent work,[4] appears useful as a point of departure for reflection on hermeneutics and anthropology precisely because this critique is put forward by Rorty in the framework of a fundamental adherence to the work of Heidegger and Gadamer – and thus to the point of view of hermeneutics itself. It attests to a sort of hermeneutical vocation for entering into an extremely close relationship with cultural anthropology, or rather, for dissolving itself into the latter. As is well known, even Habermas and Apel claim to be the rightful heirs of Heidegger's hermeneutics; Apel, in particular, claims to liberate the latter from its own internal limits by regrounding it in the perspective of a theory of unlimited communication, understood as a Kantian *a priori*. But, if it wishes to remain faithful to its Heideggerian origins, hermeneutics must reject any attempt to restore to it a transcendental perspective. Kantianism and neo-Kantianism are moments of that very same metaphysical way of thinking beyond which Heidegger tries to move by developing a concept of the finiteness of Dasein articulated around the notion of *Geworfenheit*.[5] This latter notion appears as the always radically contingent qualified-ness of the project within which things are given to Dasein as the world. When not abstractly theorized – as might still seem to be the case in *Sein und Zeit*, with the corollary possibility of founding a Heideggerian 'philosophical anthropology' – but instead granted all those historical and *geschicklich* qualifications that identify the 'thrown-ness' of the project with its 'being arranged' in a historically determinate language (which Heidegger discovers in his works of the 1930s), *Geworfenheit* is precisely that which is only open to an anthropological consideration in the broad, but still quite specific, sense that Rorty gives it in the passage quoted above. Metaphysical anthropology consists in the description of the universal structures of the occurrence of the human phenomenon. If we want to avoid this because we take seriously the historical/ *geschicklich* 'thrown-ness' of Dasein, then we must develop our thought in the direction of cultural anthropology. According

to Habermas's text (which may also be read in a Heideggerian
sense), cultural anthropology considers cognitive interests –
that is, projects that function as an *a priori* of every
relationship between humanity and the world – as the result of
natural history. More generally speaking, though, they are the
result of history *tout court*, for it is likely that – outside a
transcendental perspective – even the distinction between
natural history and 'history' no longer has any meaning. We
may say, then, that cognitive interests are events within the
Geschick. In emphasizing this sort of hermeneutical vocation
for cultural anthropology, Rorty surely isolates one of the
meanings that anthropology has assumed in the course of its
history. This meaning is perhaps its most remote and
problematic one, as we shall see; but it is probably its most
characteristic one as well. Cultural anthropology is, in fact,
considered here as a discourse on 'other' cultures, and the
anthropologist – to cite Remo Guidieri[6] – 'goes as far (away) as
possible'. Anthropological discourse appears in the history
of our culture in other ways, such as the individuation
of extremely general structures common to cultures and
civilizations, or as the discourse on the archaic. But it is likely
that these are derived from the first and most fundamental
way in which anthropological discourse appears, namely
as the experience of an encounter with *other* civilizations (an
experience that has become culturally relevant in the modern
age in particular). This alterity becomes to some degree
'regulated', or as it were exorcised, through the metaphysically
inspired appeal to a common humanity and to a suprahistorical
essence within whose confines all human phenomena – no
matter how different they may appear – may be situated.
Either as an alternative to this appeal, or in connection with it,
another way of considering 'other' cultures arises: that
which designates them as primitive or archaic. This implies
either that a common human essence may be found only if in
some way we return beyond the historical differentiations that
have distanced us from the primitive 'other' culture in the first
place, or that 'other' cultures are simply more ancient phases

of the one true human civilization, which is that civilization in which cultural anthropology acquires for the first time the dignity of a scientific discourse. In any event, whatever may be the historical relationship between these three principal modes of cultural anthropology, hermeneutics (at least in the way in which Rorty would have it function) takes the first of these to be central and determinant, namely that mode which sees anthropology as a discourse on cultures which are *other*. This is legitimated not only by theoretical arguments linked to a certain definition of hermeneutics, to which I shall return shortly, but also – however implicitly – by a wholesale rejection of ethnocentric or Eurocentric prejudices. For these prejudices are operative not only in the most simplistic notions of the primitive as a backward phase of the one true civilization, but perhaps also, though less explicitly, in descriptive and structural anthropology. On the one hand, in fact, it is likely that the very notion of the description of a culture cannot appear as a 'neutral' or transcultural notion, linked as it is to the epistemology of the Western tradition. On the other hand, it is also likely that the conceptual schemes on the basis of which such a supposedly neutral description of a culture could be made – starting with kinship structures, for instance – would bring to the forefront, as the basic elements of description, structures and relations which are again always basic in *our* own culture and experience.

Rorty's position thus privileges a certain way of understanding anthropology, or, better still, makes this choice on the basis of a notion of hermeneutics which needs to be made clearer. Hermeneutics is defined in opposition to epistemology in *Philosophy and the Mirror of Nature*, a work whose principal theme is the critique of the foundational model of Western philosophy which culminates in the modern era in a progressive identification of philosophy and epistemology (understood as the theory of foundational knowledge – founded, that is, in the mind's capacity to mirror nature accurately, or in any event to function according to a stable or natural scheme). Although Rorty occasionally varies in his use of the term 'epistemology', the opposition on the basis of which he defines hermeneutics is clear. Epistemology is founded on the presupposition that all discourses are commensurate with and translatable among each other, and that the foundation of their truth consists precisely in this translation into a basic language, that is, the one which mirrors facts themselves. Hermeneutics instead admits that there is no such single unifying language, and tries to appropriate the language of the other rather than translate it into its own tongue. Hermeneutics is a bit like getting to know a person, rather than the development of a logically constructed demonstration.[7] Epistemology and hermeneutics are not reciprocally exclusive, but – at least in one of the senses that Rorty attributes to the two terms – are applicable to different fields. Epistemology is the discourse of 'normal science', while hermeneutics is the discourse of 'revolutionary science'.[8] 'We will be epistemological', Rorty notes, 'when we understand perfectly well what is happening but want to codify it in order to extend, or strengthen, or teach, or "ground" it. We must be hermeneutical where we do not understand what is happening but are honest enough to admit it. . . .'[9] Hermeneutics is 'discourse about as-yet-incommensurable discourses'.[10] It seems clear enough from this that the typical hermeneutical condition for Rorty is the one which – in Quine's terms – could perhaps be called 'radical translation', even if it is not a matter of translation at all, but rather of 'assimilating' oneself to the discourse of the other, an act whose nature is intuitive (which links Rorty to a perhaps overly Romantic notion of hermeneutics).

With his insistence on the radical alterity that constitutes the point of departure for hermeneutic discourse, Rorty surely individuates one of the characteristic aspects of the theory of interpretation. Even in historical terms, it could be maintained that hermeneutic theory appears as a specific discipline in European culture precisely at the moment when, with the collapse of the unity of Catholic Europe, the problem of *Missverstehen* acquires a decisive importance at the level of society and culture – while at the same time a parallel and interconnected process affects the relationship with classical tradition.[11] In contemporary hermeneutic ontology, the centrality of the initial condition of *Missverstehen* is transformed instead into a fully empowered concept of Being, to which are attributed the traits of eventuality and alterity. Being occurs, according to Heidegger, only as *Zwiefalt*, or as 'unfolding'.[12] It is likely that one of the ways in which *Zwiefalt* occurs – or rather, perhaps *the* very way in which *Zwiefalt* occurs – is precisely the interpretive situation, that is, the arising of the text, or of the other in general, as alterity (and this reading would eliminate some of the points of conflict between the work of Heidegger and that of E. Lévinas[13]). It could be said that, unless we want to run the risk of falling back into a reified notion of Being, ontological difference can be thought of only as 'interference' or, in what amounts to the same thing, as dialogue. There is no other experience nor other mode of occurrence of Being (which is, moreover, nothing other than this event), if not that of the initial shock of *Missverstehen* which occurs as an encounter with the other. If this line of theoretical inquiry is to be developed further, it must be kept in mind that this experience of alterity, as an experience of the alterity of the *interlocutor* in a dialogue and not merely as the otherness of a particular objective setting, is also defined in our culture by the development of metaphysics, experimental science (which is determined by metaphysics), and epistemology (which is connected to it as well): we no longer refer to nature as a form of 'alterity', since experimental science and epistemology have made us aware of the fact that this apparent alterity is in reality only the object-ness of the object. A more careful analysis could show how hermeneutics is also positively linked to the process of becoming of metaphysics and science.

If hermeneutics does indeed feel called upon to dissolve itself into anthropology, as Rorty's theory seems to suggest, this nevertheless presents numerous problems. First of all, it is not clear that hermeneutics could indeed be defined in the terms that Rorty proposes, nor that anthropology could truly be that science of the alterity of cultures which Rorty envisions (although with good reason). This proposal cannot be understood purely in terms of theoretical definitions, as though it were possible to demonstrate that hermeneutics is *not* 'this' but rather something else, or that anthropology is *not* 'that' but something else again. More probably, we are confronted here by the specific historical determinations – as a particular *Wesen*, as an historical/*geschicklich* formation – of both 'disciplines'. If we recognize that this *Wesen*, in the long run, does not coincide with the same definitions from which such a discourse originally begins, this may in turn signify much more than the correction of a theoretical error: for we may here find ourselves face to face with an aspect of the *Geschick* itself.

There are, in short, a number of potential difficulties to be found in Rorty's theory. In regard to hermeneutics in particular, they may be considered in the light of one of the key points made by Heidegger in his dialogue on language with his Japanese interlocutor (published in *Unterwegs zur Sprache*). This dialogue, moreover, is particularly pertinent to our concerns here, for this is perhaps the text of Heidegger's that is most clearly engaged in an effort at trans-cultural understanding, and is thus a sort of anthropological adventure. One of the experiences that Heidegger encounters, and thematizes, in his dialogue on language (and on the term *Iki*, etc.) with his Japanese interlocutor, is that the very possibility of such a dialogue with cultures that are truly other is constantly menaced by the 'complete Europeanization of the earth and of man'; as a result, Heidegger observes, a 'delusion is growing' which risks destroying and silencing at its source 'everything that is of an essential nature',[14] that is, every originary occurrence of *Wesen*. The anthropologist, for his part, seems ever more often to find himself becoming aware of a condition that is perhaps specific to all Western anthropology since its inception, but that today has reached its culmination because, as Remo Guidieri notes, 'the Westernization of the world has now reached its end'[15] – even if this does not mean that all cultures that are other have actually disappeared, as we shall shortly see. Westernization occurs first of all at the level of the expansion of political domination, and especially at that of the diffusion of cultural models. This political and cultural aspect, however, is accompanied by another more scientific and methodological one: the fact that so-called primitive societies are regarded as the objects of a kind of knowledge that is completely dominated by 'Western' categories. This is not to take anything away from the scientific nature of cultural anthropology; on the contrary, it is only through the use of these profoundly Western categories that anthropology becomes a science, or, put another way, a part of the metaphysical enterprise of reducing the world to a measurable object-ness. However, this in turn raises doubts about the possibility of thinking about anthropology as a discourse on cultures that are other. Again, such an observation is not meant to detract from the scientific validity of field-work, for instance; indeed, it is thanks to its being framed within a scientific conceptuality possessed of metaphysical rigour that we are able to distinguish it from mere curiosity about the exotic, from simple individual intuition, or from a taste for day-dreaming about enchanted worlds.

In this situation, which occurs both in the experience of philosophical thought and in that of anthropological research, does a distinction between a 'classical' hermeneutics and an 'ethnographic' one (which has been recently put forward by one anthropologist[16]) still make any sense? The former may be understood as the situation in which we interpret a text which is remote and alien but still within a certain tradition, and here the term 'classical' may also be taken in its literal sense. The latter, on the other hand, has nothing to do with the understanding of texts, but rather global con-texts (which are often, moreover, devoid of any real written texts), and thus proposes something similar to Quine's 'radical translation'. There is undeniably a basic difference between these two kinds of interpretive work, in terms of both the practical and the methodological difficulties that they face. It is doubtful, though, that this could be called a particularly radical difference. Once again, it is not a matter of recognizing a terminological or conceptual error, but rather of becoming aware of an event that can and must be read in terms of *Geschick*, that is, as the history and destiny of Being. Westernization *probably* was under way even at the inception of cultural anthropology, but it is *certainly* still occurring today. If this holds true, then we must consequently recognize that in all anthropological field-work there is always already a context that places the anthropologist in a certain relation to his field of observation (although this relation may also be a negative one that places obstacles in the anthropologist's way). Above all else, this is a context of political relation (colonial, post-colonial, etc.) which also translates into a series of thought-contents belonging to both the anthropologist and the culture/object. This is in fact the condition in which the cultural anthropologist has always worked; the situation of having to encounter an other who is 'totally other' is exposed as an ideal – or even ideological – condition.[17]

The condition of encountering radical cultural alterity represents the basis of the notion of ethnographic hermeneutics, and even that of anthropology itself as Rorty depicts it. If we recognize that this condition is in reality an ideal charged with ideological determinations, this allows us to go one step further in our argument, beyond the mere recognition of Westernization as a deplorable event triggered by the triumph of imperialistic capitalism in alliance with science and technology in the era of an accomplished metaphysics. As anthropology raises well-founded doubts about the ideological nature of the ideal of an encounter with cultures that are radically other, so hermeneutics also experiences the dream of radical alterity as something which has been definitively *ausgeträumt* at both a theoretical and historical/*geschicklich* level. At a theoretical level, we must recall the connection – which recurs over and over again in Heidegger's work – between dialogue and sameness (*das Selbe*). This connection is emblematically expressed in the lines of verse by Hölderlin upon which Heidegger first comments in his 'Hölderlin und das Wesen der Dichtung' (1936): 'Viel hat erfahren der Mensch./Der Himmlischen viele genannt,/Seit ein Gespräch wir sind/ Und hören können voneinander.'[18] Heidegger specifically thematizes the *ein*, or the fact the dialogue can only be *one*. The question of the relationship between alterity and sameness cannot be simplistically resolved by isolating these two poles, making the former the beginning, and the latter the conclusion, of the dialogue. This is clearly shown by the ever renewed insistence of the theory of interpretation on the hermeneutic circle itself.

Let me raise two questions here. First of all, how can Heidegger's insistence on sameness or on *das Selbe* fit together with the hermeneutic notion of Being as eventuality and alterity? Secondly, what is the relationship between the hermeneutic discovery of sameness at the bottom of every dialogue and the unification of the world which is displayed in the Europeanization of the earth and of the very essence of man?

These two questions can probably not be answered separately. Hermeneutics, as a technical discipline, arises in the era of the collapse of the unity of European tradition, that is, the Reformation, which also corresponds more or less to the beginning of the encounter with cultures that are other – or at least to the moment in which this encounter is no longer seen solely as an experience of the fantastic, or in terms of a horror of barbarism. Yet, as a philosophical theory, it develops instead in an era not of radical alterity but of a fully unfolded metaphysical and scientific-technological unification of the world. The two questions raised above must be understood in relation to these facts; for the two poles between which hermeneutics moves (or the two sets of needs to which it responds) are radical alterity and belonging, which cannot be thought of as the separate moments – as beginning and end – of a process, because they stand instead in a circular relationship.

The first question concerning how the eventuality and alterity of Being may be combined in hermeneutic ontology with the sameness which is the basis of all dialogue may perhaps be resolved in theoretical terms without too much difficulty, for we may attribute to the Heideggerian Same – and not only as an act of provocation – the status of a chain of family resemblances *à la* Wittgenstein (a type of solution to which a hermeneutic thinker like Rorty might well subscribe). But a more complete discussion of the problem requires that the two questions be considered together.

Let us start from the not completely unfounded hypothesis that hermeneutics as a specific philosophical position (hermeneutic ontology, as it were) develops in an historical and cultural situation in which dialogue is in fact rendered difficult, not by an overwhelming distance between the interlocutors, but rather by the occurrence of a homologation that makes it insignificant and superfluous. It is no coincidence that, among the different branches of contemporary philosophy, hermeneutic ontology is the most attentive of all to the philosophical (and not only historical and political) significance of the process of homologation which dominates our civilization, as Heidegger would argue. This may not only be explained in terms of a desire to oppose a possible ideal condition of 'authentic' dialogue to the condition of dehumanization in which 'the desert grows' because of Westernization and homologation. Such an ideal condition of dialogue would in this perspective be found when, at the end of the interpretive process, the initial experience of radical alterity is transformed into a new unity, identified with the very event of Being. Such a simplification of ontological and hermeneutic theory, however, is undermined by the ambiguous interrelationship of dialogicity and sameness which has its roots in the hermeneutic circle. The eventuality of Being is not separable from its aspect as *Geschick*. The metaphysical homologation of the Western world belongs to the *Geschick* (or destiny) of Being, which is therefore not describable only as a condition of alienation in relation to a supposed – and metaphysically described – condition of authenticity.

Hermeneutics cannot be thus understood (not even on the basis of other, more extensive treatments of the problem) in terms of a theory of the radical novelty of Being which would be set over and against its 'alienated' occurrence within the condition of the metaphysical homologation of the world.

It is, then, possible that the two questions raised above gesture in the direction of a more complex mode of thought. For if hermeneutics is on the one hand defined by a constitutive ambiguity between newness and sameness, and on the other, if the recognition that the metaphysical homologation of the world cannot be simplistically seen as the destruction of the authentic condition of all dialogue, but instead perhaps constitutes a 'condition' for it (both as a state of fact and as a condition for the possibility in which it in effect arises), then perhaps hidden beneath these two related points is the emergence of the fact that hermeneutics itself *is a form of the dissolution of Being* in the era of an accomplished metaphysics.

Hermeneutics experiences anthropology (trying, as we saw in Rorty's work, to find at once a sort of identification with and dissolution in the latter) in a manner that turns out to be, from this point of view, disappointing. Yet this disappointment in turn leads to a new maturity for hermeneutics: for although it tries to see anthropology as the discourse of radical alterity, anthropology in fact can no longer be interpreted as a locus of alterity, and defines itself instead as an internal aspect of the general process of Westernization and homologation; and this process appears as a process of loss, moreover, only in the perspective of the loss of an ideal that has been exposed as purely ideological in nature. Anthropology thus functions for hermeneutics only as a further reason to reflect in a less grandiose or 'metaphysical' manner on the problems raised by the interdependence of the two questions posed above. Hermeneutics starts out by trying to see anthropology as an ideal site for verifying its own notion of

Being as eventuality and alterity, but ends up by returning to reflect upon the significance of sameness, and on the relation between the latter and the metaphysical homologation of the world.

There is, in turn, something ambiguous about this relation, just as the experience of the anthropologist who wishes to reject both the (Euro- or ethnocentric) evolutionary perspective and the illusion of a possible dialogue or interplay between different cultures is itself a deeply ambiguous one. This relation is, one might say, the essential meaning that contemporary anthropological experience has for philosophy. The ideal of an anthropology which would be the locus of an authentic encounter with the other – in accordance with a model which, in an over-simplistic and optimistic fashion, would make anthropology the rightful heir to philosophy after the end of the metaphysical epoch, when the hermeneutic perspective predominates – cannot be set in opposition to the notion of anthropology as a scientific description of the constants of all cultures, a notion that has been deeply conditioned by the metaphysical idea of science and, at a practical level, by Western domination of the planet. Any hermeneutics that understands things in these terms fails to take into account the way in which anthropology experiences itself. Above all, though, such a hermeneutics betrays its own theoretical vocation, which implies a far more complex link between eventuality/alterity and sameness, a link that demands a less superficial consideration of the metaphysical homologation of the world.

The dialogue between hermeneutics and anthropology, as well as referring us back to the problem of the nexus between eventuality and sameness, has perhaps something else to say as well. For if we are in fact able to understand what happens to the object of anthropology in the situation of a general homologation of the planet – a situation in which, lest we forget, even the descriptive scientificity of the discipline appears irremediably bound to both the horizon of metaphysics and the Western domination of the world – perhaps we may also obtain some indication concerning the proper way to consider the exercise of hermeneutic thought in the epoch of the end of metaphysics, as Heidegger tries to do in his dialogue with his Japanese interlocutor.

Let us once again take Guidieri's brief text as our point of departure. Referring to current anthropological research, Guidieri calls attention to the fact that Westernization does not entail the simple disappearance of cultures that are other. This distinguishes his approach from that of most philosophers (especially Heidegger) concerning the forms of Westernization of the planet. He remarks:

> those who have lamented the deaths of cultures have neither known how to see, nor wanted to see, that these same cultures – which are as obsessed as we are with the myth of abundance – have nevertheless produced their own specific way of entering into the Western universe. Although they may be paradoxical, irrational, or even caricatural, these modalities are just as authentic as the ancient ways, tributary as they are to the cultural forms from which they derive their condition of possibility. The non-Western contemporary world is an immense construction site of traces and residues, in conditions which have still to be analysed.[19]

In taking this situation into account, ethnology also shows, in some areas, an ideologically conditioned tendency to reject this world of traces and residues as an object of study, and instead continues to idealize the phantom of the purely 'primitive' which it has constructed as the 'bearer of values that it cultivates and defends [and which in fact are absent in the West]: proportion, order, security, thrift, etc.' Ethnology is committed to the defence of the authenticity of cultures that are other in the belief that it is also defending their values. Instead, what we see today is an ensemble of contemporaneous 'swerves' of the primitive, 'hybrid traces and residues contaminated by modernity, the margins of the present which embrace both Third World societies and the ghettoes of industrial societies'.[20]

Here, perhaps, is that something extra (beyond a mere

referral to certain of its own theoretical contents) which hermeneutics may derive from its dialogue with anthropology. This consists in a decisive change in its somewhat mannered portrayal (although its creators include Spengler, Weber and Gehlen) of the Europeanization of the planet in the epoch of the triumph of metaphysics. For we are confronted by 'an immense construction site of traces and residues', not by the total organization of the world in rigid technological schemes. The former, interacting with the unequal distribution of power and resources at the global level, gives rise to the growth of marginal situations that are the truth of the primitive in our world. The hermeneutic – but also anthropological – illusion of encountering the other, with all its theoretical grandiosity, finds itself faced with a mixed reality in which alterity is entirely exhausted. The disappearance of alterity does not occur as a part of the dreamed-for total organization of the world, but rather as a condition of widespread contamination. Hermeneutics first emerges as a technical discipline in Europe in the age of the collapse of traditional Christian unity, but it is perhaps in this condition of contamination that hermeneutics instead develops into an *ontology*. The questions that I have asked about the possible nexus between the sameness of hermeneutic dialogue and the metaphysical homologation of the world must take this into account, if only because one of the two terms under investigation – homologation – is transformed by it. Indeed, we should say that it is decisively transformed by it, since the one form of sameness that can be allowed – within the horizon of an ontology of eventuality and alterity – without relapsing into a metaphysical identification of Being with an entity is precisely this sameness in a weakened and contaminated form; it possesses neither the iron-clad unity of the total organization of the metaphysical and technological world, nor some sort of 'authentic' unity which could be diametrically opposed to the former. Contemporary cultural anthropology is aware that in our world it must deal with the marginality of the primitive, and of every culture that is other.

In this self-awareness we perhaps experience the ambiguity of the Heideggerian *Ge-Stell* as a site of extreme danger but also of a first 'flashing up of the *Ereignis*'.[21]

Having made these observations on the basis of the experience of anthropology (treated in only very general terms), we may now return to the dialogue between Heidegger and his Japanese interlocutor. In this dialogue, the effort to think without falling into the trap of metaphysics is visible as a renunciation of concepts and numbers, and as an attempt to follow instead *Winke and Gebärde*, that is, signs and gestures. The metaphysical way of thinking is still, to a certain degree, 'inevitable'; to pursue signs and gestures appears as a *Seitenpfad* or lateral path as regards metaphysics. All this searching for non-metaphysical modes of meaning (which are not signs in the sense of 'pure denotation') takes up a great deal of space in *Unterwegs zur Sprache*, and appears as clearly irreducible to a certain mystical tendency of Heidegger's.[22] Nor, however, can it be connected to a strong notion of *Selbigkeit* or sameness, which would be visible only through a 'sign' and which would appear as the authentic pole in relation to the inauthentic one constituted by the making of the world into a desert by the West. Signs and gestures are the modes of signification – and here there is no need to be faithful at all costs to the letter of Heidegger's text – which correspond to the world where, in the ambiguity of the *Ge-Stell*, the sameness of the ontological *Geschick* and the late-metaphysical homologation of humanity in terms of a 'construction site of traces and residues' are more and more difficult to distinguish from each other. Instead these constitute in their union (the *Geschick*) the destiny and the transmission in which Being, dissolving itself in its strong sameness, truly takes leave of metaphysics and – to a certain extent – of itself as well.

In this world, the difficulty encountered in distinguishing classical hermeneutics from ethnographic hermeneutics emerges as something other than a simple theoretical difficulty. Rather, it too appears as an aspect of the problem of destiny. In the process of homologation and contamination, the texts belonging to our tradition, which have always served as the measure of our humanity (the 'classics' in the literal sense of the term), progressively lose their cogency as models and become part of this vast construction site of traces and residues, just as the condition of radical alterity of cultures that are other is exposed as an ideal which has perhaps never been realized, and is certainly unrealizable for us. It is a process that, certainly, could be exaggerated and mythified by theory, but its general tendencies are unquestionably the ones that I have examined. They require more careful study, but for now we must still take them into account. The problematic of the second of Nietzsche's *Untimely Meditations*[23] appears here once again as decisive for the determination of the historical/ *geschicklich* place of European culture. The vast 'construction site of traces and residues' is not very different from the warehouse of theatrical costumes which Nietzsche compares to that 'garden of history' in which nineteenth-century humanity wanders without discovering any strong identity, but only an array of 'masks'. All this can be accepted if we keep in mind the experience of anthropology and the condition of the primitive as ghetto and as margin, without discovering it in the slightest implicit 'Dionysian', ludic, or (it might be added) Deleuzian meaning. The world of hermeneutic ontology (in the subjective and objective meaning of the genitive) is neither the 'iron cage' of total administration and regulation, nor is it Deleuze's glorification of simulacra.[24] It is instead the world of an active nihilism, where Being has an opportunity to re-occur in an authentic form only through its own impoverishment. This is not the poverty of ascesis, which is still committed to the myth of finding – at the end – the shining kernel of true value, but rather the poverty of the inapparent and the marginal, or of contamination lived as the only possible *Ausweg* from the dreams of metaphysics, no matter how they may be disguised: perhaps cargo cults too are 'a first flashing up of the *Ereignis*'.[25] Neither anthropology nor hermeneutics is either an encounter with radical alterity or the scientific and systematic description of the human

phenomenon in terms of structure. Anthropology may probably
fall back into its form as a dialogue with the archaic (the third
of the forms that our culture has historically assigned to it),
but this *arché* gives itself in the only way that is possible in the
epoch of an accomplished metaphysics, namely in the form of
survival, marginality, and contamination.

NOTES

1 Cf. Richard Rorty, *Philosophy and the Mirror of Nature* (Princeton: Princeton UP, 1979).
2 Cf. Rorty, *Philosophy and the Mirror of Nature*, p. 380; and cf. J. Habermas, *Erkenntnis und Interesse*, 2nd edn (Frankfurt: Suhrkamp, 1973), p. 410. Habermas's 'Nachwort' has been translated into English as 'A Postscript to *Knowledge and Human Interests*', trans. Christian Lenhardt, *Philosophy of the Social Sciences*, 3 (1973), pp. 157–89. The first edition was translated as *Knowledge and Human Interest*, trans. Jeremy J. Shapiro (Boston: Beacon Press, 1971).
3 Cf. Rorty, *Philosophy and the Mirror of Nature*, p. 381.
4 On this point see my *Al di là del soggetto* (Milan: Garzanti, 1981), chapter 4.
5 For this, as for other of Heidegger's concepts alluded to in this chapter, see my *Introduzione a Heidegger*, 3rd edn (Bari: Laterza, 1982).
6 Cf. R. Guidieri, 'Les sociétés primitives aujourd'hui', in *Philosopher: les interrogations contemporaines*, ed. Ch. Delacampagne and R. Maggiori (Paris: Fayard, 1980).
7 Cf. Rorty, *Philosophy and the Mirror of Nature*, pp. 318–19.
8 Cf. Kuhn, *The Structure of Scientific Revolutions*.
9 Cf. Rorty, *Philosophy and the Mirror of Nature*, p. 321.
10 Cf. ibid., p. 343.
11 It is this that explains the centrality and fundamentality, for Schleiermacher's hermeneutics, of *Missverstehen* ('misunderstanding') as the normal point of departure for all understanding. Cf. P. D. Schleiermacher, *Hermeneutics*, ed. Heinz Kimmerle, trans. James Duke and Jack Forstman (Missoula, Montana: Scholars Press (American Academy of Religion), 1977).

12 For the term *Zwiefalt*, see *Vorträge und Aufsätze*, and *On the Way to Language*, trans. Peter D. Hertz (New York: Harper and Row, 1971).

13 See E. Lévinas, *Totality and Infinity*, trans. Alphonso Lingis (The Hague: M. Nijhoff, 1979); and *Otherwise than Being*; *or*, *Beyond Essence*, trans. Alphonso Lingis (The Hague: M. Nijhoff, 1981).

14 Cf. Heidegger, 'A Dialogue on Language', in *On the Way to Language*, trans. Hertz, pp. 15–16.

15 Cf. Guidieri, 'Les sociétés primitives', p. 60. On the 'marginality' of cultures that are other (or 'ethnographic' cultures) in the contemporary world in relation to the need for identity, see F. Pellizzi, 'Misioneros y cargos: notas sobre identidad y aculturación en los altos de Chiapas', *América indígena*, 42, p. 1.

16 I refer here to an unpublished lecture by R. Guidieri given at the University of Turin in May 1982.

17 Cf. Guidieri, 'Les sociétés primitives', pp. 62–3.

18 'Much has man learned/Many heavens has he named/Since we are a dialogue/And we may listen to each other': *Erläuterungen zu Hölderlins Dichtung*, 3rd edn (Frankfurt: Klostermann, 1963), p. 33.

19 Cf. Guidieri, 'Les sociétés primitives', p. 60.

20 Ibid.

21 According to a well-known passage in *Identity and Difference*, trans. Joan Stambaugh (1969; repr. New York: Harper and Row, 1974), p. 38.

22 For all the allusions in these lines, see 'A Dialogue on Language', in *On the Way to Language*, trans. Hertz, pp. 23–8.

23 Friedrich Nietzsche, 'On the Uses and Disadvantages of History for Life', in *Untimely Meditations*, trans. R. J. Hollingdale (Cambridge: Cambridge UP, 1983), pp. 57–123.

24 See, for instance, Gilles Deleuze's *Différence et répétition* (Paris: PUF, 1968).

25 Both my *Introduzione a Heidegger* and *Le avventure della differenza* (Milan: Garzanti, 1979) offer suggestions on the interpretation of those terms of Heidegger's that are discussed in this chapter.

10

Nihilism and the Post-modern
in Philosophy

I

In order to examine the question of the post-modern in philosophy in a way that avoids making a rhapsodic comparison between contemporary philosophy and the apparent traits of post-modernity in other fields, such as architecture, literature, and criticism, we must turn to a term which Heidegger first introduces into philosophy: *Verwindung*. Heidegger uses this term sparingly in his works; it appears at one point in the *Holzwege*, in an essay in *Vorträge und Aufsätze*, and, most importantly, in the first of the two essays in *Identität und Differenz* (entitled 'Der Satz der Identität'). *Verwindung* indicates something analogous to *Überwindung*, or overcoming, but is distinctly different from the latter both because it has none of the characteristics of a dialectical *Aufhebung* and because it contains no sense of a 'leaving-behind' of a past that no longer has anything to say to us. Precisely this difference between *Verwindung* and *Überwindung* can help us to define in philosophical terms the 'post-' in 'post-modernism'.

The first philosopher to speak in terms of the possibility of *Verwindung* – even if, of course, he does not use the word itself – is not Heidegger but Nietzsche. It could legitimately be argued that philosophical post-modernity is born with Nietzsche's work, in the space that separates the second of the *Untimely Meditations* ('On the Uses and Disadvantages of

History for Life' (1874)) from the group of works published a few years later, ranging from *Human All Too Human* (1878) to *Daybreak* (1881) and *The Gay Science* (1882). In his 1874 text, Nietzsche poses for the first time the problem of the sense of being an *epigone*, that is, the problem of an excess of historical consciousness that plagues nineteenth-century humanity (or, we might say, humanity at the beginning of late modernity) and prevents it from producing a truly new history. In particular, this excess of historical consciousness prevents nineteenth-century European civilization from developing a specific style of its own, and consequently requires it to derive the forms of its art, architecture, fashion and so on from the vast warehouse of theatrical masks and costumes that the past has become for it. Nietzsche calls this a 'historical sickness' and, at least around the time of 'On the Uses and Disadvantages of History for Life', argues that it can be cured with the help of the 'suprahistorical' or 'eternalizing' forces of religion, art and, above all else, Wagnerian music. *Human All Too Human* marks the end of Nietzsche's belief in Wagner and in the reformative power of art. But, beginning with this work, his position concerning the nineteenth-century 'historical sickness' also undergoes profound changes. If in 1874 Nietzsche views with horror nineteenth-century humanity's appropriation of the styles of the past through an arbitrary use of them as theatrical masks in order to stylize its own environment and its own works, he writes to Burckhardt from Turin at the beginning of January 1889 (in one of the brief letters from the period of his insanity) that 'I am all the names of history.' Although this statement is made in the context of Nietzsche's mental collapse, from which he would never recover, it may still be considered a coherent expression of the position in regard to history that he had been developing since *Human All Too Human*.

In this work, the problem of how to escape from the historical sickness or, more accurately, the problem of modernity as decadence, is posed in a new way. While in his 1874 text Nietzsche proposes a recourse to suprahistorical and eternalizing forces, *Human All Too Human* brings into play a true dissolution of modernity through a radicalization of its own constitutive tendencies. Modernity is defined as the era of overcoming and of the new which rapidly grows old and is immediately replaced by something still newer, in an unstoppable movement that discourages all creativity even as it demands creativity and defines the latter as the sole possible form of life. If this indeed is the case, as Nietzsche claims, then no way out of modernity can possibly be found in terms of an *overcoming* of it. His recourse to eternalizing forces signals this need to find another way to resolve the problem. In his 1874 essay Nietzsche already very clearly sees that overcoming is a typically modern category, and therefore will not enable us to use it as a way out of modernity. Modernity is not only constituted by the category of temporal overcoming (the inevitable succession of historical phenomena of which modern man becomes aware because of an excess of historiography), but also by the category of critical overcoming. Nietzsche's 1874 text associates the kind of relativistic *Historismus* which envisions history in terms of pure temporal succession with the Hegelian metaphysics of history, which understands the historical process as a process of *Aufklärung*, that is, a progressive enlightenment of consciousness and increasing absoluteness of the spirit. This is probably the reason that Nietzsche, in 'On the Uses and Disadvantages of History for Life', cannot imagine a way out of modernity as the effect of critical overcoming, and must instead have recourse to myth and to art. *Human All Too Human* remains faithful in principle to this notion of modernity. It no longer, however, imagines that a way out of modernity could be discovered through recourse to eternalizing forces, and instead seeks to dissolve modernity through a radicalization of its own innate tendencies.

This radicalization consists in the following: *Human All Too Human* starts off by proposing to perform a critique of the higher values of civilization through a 'chemical' reduction (see I.1, aphorism 1) of these values to the elements of which they are composed prior to any sublimation. This programme of chemical analysis, when pursued rigorously, nevertheless leads to the discovery that truth, in the name of which this chemical analysis claims its own legitimacy, is a value which dissolves by itself. The belief in the superiority of truth over non-truth or error is a belief which arises in specific vital situations (insecurity, *bellum omnium contra omnes* in the more primitive phases of history, etc.); it is founded, moreover, on the conviction that man can know things 'in themselves'. Yet the chemical analysis of the process of knowledge reveals that this is impossible because it is nothing other than a series of metaphorizations. This series goes from the thing to the mental image, from the image to the word which expresses the individual's state of mind, from this to the word which social conventions determine to be the 'right' one, and then once again from this canonical word to the thing, which we now see only in terms of the traits which may most easily be metaphorized in the vocabulary that we have inherited. . . . As always, this analysis occurs in Nietzsche's work both at the level of an *Erkenntniskritik* (based on a 'positivistic' version of Kant) and at an anthropological and phylogenetic level. Through the 'discoveries' made by chemical analysis, the very notion of truth is dissolved: or, in what amounts to the same thing, God 'dies', slain by religiosity and by the will to truth which believers have always had, and which now leads them to recognize God himself as an error which one can do without.

Nietzsche argues that this nihilistic conclusion offers us a way out of modernity. Since the notion of truth no longer exists, and foundation no longer functions (insofar as there is no longer a foundation for the belief in foundation, that is, in the fact that thought must 'found'), there can be no way out of modernity through a critical overcoming, for the latter is a part of modernity itself. It thus becomes clear that an alternative means must be sought, and this is the moment that could be designated as the moment of the birth of post-modernity in philosophy. Like the death of God announced in *The Gay Science* (aphorism 125), this is an event whose meaning and consequences we have not yet fully fathomed. In *The Gay Science*, where Nietzsche speaks for the first time of the death of God, the idea of the eternal return of the Same also first appears; this marks, among other things, the end of the era of overcoming, namely that epoch of Being conceived under the sign of the *novum*. Whatever other (and rather problematic) meanings it may have in a metaphysical perspective, the idea of the eternal return surely can be said to have at least this 'selective' meaning (this is Nietzsche's own adjective). This idea, for us, exposes the essence of modernity as the epoch in which Being is reduced to the *novum*. As examples of this reduction, we might mention here both the avant-garde artistic movements of the early decades of the twentieth century (particularly Futurism) and such philosophers as Bloch, Adorno and Benjamin. We might also add that, from the point of view of ethics, the one value that seems to be most generally – and tacitly – accepted today is that of 'development': the good is that which more or less explicitly opens up the possibility for further development of one's personality, one's life, etc. The 'epochal' nature of this phenomenon may also be seen in the fact that we cannot easily find another value to take its place, even though we must recognize (together with Nietzsche and Heidegger) that ethics cannot be founded on such a value. Post-modernity is only at its beginning, and the identification of Being with the *novum* – which Heidegger understands to be expressed in an emblematic way, as we know, by Nietzsche's notion of the will to power – continues to cast its shadow over us, like the defunct God that *The Gay Science* discusses.

Aufklärung, or the progressive unfolding in history of the force of the foundation, does not end with the destruction of the ideas of truth and foundation. This destruction denies all meaning to historical novelty, which from the perspective of *Aufklärung* is still the one connotation of metaphysical Being in modernity, because it defines the latter as the era of overcoming, criticism, and even – at a lower level – fashion (I am thinking here of Georg Simmel's famous essay[1]). But the task of thought is no longer what modernity has always considered it to be, namely to return to foundations and, *via this route*, to rediscover the *novum*/Being/value. The latter, in unfolding ever further in history, confers a meaning on history: this is apparent in every renaissance of Western art and culture, which always takes its inspiration from a return to the origin, to the 'classical', etc.

'The insignificance of the origin increases with the full knowledge of the origin.'[2] This aphorism in *Daybreak* summarizes at least in part the destiny of the foundation, truth, or *Grund* in the chemical analysis of *Human All Too Human*. Not only is the idea of foundation 'logically' dissolved from the point of view of the foundation of its claims to be the norm for true thought; but it also appears empty (as it were) in terms of its content. The insignificance of the origin increases when the origin becomes known, and, as a consequence, 'the nearest reality, that which is around us and inside of us, little by little starts to display colour and beauty and enigma and a wealth of meaning – things which earlier men never dreamed of.'[3]

This comparison between the insignificance of the origin and the wealth of colour in the reality at hand, more than anything else, gives us a sense of what Nietzsche sees as the task of thought in the epoch where both the foundation and the idea of truth have been dissolved. What he calls in *Human All Too Human* a 'philosophy of morning' is precisely a kind of thought that is oriented towards proximity rather than towards the origin or foundation. This way of thinking about proximity could also be defined as a way of thinking about error, or better still, about erring. The latter emphasizes that it is not a question of thinking about the non-true, but rather of examining the process of becoming of the 'false' constructs of metaphysics, morality, religion and art, that is, the entire tissue of erring that alone constitutes the wealth or, more simply put, the *essence of reality*. As *The Twilight of the Idols* was later to argue, the real world has become a fiction and even the 'apparent' world has dissolved along with it. Given that there is no longer a truth or a *Grund* that could contradict or falsify the tissue of erring, all these errors are to be understood as kinds of roaming or wandering; for they embody the process of becoming of spiritual formations whose only rule is a certain historical continuity that is in turn devoid of any relationship to a fundamental truth.

The chemical analysis begun in *Human All Too Human* in this fashion loses all semblance of a 'critical' analysis as well. Rather than unmask and liquidate error, thought must attempt to see error as the very source of the wealth that constitutes us and that gives interest, colour, and *Being* to the world.

All the works of the period that begins with *Human All Too Human* (principally *Daybreak* and *The Gay Science*) represent an effort to determine the idea of this philosophy of morning. Even the apparently more 'metaphysical' concerns of the later writings and the posthumous fragments found in *Der Wille zur Macht* ought to be read, far more than is usually done, in relation to this effort. This is the case, for example, with such ideas as the eternal return of the Same or that of the *Übermensch*. What exactly does it mean, though, to say that the philosophy of morning 'historically' – since this is another of the methodological rules set down in *Human All Too Human* – pursues the paths of metaphysical and moral erring with what we might call a deconstructive intent, rather than with the aim of performing a critical dissolution? In order to answer this question, Nietzsche employs a number of 'physiological' metaphors: for the man who is capable of following the philosophy of morning is the man of good temperament who has nothing of 'snarling or sullenness – those familiar tedious qualities of old dogs and men who have long been kept on the leash'.[4] The rather frequent allusions (which have a biographical motivation as well) to health and convalescence that fill Nietzsche's texts of this period share this same meaning. Once again, as it was in 'On the Uses and Disadvantages of History for Life', we are confronted by an effort to think of a way out of metaphysics in a form which is not bound to a critical overcoming. Here, as a result of the radicalization of Nietzsche's chemical analysis, we know that it is not a question of making recourse to 'suprahistorical' values, but of living completely the experience of the necessity of error and of raising oneself for an instant above that process; or, to put it another way, of living the errant in the light of a fundamentally different attitude. We know in particular that the content of the philosophy of morning is nothing other than the very errancy of metaphysics, but seen from a different point of view, that of the man of good temperament, who possesses a firm, mild, and, at bottom, cheerful soul.

II

The essential meaning of this attitude may be found in its referral to the history of metaphysics (and thus also to modernity as the end result of metaphysics and Platonic/ Christian morality). For it refers to this history in a way which is neither an acceptance of its errors nor a critique that tries to overcome them but merely ends up by prolonging them instead. Nietzsche conceives of this in terms of convalescence and good temperament, as we have seen; but in order to describe such an attitude more accurately we must have recourse to Heidegger's notion of *Verwindung*. In those (few) works by Heidegger mentioned at the beginning of this chapter, the term *Verwindung* indicates a sort of improper *Überwindung*, an overcoming which is an overcoming neither in the usual sense nor in the sense of a dialectical *Aufhebung*. Heidegger's least ambiguous text in this regard is the first essay in *Identität und Differenz* (as it appears in the 1957 fourth edition). In this essay he discusses the *Ge-Stell*, or the world of modern technology, as an ensemble (*Ge-*) of *stellen* ('placing'/'arranging'/'imposing'/etc.). He observes that 'what we experience in the *Ge-Stell* . . . is a prelude to what is called the *Er-eignis* [event of appropriation]. This event, however, does not necessarily persist in its prelude. For in the *Ereignis* the possibility arises [*sprich . . . an*] that it may overcome the mere dominance [*Walten*] of the *Ge-Stell* to turn it [*verwindet*] into a more original *Ereignis*'. It becomes clear later in the same text that the *Ge-Stell*, or the world of technology, is not only the place where metaphysics reaches its climactic moment and its highest and most complete unfolding, but also the one where we witness for this very reason 'a first flashing up of the *Ereignis*'.[5] I shall return to this text shortly; for now, it is enough to see how the term *Verwindung* helps us to define what it is that Nietzsche understands as the 'philosophy of morning' and that constitutes the essence of philosophical post-modernity itself.

How, then, should the term *Verwindung*, as it appears here in *Identität und Differenz* (and, allowing for necessary variations, in Heidegger's other works), be translated? We know from what Heidegger told the French translators of *Vorträge und Aufsätze*, where the term appears in an essay concerning the *Überwindung* – overcoming – of metaphysics, that it indicates a going-beyond that is both an acceptance and a deepening. The lexical meaning of the term in German provides two other shades of meaning: it is a convalescence (in the sense of '*ein Krankheit verwinden*': to heal, to be cured of an illness) and a distorting (although this is a rather marginal meaning linked to '*winden*', meaning 'to twist', and to the sense of a deviant alteration which the prefix '*ver-*' also possesses). The notion of 'convalescence' is linked to another meaning as well, that of 'resignation'. Not only can one *verwinden* from an illness, but one can also be *verwunden* to a loss or to pain. If we now return to the *Verwindung* of the *Ge-Stell*, or even to that of metaphysics (of which the *Ge-Stell* is the final form), we find that for Heidegger the possibility of a change that would lead us towards a more initial *Ereignis* – or, in other words, outside and beyond metaphysics – is linked to a *Verwindung* of metaphysics. Metaphysics, to put it another way, is not something which can 'be put aside like an opinion. Nor can it be left behind us like a doctrine in which we no longer believe';[6] rather, it is something which stays in us as do the traces of an illness or a kind of pain to which we are resigned. Besides these meanings of the term, there is that of 'distortion' to consider as well; this can already be seen to be present in the notion of 'convalescence/resignation': for metaphysics can never be simply accepted, any more than the *Ge-Stell* can ever be accepted without reservation, since it is the system of technological domination. Metaphysics and the *Ge-Stell* may be lived as an opportunity or as the possibility of a change by virtue of which both metaphysics and the *Ge-Stell* are twisted in a direction which is not foreseen by their own essence, and yet is connected to it.

Verwindung, when seen in all these ways, defines Heidegger's basic position and understanding of the task of thought at the moment in which humanity finds itself today, namely at the end of philosophy in the form of metaphysics. For Heidegger, as for Nietzsche, thought has no other 'object' (if we may even still use this term) than the errancy of metaphysics, re-collected in an attitude which is neither a critical overcoming nor an acceptance that recovers and prolongs it. It should be kept in mind here that the problem of the *Wiederholung*, which is linked to the distinction between *Tradition* and *Überlieferung* as different ways of looking at the past, is already central in *Sein und Zeit*.

The importance that the notion of *An-denken* (re-collection) acquires in the late Heidegger, for whom post-metaphysical thought is defined as a recollection, a recovery, a re-thinking, etc., places his work in substantial proximity to Nietzsche's philosophy of morning. It is true that the point of departure of *Sein und Zeit* seems to assign to thought the task of reproposing the problem of the meaning of Being. This task appears as an alternative to the attitude which for centuries had been at the basis of metaphysics, namely the forgetting of Being as such. In *Sein und Zeit*, however, an essential part of this task is already defined by the 'destruction of the history of ontology', and the development of Heidegger's work from the 1930s on leads him in the end to identify the task of thought ever more closely with that work of destruction or, better still, of deconstruction.

The 'turning-point' (*Kehre*) in Heidegger's work is the passage from a level in which there is only the human subject (humanistic existentialism *à la* Sartre) to a level in which there is principally Being, as he states in 1946 in his text on humanism. This, however, also means that, among other consequences, the forgetting of Being which constitutes metaphysics cannot be thought of as just another human error, from which the subject could escape through an act of will or a more rigorous methodological choice. Metaphysics is not, for this reason, simply the destiny of humanity in the sense that it belongs to us and constitutes us, and in the sense that we can only *verwinden* it. At least in a certain sense, the forgetting of Being is also inscribed in Being itself (since this forgetting does not even depend on us). Being can never completely arise as presence.

Recollection too, by the same token, can never lead us to grasp Being as an object which is given before us. What do we think, then, when we re-collect Being? We may think of Being only as *gewesen*, only as what is not present (any longer). Heidegger's perpetual return to the history of metaphysics in his post-*Sein und Zeit* writings has itself the structure of a *regressus in infinitum* that is, for instance, typical of etymological reconstructions. This does not take us anywhere, except to the memory of Being as that from which humanity has always already taken leave. Being arises here only in the form of the *Ge-Schick* (the whole of the 'dispatching') and the *Überlieferung* (or 'trans-mission'). In Nietzsche's terms, thought does not return to the origin in order to appropriate it; all that it does is travel along the multiple paths of errancy, which is the only kind of wealth and the only kind of Being that is ever given to us.

The different stages in Heidegger's intellectual itinerary can thus quite clearly be set in proximity to Nietzsche's. The nihilistic effect of the (self-)dissolution of the notions of truth and foundation in Nietzsche has its parallel in Heidegger's 'discovery' of the 'epochal' nature of Being. For in Heidegger's work as well as in Nietzsche's, Being cannot function (any longer) as a *Grund* either for things or for thought itself. Heidegger notes in his lecture on 'Time and Being', which is in theory meant to complete the work of *Sein und Zeit*, that in order to prepare a way out of metaphysics we must 'relinquish Being' as *Grund*.[7] Being cannot be remembered; for we can do nothing except re-think – from the point of view of the *Ge-Schick* – the same history of metaphysical errancy that constitutes us and that 'constitutes' Being as *Überlieferung*. In its sense of 'distortion', *Verwindung* indicates that this repetition of metaphysics does not seek to accept metaphysics as it is. For instance, Plato's work cannot be rethought today in terms of whether the doctrine of Ideas is true or untrue, but only in terms of trying to recollect the *Lichtung* or preliminary *geschicklich* opening within which something like the doctrine of Ideas is able to appear. Heidegger notes in *Der Satz vom Grund* that such an attitude is an emancipatory one: for to think from the point of view of the *Ge-Schick* of Being means to entrust oneself to the liberating bond of the *Überlieferung*.[8]

In what terms may we provisionally understand this emancipatory effect of *Andenken*, which would appear to constitute the meaning of *Verwindung* as 'distortion'? Metaphysics must be seen as *Ge-Schick*, dispatching, historical 'trans-mission', if we are to strip all force from its claims to cogency. This in turn leads to a kind of historicist relativism, for there is no *Grund* or ultimate truth; there are only historically destined or historically dispatched overtures from a *Selbst* or Same, which gives itself to us only in and *through* these overtures (by traversing them rather than by using them as a means). This historicism is nevertheless tempered and *verwunden* by an awareness that the history of such overtures is not 'only' the history of errors, which may be revealed as such by an otherwise accessible *Grund* of some sort, but rather is Being itself. This, as Nietzsche underlines in his metaphor of the man of 'good temperament', makes a profound difference to us. The word that best defines this approach to the past and to everything that is transmitted to us (even in the present) is *pietas*.

In this way, *Andenken* and *Verwindung* make clear in what sense Heidegger's philosophy needs to be understood as a hermeneutics. It is not a technical theory of interpretation, nor even a philosophy that, in its description of human existence, grants special importance to the interpretive phenomenon. Rather, it needs to be understood in a more radically ontological sense: Being is nothing other than the transmission of the historical/*geschicklich* opening that constitutes for every historical being, *je und je*, the specific possibility of access to the world. The experience of Being is always an *Andenken* and a *Verwindung*, inasmuch as it is an experience of the reception of, and response to, these transmissions.

III

Nietzsche and Heidegger, in their 'continuity' (which can be recognized only by an explicit 'distortion' of the Heideggerian interpretation of Nietzsche),[9] provide the basis for at least some further steps towards the definition of what a post-modern philosophy might be.

These steps, which I will define below, will serve as the provisional conclusions of the present work.

(a) Both the notions of *Verwindung* and *Anaunken*, and the similar notion of 'the philosophy of morning' in Nietzsche, seem to point out that post-metaphysical thought can only be a sort of 'revised' (*verwunden*), distorted form of historicism. This is very clear in Nietzsche's proclamation of the death of God. This is in no way comprehensible as a metaphysical assessment of the non-existence of God (as if there were a 'structure' of Being in which God cannot exist); it is a real announcement, the 'narration' of a 'fact' or, at least, of an experience that humanity, or Western culture, has undergone. This 'fact' proves nothing in the strictly logical sense of the word; it is cited as a rhetorical appeal, as a way to persuade by referring to an experience which everyone is assumed to have had. (We may recall Kant's arguments for aesthetic validity in his *Critique of Judgement*.) This appeal to fact and experience implies a sort of paradoxical historicism, as if one were to say that we must think this or that because an event, the death of God, has occurred. If God is dead, that is, if foundational thought has been dissolved by the experiences of philosophical reason in the course of history, then the only way of 'proving' a thesis is to appeal to these experiences. In a sense, then, we have to conform to a 'logic' which is inscribed only in the course of events, to which we cannot object in the name of some different legitimacy.

But why should we take seriously and conform to the development of Western thought in which, ultimately, God is dead? Precisely because this development has dissolved any other point of reference, any other basis of certainty except the cultural heritage. When the origin has revealed its insignificance, as Nietzsche says, then we become open to the meaning and richness of proximity; or, in other words, we become capable of playing those language games which constitute our existence upon the sole basis of our belonging to a particular historical tradition, which we have to respect in the same way in which we feel respect for monuments, tombs, traces of past life, or even family memories.

(b) But if we follow Heidegger's indication that modern science and technology really characterize the metaphysics we are supposed to 'overcome', then the 'objects' towards which the *verwindend* and *andenkend* attitude of post-metaphysical thought turns itself are not exclusively the messages of the past. Metaphysics is not only transmitted to us in the contents of the *Geisteswissenschaften*, in the humanistic heritage of our culture; it is 'realized' in the *Gestell*, the scientific-technological organization of the modern world. Hermeneutics, as *verwindend-andenkend* thought, must also interpret the 'messages' of science and technology, and even the messages of the mass media system, which represent a sort of distorted synthesis of the cultural tradition and of modern technology. Although Heidegger has repeatedly said that science does not think, it is difficult to maintain that hermeneutics (seen here as the characteristic form of post-metaphysical thought) has solely the task of re-collecting messages which used to be the contents of the *Geisteswissen-schaften*. Even Gadamer, who would certainly prefer the 'humanistic' orientation of hermeneutics, has more and more often emphasized, in recent works such as *Vernunft im Zeitalter der Wissenschaft* (1976), the ethical and political implications of hermeneutics, which surely require a *Verwindung* of the scientific and technological languages that tend to dominate our society. Of course it is not easy to see what a *verwindend* recollection of the 'messages' of science and technology would be: the reconstruction perhaps of a *Weltanschauung*, of a unified view of the world, out of the manifold information provided by the natural and human sciences. Because of the predominantly operational and manipulative character of the modern sciences, it is likely that the construction of such a unified *Weltanschauung* will reveal itself to be very difficult, or even impossible; but the continuity of experience which the hermeneutic act of recollection aims to reconstruct cannot be reached without some sort of unification of the information provided by the sciences. This unifying reconstruction cannot be pursued only in the form of ethics (as Gadamer seems to believe), that is, solely by putting science and technology under the control of moral imperatives related to our cultural heritage. A theoretical or cognitive reconstruction is needed: this may be the distorted recollection of the ancient idea of metaphysics as the *prote philosophia*, the first science. Post-metaphysical philosophy can no longer unify the different knowledges of the world provided by the sciences from the point of view of the foundational grasping of Being *qua* Being, as Aristotle put it, or from the point of view of a transcendental or methodological reflection on the conditions of possibility of the sciences (as Kant or the neopositivists thought). What philosophy, in its present form, can do is perhaps only to propose a 'rhetorically persuasive', unified view of the world, which includes in itself traces, residues, or isolated elements of scientific knowledge. As a matter of fact, our everyday language regularly incorporates and uses terms originally belonging to specific sciences like psychoanalysis, physics, etc. In such a philosophic, unifying discourse, not only metaphysics but also its final form, that is, science and technology, would be *verwunden*: recollected, distorted, accepted as a destiny.

(c) *Verwindung*, which we experience as the sole possible form of post-metaphysical thought, is not only a matter of thought: rather, it concerns Being as such. This is another clear implication of the thought of both Nietzsche and Heidegger: nihilism is not only an 'error' of the mind but a destiny of Being itself. The history which we recollect has itself the structure of the *Verwindung* of recollection and distortion. This may appear to be a very abstract generalization, but it is no longer so if we translate *Verwindung* into a term which is much more familiar to historians of Western civilization, namely the term 'secularization': I am thinking here of Max Weber, but also of Norbert Elias and of Réné Girard. Taken in the connotations it has for these authors, secularization/ *Verwindung* would describe the course of history not as a linear progression or as decadence, but as a course of events in which emancipation is reached only by means of a radical transformation and distortion of its very contents. Thus, for instance, Nietzsche and Heidegger, or more recently Foucault, suggest that 'humanity' can be fulfilled in history only through a profound revision and transformation of the very notion of humanism. Or, to cite another example, is it not true that the scientific-technological society may be described as the absolute spirit imagined by Hegel, but in a distorted way, as Adorno has suggested? It is very likely that the idea of thought's progress and emancipation through 'critical overcoming' is closely related to a linear conception of history;

when critical overcoming is 'distorted' into the notion of *Verwindung*, history itself can no longer appear in a linear light. History reveals its 'ironic' essence: interpretation and distortion, or dis-location, characterize not only the relation of thought to the messages of the past but also the relation of one 'epoch' to the others. Perhaps this was one of the meanings Heidegger had in mind when he spoke of the 'epochal' essence of Being (in the essay on Anaximander in his *Holzwege*): in its event, Being reveals itself only insofar as it also conceals itself, so that one cannot speak in terms of a progressive revelation of Being (nor, of course, in terms of a 'regressive' concealing of it).

This last implication of 'the philosophy of morning' and of the *verwindend* 'essence' of thought is especially pertinent, though it entails many problems related to the question of the possibility of a 'philosophy of history'.[10] Like the death of God in *The Gay Science*, the *Verwindung* too is an 'event' whose consequences we have just begun to comprehend.

NOTES

1   G. Simmel, 'Fashion', in *On Individuality and Social Forms*, ed. Donald N. Levine (Chicago: Chicago UP, 1971), pp. 294–323.
2   Friedrich Nietzsche, *Daybreak*, trans. R. J. Hollingdale (Cambridge: Cambridge UP, 1982), aphorism 44.
3   Ibid.
4   Friedrich Nietzsche, *Human, All Too Human*, vol. I, trans. R. J. Hollingdale (Cambridge: Cambridge UP, 1986), aphorism 34.
5   Martin Heidegger, *Identity and Difference*, trans. Joan Stambaugh (1969; repr. New York: Harper and Row, 1974), pp. 32–3, 36–7.
6   Martin Heidegger, *Vorträge und Aufsätze* (Pfullingen: Neske, 1954), p. 71.
7   Martin Heidegger, *On Time and Being* (1967), trans. Joan Stambaugh (New York: Harper and Row, 1972), pp. 6–7.

8 Martin Heidegger, *Der Satz vom Grund* (Pfullingen: Neske, 1957), p. 187.

9 Heidegger's view of Nietzsche is set forth in the four volumes of *Nietzsche*, trans. David F. Krell (New York: Harper and Row, 1979–84).

10 I have tried to develop these themes in 'Myth and the Fate of Secularization', trans. Jon R. Snyder, *Res*, no. 9 (1985), pp. 29–35, and in the paper 'The End of the Story', presented at the International Symposium on Post-modernism held at Northwestern University in Evanston, Ill., October 1985.

Bibliographical Note

The great majority of the chapters of this book were originally written as lectures, introductions to seminars, or papers for scholarly meetings, and were first published in journals or anthologies. I wish to thank the editors and publishers of the various publications mentioned below for their permission to reprint these texts.

'An Apology for Nihilism' ('Apologia del nichilismo'), in *Problemi del nichilismo*, ed. C. Magris and W. Kämpfer (Milan: Shakespeare and Co., 1981).

'The Crisis of Humanism' ('La crisi dell'umanismo'), in *Teoria*, 1 (1981).

'The Death or Decline of Art' ('Morte o tramonto dell'arte'), in *Rivista di estetica*, 4 (1980).

'The Shattering of the Poetic Word' ('L'infrangersi della parola poetica'), trans. Thomas Harrison, in *The Favorite Malice*, ed. Thomas Harrison (New York: Out of London Press, 1983).

'Ornament/Monument' ('Ornamento monumento'), *Rivista di estetica*, 12 (1982).

'The Structure of Artistic Revolutions' ('La struttura delle rivoluzioni artistiche'), *Rivista di estetica*, 14–15 (1983).

'Truth and Rhetoric in Hermeneutic Ontology' ('Verità e retorica nell'ontologia ermeneutica'), in *Linguaggio, persuasione, verità*, Atti del XXVIII Congresso nazionale di filosofia (Padua: CEDAM, 1984).

'Hermeneutics and Anthropology' ('Ermeneutica e antropologia') first appeared in a somewhat different English-language version in *Res* (Autumn 1982).

'Nihilism and the Post-modern in Philosophy' ('Nichilismo e

postmoderno in filosofia'), in *Aut Aut*, 202 (1984), with the title
'The Philosophy of Morning' ('La filosofia del mattino'); later, in a
rather modified version, in *SubStance*, 16, no. 2 (1987). The third
section of the paper printed here does not correspond to the one
published in Italian, but to the English version which appeared in
SubStance. For the translation of this section I am solely
responsible, with the kind assistance of Richard D. Palmer and
Kealla Jewell, whom I wish to thank.

Index

Index by Mandy Crook